HISPANIC-SERVING INSTITUTIONS

Despite the increasing numbers of Hispanic-Serving Institutions (HSIs) and their importance in serving students who have historically been underserved in higher education, limited research has addressed the meaning of the growth of these institutions and its implications for higher education. *Hispanic-Serving Institutions* fills a critical gap in understanding the organizational behavior of institutions that serve large numbers of low-income, first-generation, and Latina/o students. Leading scholars on HSIs contribute chapters to this volume, exploring a wide array of topics, data sources, conceptual frameworks, and methodologies to examine HSIs' institutional environments and organizational behavior. This cutting-edge volume explores how institutions can better serve their students and illustrates HSIs' changing organizational dynamics, potentials, and contributions to American higher education.

Anne-Marie Núñez is Associate Professor of Educational Leadership and Policy Studies in the Higher Education program at the University of Texas at San Antonio.

Sylvia Hurtado is Professor of Higher Education in the Graduate School of Education and Information Studies at the University of California, Los Angeles.

Emily Calderón Galdeano is Director of Research for *Excelencia in Education* and formerly served as the Director of Research and Information for the Hispanic Association of Colleges and Universities (HACU).

HISPANIC-SERVING INSTITUTIONS

Advancing Research and Transformative Practice

Edited by
Anne-Marie Núñez
Sylvia Hurtado
Emily Calderón Galdeano

Routledge
Taylor & Francis Group

NEW YORK AND LONDON

First published 2015
by Routledge
711 Third Avenue, New York, NY 10017

and by Routledge
2 Park Square, Milton Park, Abingdon, Oxon, OX14 4RN

Routledge is an imprint of the Taylor & Francis Group, an informa business

© 2015 Taylor & Francis

The right of the editors to be identified as the authors of the editorial material, and of the authors for their individual chapters, has been asserted in accordance with sections 77 and 78 of the Copyright, Designs and Patents Act 1988.

All rights reserved. No part of this book may be reprinted or reproduced or utilised in any form or by any electronic, mechanical, or other means, now known or hereafter invented, including photocopying and recording, or in any information storage or retrieval system, without permission in writing from the publishers.

Trademark notice: Product or corporate names may be trademarks or registered trademarks, and are used only for identification and explanation without intent to infringe.

Library of Congress Cataloging-in-Publication Data

CIP has been applied for

ISBN: 978-1-138-81430-1 (hbk)
ISBN: 978-1-138-81431-8 (pbk)
ISBN: 978-1-315-74755-2 (ebk)

Typeset in Bembo
by Apex CoVantage, LLC

CONTENTS

FOREWORD: THEN AND NOW

Michael A. Olivas

When I was asked to undertake this Foreword, it was an easy decision, for several reasons. First, two of the editors are friends and colleagues who have real bite and vision on the subject. Second, as the historiographic introductory essay reveals, I have labored for many years in this vineyard, although other subjects have since overtaken my attention span, so I was glad to revisit the field and was astonished to see how far the boulder has been pushed up the hill since my fledgling efforts more than thirty years ago. Indeed, returning full circle has also served as a template for how far the academic lot of Latina/o scholars has improved, particularly in higher education as a field of study. While these scholars have increased almost across the board—though still woefully inadequate in all disciplines—it is my sense that the three fields that have attracted the most and the most-accomplished have been my own: higher education, law, and my "accidental" field, history. Third, my very early scholarly focus and, for that matter, full-time employment, was with ethnic and racial enterprises: my first postdoctoral position was as a Senior Fellow and Assistant Director for a research institute at Howard University, the premier Historically Black Institution, and my second was as Director of Research with the League of United Latin American Citizens (LULAC) National Educational Service Centers, also in Washington, DC. I held these positions while in law school at Georgetown University Law Center, which I attended at night, working full time by day in these organizations. Doing so before I became a professor of Higher Education and Law cemented my loyalty and admiration for those who devote their lives to these missions.

Although I have known Professors Anne-Marie Núñez and Sylvia Hurtado, I have not made the actual acquaintance of the other, rising scholars who have contributed to the editing and scholarship in the volume. Many years ago, certainly when I edited the first full-length scholarly book on Latina/o college students, cleverly titled *Latino College Students*, I personally knew virtually every scholar who wrote in the area—or whom I identified as being able to do so for the edited volume—and involved them all in the project. Of course, inasmuch as I have not remained at the front end of this field, it is not surprising that I do not know the scholars writing in this volume, but I will say this: they are better trained than we were for this, predominantly by that first and second wave of Chicana/o scholars, with a few other Latina/o subgroup members. Sylvia Hurtado is chief among them, having studied with Walter Allen and Alexander Astin at UCLA, and then moving to two of the more productive venues in higher education studies, the University of Michigan and a return to UCLA, where she has directed the Higher Education Research Institute, trained many students and scholars in the use of HERI data, and produced dozens of the best Latina/o doctoral graduates, now making their way through the various institutions where they serve on faculties, replicating and extending the DNA chain.

Anne-Marie Núñez, a UCLA doctoral graduate who studied with Professor Hurtado, teaches at UT San Antonio (a major Hispanic-Serving Institution, or HSI), and has carved out what is among the preeminent research careers studying Latina/o students and HSIs. While it might be true, as pointed out in Chapter 1, that my 1982 article was one of the earliest treatments of these fledgling and marginal, predominantly Latina/o colleges, I was simply being descriptive and decidedly first-generation in my observations. If you wish to see the arc of the improved trajectory from early to later generations, read the work of Núñez. She has published in major journals and has been actively involved in the work of *The Review of Higher Education*, housed at UTSA under the direction of my own first doctoral advisee and postdoctoral fellow, Amaury Nora.

When I first attended the Association for the Study of Higher Education (ASHE), in the 1970s—when it was still the Association of Professors of Higher Education, housed by the AAHE—I was the only Mexican American graduate student, then law student, then faculty member. Little by little, the numbers grew, and as of today, ASHE has had four Latina presidents (including Sylvia Hurtado). In a Walter Mitty/Harold Stassen-kind of way, I blocked and tackled for them, having been a candidate for the ASHE presidency a frustrating four times, but no cigar. I recount this insider-baseball history of ASHE only because the success enjoyed by Latina presidents and the many other award-winning ASHE members at all levels is testimony to how far we have come in this important and mainstream organization and field of study.

And there has been similar success in my other fields of study as well, especially the Association of American Law Schools, where we have had five Mexican American presidents in a decade, including myself, and two other who succeeded me, two years in a row. It is surely not your father's AALS, as has been pointed out to me by a number of observers. From a base of twelve Latina/o law professors in 1982, the year I began teaching law at the University of Houston, we have grown to well more than 250 and have succeeded across fields and subspecialties—well beyond the progress any of us dared hope for in that sturdy bunch that first assembled, when I snagged a small Ford Foundation grant to get us together. While the higher education faculty increases grew organically, as the number of Latina/o students grew across institutions, it was a tougher slog in the law teaching field, where more elite criteria and active resistance played out more slowly. An organized plan of identifying candidates and shaming law schools slowly led to results, although progress has slowed, as the field of law teaching and legal education generally has slowed. And, of course, Latinas/os have moved into most major institutions across other disciplines, leading to breakthrough successes in many fields of study, particularly History and Sociology. Even as these numbers and evident successes have surfaced, the rise of contingent faculty, the overexpansion of many undergraduate and graduate programs, and legal threats to affirmative action have taken their toll and slowed the pace of Latina/o faculty hiring.

As this book shows, however, if there is a sector where the growth has continued, it is surely the HSIs and other Minority-Serving Institutions. Indeed, the very definitional and conceptual framework that has defined and determined "minority" status has shifted. A mere 30% of the school enrollment in Texas is White, approximately the same as in California and other states with substantial Latina/o populations. As is noted in several of the more demographic sections of this volume, this growth has not led to proportional progress by various Latina/o subgroups, especially the largest group, Mexican Americans. The numbers have been predominantly U.S. Birthright citizens, but in addition, the immigration figures have replenished the slowed birthrates, and the important policy development of Deferred Action for Childhood Arrivals (DACA) has been a boon to the formerly undocumented college students, even in the absence of comprehensive immigration reform.

While the qualitative scholarship in this book is quite interesting, I will reveal my own institutional case study of the institutional effects of being in an HSI upon faculty, particularly Mexican American faculty. As a participant observer, I will share some experiences about my own institution's experience in HSI-status, and the odd transformation to this status. The University of Houston has slowly been becoming more Mexican American—not by design or plan—but by propinquity, being located near the downtown of the fourth largest city in the United States, which is becoming predominantly Latina/o and Mexican American. If you use a search engine to access Houston demographic data, you are led to the website of the City of Houston Planning and Development Department, which reveals that the 2010 Census date counted 2,099,451 persons in Houston, with 919,668 "Hispanic or Latino" residents, of whom 673,093 were Mexican origin, and the remaining originating from across all Latin countries. In percentage terms, the city's population is 44% Latina/o, and 32% Mexican-origin. The school data from the almost twenty school districts reveal an even larger percentage of the school children are Latina/o, again, predominantly Mexican American.

Thus, inasmuch as the University of Houston (UH; 39,000+plus students on the main "Central" campus) draws its undergraduates primarily from the region, UH has become an HSI, one of the three in this cohort with a law school, and one of the few with the full range of doctoral and professional programs. Traditionally, HSIs are at least one-quarter Latina/o in their enrollments, and UH at 25.8% is somewhat under the area's ethnic percentage, and substantially under the Houston Independent School District Latina/o enrollment. (All four of the established UH System campuses are HSIs and members of the HACU, the service organization for HSIs.)

That said, UH institutional leadership has focused instead on an inchoate "Tier One" status as its golden fleece, a somewhat-artificial designation with lofty connotations: "Tier One," "Top Tier," and "Nationally Competitive Research University" are terms used interchangeably to refer to universities known for world-class research, academic excellence, an exceptional student body, and the highest levels of innovation, creativity and scholarship. Because of these accomplishments, these universities enjoy a national 'brand,' recognition and prestige. Not a publication comes out that does not highlight the "Tier One" status claimed by UH, although it is difficult to find a reference anywhere to the newly acquired HSI status. I cannot find a reference to the University of Houston's HSI status in a single online article or website.

Indeed, one of the casualties of becoming a larger and "Tier One" institution is that it actually has become more tiered, in the traditional sense, which means that different components of the overall UH System have differentiated and segmented academic admissions requirements, allowing the UH campus flagship to take the more high-achieving students, while the other campuses take students who are not admissible by the tiered requirements. As the UH publicity materials note, very carefully and diplomatically: "Not all students, however, will be academically prepared and not all will find the flagship campus the right choice for their interest, aptitude or learning style. Fortunately, UH is a system of four independent universities and a number of teaching centers. It is our commitment that the UH System will have a place for all students, but some may begin their college education in a community college or another UH System university where class size, academic programs and modes of delivery are more conducive to their learning style." This is assuredly not the academic signaling that most HSIs make to attract first generation, first time, and immigrant students. And choosing one signal over the other deracinates the actual campus achievement, one where Whites are only 30.7% of the enrolled students, in the 2013 count.

In this welter of messages, the Tier One mythology and ethos are naturally stressed, while the more mundane HSI achievement is not touted or advertised, lest UH seem more Mexican than it is. (One only need examine the poor Mexican American records in faculty hiring and administration personnel to see how underachieving it is on these measures.) While I do not know how eager other new HSI institutions are to embrace their actual or ascribed Latina/o identity and advertise themselves as such, I know from personal experience and considerable interaction how little my own University wishes to advertise and celebrate and embrace this dimension of its institutional saga and trajectory. Yet UH's future is assuredly that of its students of color, not its declining White population. Demography is destiny, and supply.

Given my own head-banging on this regrettable institutional reluctance to acknowledge its provenance and birthright, I am somewhat chagrined at the volume's evaluation that I am behind the eightball. Chapter 1 notes, "From a historic and legal standpoint, [Olivas] accurately foretold that the model for institutions that might serve Latinas/os would not develop in the same manner as it had for those whose missions focused on serving Blacks and Native Americans. However, he did not anticipate the Latina/o population growth that would coincide with the recognition of HSIs, many of which were transformed from broad access predominantly White institutions (PWIs) to institutions with HSI status." On this point, I can say this: if it is correct that I did not see it in 1982, when I joined the UH faculty, I certainly see it today, 33 years later.

As I read through the various chapters in this volume—all of them interesting and thoughtful—I was inevitably drawn back to my earlier experience in editing *Latino College Students*. I was pleased with the results of that enterprise, and in many respects it broke new ground. Indeed, I have been approached by SUNY Press people and by others over the years to update or revisit it, but my research interests have moved on, like light from a star that had moved to a different place in the cosmos. This is not to say that I ever abandoned my interest in these students, but as my law professor career moved to the fore, I began to concentrate upon the legal issues that virtually no Chicano legal scholars had interest in exploring: undocumented students and immigrant students generally, residency requirements and how we apportion benefits on the basis of where we live and for how long we live there, financial aid for the undocumented, and a number of other higher education subjects informed by my legal training and interests.

This has been a good bend in the river for me, and I have tended to my fly-casting and fishing-form in these currents. I am delighted to see so many others fish in my old waters and follow many of the same paths I trod more than three decades ago. I tried to leave the pathways better than I found them, and they are being taken up by young and dedicated scholars who have better tools than I had, and in many respects, who are better artisans than I was. It has been rewarding to see this intergenerational effort about HSIs, which has involved a senior and mid-career scholar, as well as emerging scholar Emily Calderón Galdeano, a former student and faculty member at HSIs who has also served as a research analyst at national Hispanic advocacy organizations. I am privileged to be asked to comment upon these themes and to have learned so much at the hands of so many in this volume. And remember what a privilege it is to be a professor with so many opportunities. May your careers be as soul-satisfying and wondrous as mine has been.

Thank you all for this wonderful book. I am in your debt.

Michael A. Olivas is the William B. Bates Distinguished Chair in Law at the University of Houston Law Center and the author of 15 books, including *Suing Alma Mater: Higher Education and the Courts*, published by Johns Hopkins University Press. He hosts a weekly NPR radio show, *The Law of Rock and Roll*.

ACKNOWLEDGMENTS

This book is the result of several years of conversations and collaborations among many scholars and educators who have met at the gatherings of national associations. We would like to thank the following organizations for providing opportunities to explore, develop, and disseminate research in this emerging field of Hispanic-Serving Institutions (HSIs): American Association of Hispanics in Higher Education (AAHHE), Hispanic Association of Colleges and Universities (HACU), and *Excelencia* in Education. HACU, in particular, has worked with many agencies over the years to provide a sustained level of financial support to build and maintain institutional capacity for HSIs and support more research related to HSIs to increase their visibility. With initial funding from Educational Testing Service (ETS) and additional funds from the Lumina Foundation, the HACU Hispanic Higher Education Research Collective (H³ERC) was created to bring scholars and HSI educators together to advance research on Latina/o higher education. H³ERC meetings were held in collaboration with the Higher Education Research Institute at the University of California Los Angeles (2006), University of Texas at San Antonio (UTSA) (2005; 2006), University of Houston (2007), Montclair State University (2008), and the Center for Research and Policy in Education at UTSA (2012). The conversations and knowledge shared at these meetings eventually culminated in the development of this book. Most importantly, we acknowledge the initial scholarship of Berta Vigil Laden, which helped alert the scholarly and policy community about the special role of HSIs and broad access institutions in American higher education. We are honored to carry on and expand her central research agenda.

We also want to acknowledge the insightful feedback from external reviewers, and of course, Heather Jarrow at Routledge, who was enthusiastic from the beginning about the prospect of a book on HSIs. We thank independent consultant Karen Jarsky, who expertly suggested edits to each chapter to help each author clarify points. Deep appreciation is also in order for the UTSA College of Education and Human Development for funds to support the development of this book.

Special thanks also go to Michael A. Olivas, Bates Distinguished Professor of Law at the University of Houston, who took the time from his busy summer schedule in Santa Fe to write the Foreword. He has been a champion of Latina/o education causes, shaping policy for decades. To us, he is also a role model in writing books to reveal good thinking. He reminds us that the issues on Latina/o education are complex and too important to remain invisible or left to the interpretation of others.

1

WHY STUDY HISPANIC-SERVING INSTITUTIONS?

Anne-Marie Núñez, Sylvia Hurtado, and Emily Calderón Galdeano

We are experiencing a unique moment in the history of higher education and institutional change. In recent decades, U.S. higher education has reached a point of providing nearly universal postsecondary education, including options in many different institutional types (Thelin, 2013; Trow, 1970). Yet postsecondary access is still significantly stratified by income and race/ethnicity (e.g., Carnevale & Strohl, 2013), even though the proportion of Americans in general and the share from populations that historically have had less access to higher education are both higher than they ever have been before (e.g., Thelin, 2013). External pressures to better serve diverse student populations are on the horizon.

At the same time, the United States has seen significant shifts in its demographic composition. The Hispanic[1] population in particular has grown at a remarkable rate, from just 4.5% of the U.S. population in 1970, to 16.3% in 2010, surpassing African Americans as the largest non-White population in this country (U.S. Census Bureau, 2010). Latina/o youth constitute more than half of K–12 students in California and Texas (Gándara & Contreras, 2009), and Latinas/os now represent the largest non-White group of college students in the country (Fry, 2011). Some projections indicate that by 2050, at least 3 in 10 U.S. residents will be of Latina/o origin (Sáenz, 2010).

In line with this demographic transformation, we are witnessing a significant trend among established institutions in American higher education: More two-year and four-year colleges and universities are serving at least a 25% Latina/o student body, and are now federally recognized as Hispanic-Serving Institutions (HSIs) (Santiago, 2006). Currently, there are 370 institutions designated as HSIs, and an additional 277 have between 15% and 24% Latina/o enrollment, and hence are known as emerging HSIs (Calderón Galdeano & Santiago, 2014). Many recently established higher education institutions are now HSIs that have been tasked to serve historically underrepresented populations in new regions (Hurtado & Guillermo-Wann, 2013). Examples include all five California State University campuses founded within the past 50 years, as well as two out of the three new University of California and University of Texas campuses established in that time frame. Furthermore, as Latinas/os settle in more diverse parts of the country, HSIs are emerging in more diverse geographic locations (Torres & Zerquera, 2012).

While many studies have focused on Latinas/os in higher education,[2] Michael Olivas (1982) and Berta Vigil Laden (1999) were the first scholars to call for specific policy and research attention to these institutions. In 1982, Olivas reported on the development of Chicana/o (Colegio Cesar Chávez) and Puerto Rican colleges (Hostos Community College and Boricua College) that had been established to serve these populations on the U.S. mainland. Based at the time on the small number of institutions with a historic mission to serve Latinas/os, he contended that, "The future of Chicanos in higher education appears to be in penetrating majority institutions [and] convincing policymakers that minority institution programs will not reach enough Chicano students" (Olivas, 1982, pp. 42–43). From a historic and legal standpoint, he accurately foretold that the model for institutions that might serve Latinas/os would not develop in the same manner as it had for those whose missions focused on serving Blacks and Native Americans. However, he did not anticipate the Latina/o population growth that would coincide with the recognition of HSIs, many of which were transformed from broad access predominantly White institutions (PWIs) to institutions with HSI status.

Once HSIs became federally recognized in 1992, Berta Vigil Laden (1999, 2001) was the first scholar to place these institutions and their stories at the center of a research agenda. When she began her scholarship in this area, she astutely acknowledged that, at the time, fewer than a handful of manuscripts had identified HSIs (Laden, 1999). As a pioneer in identifying the importance of federal recognition for these institutions, she served as a strong advocate for their support.

Since Olivas (1982) and Laden (1999, 2001) focused on and advocated for institutions that become federally designated to serve Latina/o students, limited research to date has addressed the implications of the growth of these institutions for higher education, or the institutional behaviors and changes required to address the needs of their diverse student bodies (Nora & Crisp, 2009). We do not know enough about whether changes at HSIs are evolutionary or actively managed so that institutional culture and daily practices are transformed in ways befitting their changing student populations. Moreover, we need to learn how HSIs are unique as a set of institutions that face similar changes, challenges, and external pressures. Finally, more research is needed to advance and transform practice in a way that incorporates an inclusive excellence perspective (Association of American Colleges and Universities, 2014) that integrates diversity and equity as central features.

The goal of this book is to provide new research and to advance the study of HSIs as complex organizations as they undergo change and respond to external pressures (Kezar, 2014), including demographic change, increased institutional accountability, and resource constraints. We aim to provide a better sense of the following: (1) the institutional characteristics and diversity among HSIs; (2) how HSIs are similar to or different from other higher education institutions; (3) how HSIs form organizational identities, develop organizational behaviors, and build institutional capacity to respond to diverse student bodies; and (4) why it is critical to understand HSIs' localized contexts, particularly with regard to economic resources for institutions and students.

Organizational studies of higher education in the United States have, to date, focused on the behaviors of the most elite and selective institutions, while scant research has addressed community colleges or less selective four-year institutions with relatively (or completely) open admissions policies—institutions that enroll at least 80% of college students in this country (Kirst, Stevens, & Proctor, 2010). Thus, this book addresses a critical gap in the research on these so-called broad access institutions (Bastedo, 2012; Kirst et al., 2010). In addition, this edited volume advances organizational studies in higher education by providing examples of perspectives and empirical research that employ various lenses to understand how HSIs navigate complex and challenging environments and serve diverse students. Finally, a central goal of this book is to shift assumptions and inform competing narratives about HSIs, to illustrate how these institutions play a critical role in the U.S. higher education landscape—particularly in developing the talents of many students who may not otherwise attend college and/or who face challenges in completion—and serve as critical engines of social mobility.

Universal Higher Education, Institutional Stratification, and the Role of HSIs

HSIs have resulted from broader trends, both nationally and more specifically within U.S. higher education. U.S. income inequality is currently among the highest in the world, and has increased relative to other countries (Organisation for Economic Co-operation and Development [OECD], 2011). Many countries across the globe are increasing postsecondary opportunities, as growth in average educational attainment appears to be "the single most important factor contributing not only to reduced wage dispersion among workers but also to higher employment rates" (OECD, 2011, p. 31). This has prompted President Obama to position improved college degree attainment as an important component of efforts to strengthen the U.S. economy and increase social equity, with a corresponding interest in holding institutions accountable for degree completion rates (Espinosa, Crandall, & Tukibayeva, 2014).

Indeed, universal higher education has come to be seen as an important mechanism for providing educated and skilled workers to advance the U.S. economy (Goldin & Katz, 2009). Trow (1970) noted the movement of the U.S. postsecondary system from an elite approach—providing education to a limited number of students at a handful of institutions—to a universal approach for all individuals interested in pursuing college, including at community colleges and four-year institutions of varying selectivity, in a wide variety of locations around the country. The numbers and types of postsecondary institutions in the United States have increased as a result, leading to a diverse system of institutions stratified by prestige, racial/ethnic composition, and resources (e.g., Birnbaum, 1991; Carnevale & Strohl, 2013).

Observers have noted that the movement toward universal education has posed deep challenges for higher education (Thelin, 2013; Trow, 1970). The historical trends of increasing enrollments of students from more diverse backgrounds (in many, but not all, higher education institutions) during a time of increasing resource constraints mean that, in the words of historian John Thelin (2013), "a university will be hard pressed to maintain a high graduation rate" (p. 112). Furthermore, "such quantitative changes are accompanied by fundamental qualitative changes in what the college experience is and what the American campus is" (Thelin, 2013, p. 112). These changes call upon higher education institutions to transform their organizational cultures to serve students from different backgrounds, in response to the various historical, economic, and social contexts within which they are embedded (Hurtado, Álvarez, Guillermo-Wann, Cuellar, & Arellano, 2012).

This emphasis on universal access to postsecondary education has, in fact, incorporated a movement of holding higher education institutions more accountable, with success often measured by college graduation rates (Espinosa et al., 2014; Toutkoushian & Webber, 2011). For example, the Obama administration's planned postsecondary ratings system—to be implemented in 2015—will provide students and families with information to compare the performance of institutions. The administration also proposes to tie these ratings to institutional performance funding. There is much concern, however, that such a policy could disadvantage broad access institutions (Espinosa et al., 2014), and specifically HSIs (Núñez, 2014), in their capacity to serve students.

HSIs are more likely than other institutions to educate a significant proportion of students from populations that have historically had less access to higher education, including low-income, first-generation, and underrepresented racial/ethnic minority students, as well as students who are less academically prepared for college (Hispanic Association of Colleges and Universities [HACU], 2012; Núñez & Bowers, 2011; Núñez & Elizondo, 2012). HSIs tend also to have fewer resources to support these students (HACU, 2012). Having fewer institutional resources and larger proportions of students from low-income backgrounds are both independently and negatively related to graduation rates (Bound, Lovenheim, & Turner, 2010; Titus, 2006a, 2006b, 2009; Webber & Ehrenberg, 2009). These same issues have contributed to less value being placed on the significant role of broad access institutions more generally in educating the majority of American college students (Kirst et al., 2010).

Because broad access institutions and community colleges enroll the majority of U.S. college students (Kirst et al., 2010), they clearly play a large role in educating individuals who contribute to the nation's workforce and economic growth. Likewise, given the current and expected increases in Latinas/os as a share of the overall population, any efforts to raise U.S. postsecondary degree completion and attainment must target this and other groups that historically have had less postsecondary access. Thus, considering that HSIs graduate 40% of Latina/o baccalaureates in the United States (Harmon, 2012), we see the potential for HSIs ultimately to reduce the gaps in U.S. educational and economic inequality. As described in the rest of this chapter and throughout this volume, however, HSIs face tremendous challenges in supporting the success of their students.

Distinguishing HSIs among Other Minority-Serving Institutions

HSIs are the largest and fastest growing segment of a broader group of institutions that have historically targeted underserved groups of students, including Latinas/os, African Americans, and Native Americans. Many of these institutions are part of a diverse group known as Minority-Serving Institutions (MSIs). Historically Black Colleges and Universities (HBCUs) and Tribal Colleges and Universities (TCUs) have missions to explicitly support students from specific underrepresented backgrounds due to systematic exclusion from postsecondary opportunity and historic *de jure* segregation (Olivas, 1982). Due to their classification, they automatically receive federal funding from the government. The same is not the case for HSIs. Furthermore, the number of HBCUs (100) and TCUs (33) is relatively stable, and these institutions tend to have small student enrollments (Calderón Galdeano & Santiago, 2014), while the average enrollment size for an HSI in the 2008–2009 academic year was 6,173 students (Núñez, Crisp, & Elizondo, in press).

HSIs are federally designated not by a specific mission to serve Latina/o students, but rather by their relatively high enrollment (at least 25%) of Latina/o students. The number of HSIs is more than double that of all other MSIs (Calderón Galdeano & Santiago, 2014) and only continues to grow. Notably, "Hispanic-Serving" does not mean serving *only* Hispanic students—the student bodies of HSIs are diverse. In 2012–2013, HSIs enrolled 59% of all Latina/o students in higher education, and also enrolled 28% of Asian American, 16% of Black, 14% of American Indian, and 10% of White students nationally. In fact, HSIs enroll a greater share of Black students in the United States than HBCUs (16% and 10%, respectively) and a higher share of Native American students than TCUs (14% and 11%, respectively) (Calderón Galdeano & Santiago, 2014). With compositional diversity achieved among HSIs, a continuing focus on equity requires systematic study of other elements of these colleges, such as the psychological, behavioral, and organizational dimensions of the environment (see Hurtado & Ruiz Alvarado, Chapter 2, this volume). Accordingly, studies on HSIs hold the promise of generating new knowledge about diversity and equity across higher education as well as within particular institutions.

Most of the research on HSIs to date has focused on their contributions to traditional student outcomes, such as degree attainment and persistence, but the narratives that surround these institutions are sometimes in conflict. For example, HSIs have been celebrated for the quantity of graduates they produce from low-income, first-generation, and Latina/o backgrounds (Harmon, 2012). Many students have earned undergraduate or graduate science, technology, engineering, and mathematics (STEM) degrees—only about 9% of all postsecondary institutions were HSIs during the 2008–2009 academic year, yet they produced nearly 65% of the STEM certificates, 61% of the STEM associate's degrees, and 40% of the STEM bachelor's degrees earned by Latinas/os (Malcom-Piqueux & Lee, 2011). Thus, HSIs are preparing Latinas/os for the growth of new jobs in STEM fields. At the same time, however, HSIs are also often criticized for their relatively low persistence rates in comparison to other institutions (Contreras, Malcom, & Bensimon, 2008). Part of the reason for these competing narratives is that research to date has typically not examined the institutional characteristics, resources, and activities within HSIs that could contribute to these outcomes, nor has it looked at how these institutions operate at the ground level. Given the capacity of HSIs to impact more students, there is much to be gained from expanding research on HSIs' contributions to degree attainments and many other outcomes connected to their mission.

While many HSIs are still primarily broad access and regionally focused (García, 2013; Núñez et al., 2014), they are often called upon by public agencies to broaden their organizational identities and to extend their purposes and functions. Specifically, in serving students from historically underrepresented backgrounds, HSIs must also respond to challenges to reinvigorate local economies (Vega & Martínez, 2012). This involves increasing their (1) research capacity and presence of graduate programs for underserved communities, (2) responsiveness to demands for a more highly skilled workforce, and (3) performance on traditional metrics of institutional success, such as transfer, persistence, and degree completion (Hamilton, 2010; Núñez, 2014). These external pressures to rise to new levels of performance are occurring at the same time that institutions are experiencing increasing levels of financial constraint (Ortega, Frye, Nellum, Kamimura, & Vidal-Rodríguez, Chapter 9, this volume). As such, it is especially timely to examine HSIs as developing institutions because these performance pressures begin to reflect competing priorities that play out in the daily work of faculty, staff, and administrators, and consequently shape students' college experiences.

Historical Background, Definition, and Growth of HSIs

In order to understand the evolution of HSIs in American higher education, it helps to understand how they were initially recognized. By the early 1980s, there had been some Congressional discussion of "Hispanic institutions," but no sustained effort to convert this discussion into legislation. As early as 1989, recognizing the demographic and economic shifts occurring in the country, the federal government worked with several Hispanic institutions and organizations to create a federal designation for institutions enrolling high shares of Latina/o students. Two proposed bills at that time called for $70 million in aid to colleges and universities with significant Hispanic enrollment for the improvement of educational opportunities for Hispanic students; however, neither bill made it out of committee. In 1990, President George H.W. Bush signed a Hispanic education Executive Order that encouraged federal agencies to allocate grants and contracts to significantly Hispanic institutions and community-based Hispanic organizations.[3]

The first instance of national recognition and the first legal definition of what constitutes a Hispanic-Serving Institution appeared in the 1992 Reauthorization of the Higher Education Act (HEA) of 1965, but federal funding for HSIs did not come until 1994 (Laden, 1999). In that year, under Title III of the HEA, also known as the *Strengthening Institutions Program*, an HSI was defined as an accredited, degree-granting, public or private, not-for-profit college or university with 25% or more total undergraduate Hispanic enrollment. Official HSI designation was reserved for those institutions that applied for (and were granted) a designation by the U.S. Department of Education (Laden, 1999).

This federal enrollment-based definition sets HSIs apart from HBCUs and TCUs, which were established specifically to serve the educational needs of otherwise underserved populations. Most HSIs on the U.S. mainland were not founded with a specific mission to serve Hispanic students, with the notable exceptions of the National Hispanic University (California),[4] St. Augustine's College (Illinois), Boricua College (New York), Eugenio María de Hostos Community College (New York), Northern New Mexico College (New Mexico), and Colegio Cesar Chávez (Oregon) (Calderón Galdeano, Flores, & Moder, 2012; Olivas, 1982).

When the HEA was reauthorized in 1998, HSIs were placed under Title V (Part A), also known as the *Developing Hispanic-Serving Institutions Program* (Santiago, 2006). Title V authorizes eligible institutions to apply for institutional development and planning grants in order to improve and expand their capacity to serve Hispanic and low-income students. While the official HSI designation is based on undergraduate enrollment, a graduate HSI education component was added with the 2008 HEA reauthorization. Title V (Part B) of the HEA authorizes the *Promoting Postbaccalaureate Opportunities for Hispanic Americans* (PPOHA) program, and its purpose is to expand graduate educational opportunities for, and improve the academic attainment of, Hispanics and other low-income students (20 U.S.C. §§ 1102–1102c, 1103–1103g; Higher Education Act of 1965, 2013).

Importantly, for the purposes of federal funding, other than funding given for student financial aid, an "institution of higher education" must be either public or not-for-profit (20 U.S.C. § 1001; Higher Education Act of 1965, 2013).

Therefore, proprietary (for-profit) institutions are not eligible for Title V funding and are not designated as HSIs, even though they may have high Latina/o enrollments.

The evolution of Hispanic-Serving Institutions during the past 30 years has been characterized as *de facto*, i.e., a direct result of their proximity to growing Hispanic communities (Laden, 2001). Two characteristics that have played a key role in attracting Latina/o students to HSIs are relatively inexpensive tuition and proximity to students' homes (Núñez & Bowers, 2011; Santiago, 2007). Both are major considerations for Hispanic students as they choose institutions for the pursuit of higher education (Benítez, 1998; Rendón, Dowd, & Nora, 2012; Santiago, 2007). Consequently, Latinas/os have enrolled in a disproportionately small number of institutions when compared to other student populations, with increasing numbers attending local HSIs (Laden, 2001; Santiago, Andrade, & Brown, 2004; Perna, Li, Walsh, & Raible, 2010). HSIs, by design, serve students who may be the hardest to serve, as many low-income students have historically been underprepared in K–12 (Gándara & Contreras, 2009; Oakes, Silver, Valladares, Terriquez, & McDonough, 2006).

Driven largely by Hispanic population growth, HSIs have continued to increase in number, from 189 institutions in 1994–1995 to 370 in 2012–2013 (Calderón Galdeano & Santiago, 2014). Currently, HSIs represent 11% of all colleges and universities and serve a diverse student body that constitutes 18% of all students in secondary education. These institutions offer undergraduate and graduate degrees in 15 states and Puerto Rico and enroll 59% of all Latina/o students (Calderón Galdeano & Santiago, 2014). Organizations such as *Excelencia* in Education and HACU have begun tracking institutions that are close to reaching the critical mass of 25% Latina/o student enrollment. Although there is no official federal definition for these institutions with Hispanic student enrollments of 15% to 24%, they are considered "emerging HSIs" and are located throughout the United States (Calderón Galdeano & Santiago, 2014).

Table 1.1 shows growth in the number of HSIs over a 19-year span. Three observations are worth nothing. First, the table illustrates the heterogeneity of institutional types among HSIs, at both the four- and two-year levels and in the public and private, not-for-profit sectors. Second, the number of HSIs has increased steadily in every sector of higher education. Third, Latina/o percentages fluctuate slightly as a proportion of the population of all campuses. This is largely due to expanding campus enrollments over this time period and relatively higher Latina/o enrollment mobility (Ruiz Alvarado, 2014).

In terms of resources, HSIs have been chronically underfunded in comparison to all not-for-profit higher education institutions, even while they serve an increasing number of the neediest population of college students (de los Santos & de los Santos, 2003; Malcom, Dowd, & Yu, 2010; Merisotis & McCarthy, 2005). They are typically limited in budget and endowment, and are highly dependent on state, federal, and municipal funds (Benítez, 1998; HACU, 2012; Hurtado & Ruiz Alvarado, Chapter 2, this volume; Ortega et al., Chapter 9,

TABLE 1.1 *Number of Hispanic Serving Institutions*

	1994–1995	1999–2000	2004–2005	2009–2010	2012–2013
Total	189	216	242	293	370
% of all Latina/o undergraduates enrolled at HSIs	46%	52%	53%	54%	59%
2-year institutions	103	114	119	150	193
% of all HSIs	54%	53%	49%	51%	52%
4-year institutions	86	102	123	143	177
% of all HSIs	46%	47%	51%	49%	48%
2-year public HSIs	91	101	108	137	178
2-year private not-for-profit HSIs	12	13	11	13	15
4-year public HSIs	30	43	52	62	72
4-year private not-for-profit HSIs	56	59	71	81	105
Emerging HSIs	189	146	183	204	277

Source: Based on data from the *Excelencia* in Education Hispanic-Serving Institutions Center for Policy and Practice (HSI-CP^2)

Note. Only public and not-for-profit institutions are included in this table; for-profit institutions cannot apply for HSI designation or institutional capacity-building funds.

this volume). Furthermore, they are generally underequipped, understaffed, and non-competitive with regard to employee salaries (de los Santos & Cuamea, 2010; Hurtado & Ruiz Alvarado, Chapter 2, this volume; Malcom et al., 2010; Merisotis & McCarthy, 2005; Mulnix, Bowden, & López, 2002).

On average and per student, HSIs receive just 66 cents for every dollar from all federal funding sources that not-for-profit higher education institutions receive (Calderón Galdeano et al., 2012). Villarreal and Santiago (2012) found that although the total amount of Title V funds awarded to HSIs between 1995 and 2010 increased by 875%, the number of institutions receiving these funds decreased by 9%. More specifically, in 1995–1996, 64% of all HSIs received Title V funding, but by 2010–2011, only 25% of HSIs received these funds (Villarreal & Santiago, 2012). Therefore, even though HSIs are eligible for federal funding, only a minimal proportion actually receive that funding, and it will become more competitive as the number of HSIs increase (Ortega et al., Chapter 9, this volume). Notwithstanding many of these challenges, HSIs continue to be instrumental in the development of Latina/o human capital (Harmon, 2012).

Data Issues in Studying HSIs

Researchers, practitioners, and policymakers need to become aware of some of the challenges in studying HSIs. First, as higher education enrollments change from year to year, so will the designation of institutions as HSIs. Thus, the number of HSIs will not be consistent over time. Researchers must make decisions about the sample of HSIs and a specific year to analyze, realizing their findings may differ from other studies that have opted to use a different sample from a different year. Second, the Integrated Postsecondary Education Data System (IPEDS), the source of much data about HSIs, frequently has missing data (Espinosa et al., 2014), making it difficult to capture a full range of institutional characteristics about HSIs. Third, due to the absence of an official federal list of HSIs, scholars must conduct initial analyses to determine whether or not institutions meet HSI enrollment criteria.[5]

For all of these reasons, scholars who conduct large-scale studies on HSIs may report institutional data that seem inconsistent. This is largely because of variations in HSI designation over time and different decisions about how to construct samples based on timeliness of data, amount of missing data, and other critical issues. Thus, readers of this volume may note that different authors use different years of data and report different sample sizes of HSIs. Importantly, the editors of this book have ensured the following: (1) the data analyses presented across the chapters are internally consistent within the various chapters, and (2) the authors have clearly presented their sources and the corresponding years when discussing overall data on HSIs. Readers are encouraged to consult the original sources for more information on the construction of the samples of HSIs used in those studies. It is clear that understanding how HSIs are studied is just as important as understanding why we need to study them.

A Transformative Research and Practice Paradigm for Studying HSIs

In addition to important choices regarding existing data sets that include HSIs, researchers have employed a variety of paradigms to shed light on information about these higher education institutions and their students, faculty, and staff. It is not surprising that they are subject to the normative way of conducting research in post-positivist, constructivist, and pragmatic (i.e., what works) paradigms, following the conventions of their graduate training and what is considered rigorous and trustworthy research—practices that are only reinforced in the peer-review processes (Hurtado, in press). Less training and implementation of the transformative paradigm is apparent because articulation of its principles is fairly recent, and it now serves as an umbrella for critical research focused on marginalized communities (Mertens, 2009). We provide insights into several distinctive features of the transformative research paradigm here. This is not to say that the authors in this volume have adopted all aspects of this paradigm, but we begin to see it in their work in various ways.

The transformative paradigm is characterized by unique assumptions regarding ethics and values (axiology), the nature of reality (ontology), the nature of knowledge and the relationship of the researcher to study participants (epistemology), and appropriate methods of systematic inquiry (methodology) (Mertens, 2009).

First, in terms of *ethics and values*, transformative paradigm researchers assume respect for the cultural norms of diverse communities in connection with a social justice agenda. They value inclusion and assume rigorous forms of research that advocate for improving the conditions of marginalized communities (Hurtado, in press). In these communities, they recognize not only challenges and vulnerabilities but also agency and critical resilience. Second, the assumption about the *nature of reality* is that multiple versions of reality are socially constructed, and privileged versions of reality influence what is accepted as real. Therefore, versions of reality may not have equal legitimacy. A third clear distinction is reflected in assumptions regarding the *nature of knowledge*: The researcher recognizes power relations and dynamics in broader historical, economic, and social contexts, while realizing that ways of knowing are linked with multiple social identities and positionalities. Instead of distancing themselves from the communities under study, researchers build dynamic relationships with these communities for action and empowerment. Fourth, transformative researchers often use *multiple research methods* to capture context, history, cultural norms, and structures of opportunity or inequality.

How might the transformative paradigm apply to studies of HSIs? Many students at HSIs come from distinct cultural traditions and communities, and have faced poverty and oppression, structural discrimination in education, and limited opportunities or resources. In the context of a stratified higher education system, HSIs, like their students (Valencia, 2010), face "victim blame" and being cast in "deficit" terms. Yet, as this edited volume shows, these institutions are remarkably resilient, possessing other kinds of assets that have contributed to their success. Thus, researchers must approach HSIs with a great deal of respect and appreciation for the difficult work of dedicated individuals who spend many years working at these institutions. In short, transformative researchers seek a social justice agenda for HSIs, and typically engage in studies that support policies and resource distribution that lead to institutional forms of empowerment and capacity-building.

The chapters in this book illustrate emerging research shifts in axiology, ontology, epistemology, and methodology in the study of HSIs. The shift in axiology is reflected in emphasizing the assets that HSIs have and how these institutions contribute both the individual and social benefits of higher education to society (Bowen, 1977). The shift in ontology is characterized by the abandonment of the dominant research narrative, based on selective, four-year institutions, and the transference of unquestioned assumptions about definitions of institutional "success" and the behaviors that contribute to it, in order to reflect the reality of HSI and broad access institutional contexts. Researchers employing a transformative paradigm recognize the struggle for legitimacy among HSIs—their status, mission, and perspectives—and how they serve the least privileged in the stratified system of higher education. The shift in epistemology is reflected in research on HSIs that provides insights into alternative ways of knowing, and in higher education scholarship that takes into account broad access institutions and their standpoints within the higher education field.

Creating a new perspective for understanding organizational behavior from the standpoint of HSIs, rather than using a lens that emphasizes and values the characteristics of elite or predominantly White institutions, has led many researchers to push boundaries in important ways to understand HSIs and the students they serve. They focus on elements important to knowing HSIs' working assumptions and how the realities of HSIs look and work differently than other types of higher education organizations. They ask new questions about equity within HSIs (Bensimon & Malcom, 2012), the conditions for student success in diverse learning environments (Hurtado et al., 2012), what it means when a researcher's or faculty member's identity matches that of their students (García, 2013; Núñez, Murakami, & Cuero, 2010), and how Latina/o experiences are unique at HSIs (Cuellar, 2014). They focus on how actors in HSIs make sense of their roles, responsibilities, organizational challenges, and contributions. These researchers navigate the boundaries of insider and outsider status in their work and are aware of how HSIs have typically been excluded or made to feel "less than" other institutions, while they strive to do better and do more with less. Thus, the complexity of HSIs also requires shifts in attention to methodology, and this affects how researchers collect and analyze data.

Transformative practice can be characterized as action that follows transformative research. In a model of public engagement with research, scholars can move from *informing* participants about results to *empowering* them to ask new questions and generate their own studies (Hurtado, in press). The latter stage should naturally lead to more reflective and intentional forms of practice. In short, transformative research and practice share the application of ethics, care, and respect for marginalized communities; acknowledgment of multiple realities of groups and actors on the same campus; and incorporation of different ways of knowing and different methods to reach and educate diverse student populations. The chapters in this volume illustrate the application of a transformative paradigm by demonstrating the diversity of HSIs and the extent to which HSIs are similar to or different than other higher education institutions, calling into question conceptions of student and institutional "success," and recasting how higher education institutions can achieve success.

Organization of This Volume

Now that there are greater numbers of HSIs, several senior scholars as well as a new generation of scholars are pushing the boundaries of theory, employing more advanced and rigorous research methods, and challenging common assumptions about HSIs. This book begins to lay the groundwork for conducting further studies on these institutions. As HSIs continue to provide opportunities to large proportions of historically underrepresented students to pursue a college education, it is critical that more research address these institutions as organizational contexts that are shaping the landscape of American higher education. Such research can inform not only policies and practices within HSIs and institutions that are poised to become HSIs, but it can also provide insights on how to serve students who have historically been underrepresented in higher education.

The chapters in this book primarily use an organizational lens to understand HSIs, gaining insights from constituencies (students, faculty, and leaders) within them. They fill a critical gap in understanding the organizational behavior of institutions that serve large numbers of low-income, first-generation students, and students of color. As such, they also contribute to the limited body of scholarship on broad access colleges and universities (Kirst et al., 2010) and to the study of organizational theory, culture, and behavior (Bastedo, 2012), particularly in these institutional settings. Although there has been more extensive research on the organizational behavior of elite and selective institutions, we know relatively little about the majority of higher education organizations, particularly those enrolling many underrepresented students. Thus, contributors to this volume help us understand HSIs specifically and also advance organizational perspectives on the American system of higher education more broadly.

Through empirical inquiry, this volume calls into question commonly held assumptions about HSIs, including the following: (1) HSIs are monolithic, (2) HSIs are either only "Hispanic-enrolling" or fully "Hispanic-serving," and (3) HSIs are underperforming institutions. This work suggests that these narratives are overly simplistic, and it poses alternative frames for understanding the contributions of HSIs to American higher education. The chapters address a wider array of topics, data sources, conceptual frameworks, and methodologies to examine HSIs' institutional environments and organizational behavior than are typically used to understand HSIs or (in some cases) any higher education phenomena. Collectively, the work offers diverse and complementary lenses for understanding HSIs and their contributions.

Each chapter is based on new analyses of diverse data to address the heterogeneity and complexity of HSIs and the key challenges they face. The intergenerational group of authors, all of whom are leading scholars on HSIs (and many of whom have studied at or worked in HSIs), pose an array of complementary questions to capture different angles of HSIs' organizational identities and behaviors, which collectively reveal the multiple dimensions of the evolving nature of these institutions. Accordingly, the authors utilize different types of quantitative and qualitative methods to explore how institutional conditions and actors in HSIs shape organizational contexts and student outcomes.

The quantitative methods used in various chapters include multivariate regression and the advanced quantitative technique of propensity score matching to explore the relationship between institutional characteristics in HSIs and student outcomes. The qualitative methods include case studies and interviews to explore the perspectives and experiences of organizational actors in HSIs. Data sources include large-scale national data sets from the U.S. Department of Education and UCLA's Higher Education Research Institute (HERI), as well as interviews with the faculty and administrators who shape the institutional contexts of HSIs. Accordingly, the chapters in this volume illustrate HSIs' changing organizational dynamics, potentials, and contributions to American higher education, in both a broad and more localized context.

Collectively, the empirical studies presented in this book challenge commonly held conceptions of how HSIs and, by association, broad access institutions, are transforming to serve changing student populations, local communities, and national goals of increased postsecondary attainment. Despite HSIs' success in producing large numbers of graduates from underrepresented backgrounds, one common criticism is that they are not held to a mission to truly *serve* Hispanic students, that they have not transformed beyond merely *enrolling* them. This book engages these competing narratives by delving more deeply than prior research into the organizational experiences, resources, and outcomes of HSIs. The evidence presented calls into question commonly held notions about how HSIs function as organizations, how they serve their diverse student bodies, and how they perform in both conventional and alternative metrics of success. Together and independently, the book chapters challenge traditional perspectives and provide alternative frames of reference for understanding how broad access organizations and HSIs work to meet the needs of their diverse student bodies.

The book is divided into three sections. Part I, "Contextualizing the Culture, Structure, and Identity of Hispanic-Serving Institutions," examines the diverse institutional characteristics and organizational cultures of HSIs. This section lays the foundation for understanding HSIs as organizational contexts and introduces conceptual lenses for exploring these contexts. Part II, titled, "Framing Institutional Actors and Experiences Within Hispanic-Serving Institutions," provides insights into the organizational behavior of HSIs by providing rare glimpses into the experiences of students, faculty, and administrators at these institutions. Part III, "Building Capacity and Accountability in Hispanic-Serving Institutions," offers a deeper view of HSIs' capacity to support college personnel and students. Building on insights from the previous sections, this final section also addresses the nature of organizational performance and success for HSIs, and how this may be distinct from performance and success as measured in other types of institutions.

Following this introductory chapter, in Chapter 2, Sylvia Hurtado and Adriana Ruiz Alvarado provide an overview for understanding the context of HSIs. Drawing on institutional transformation theory and a climate model that places the Latina/o student identity at the center of practice, they provide a blueprint for addressing multiple institutional areas that need greater attention in order to realize the potential of HSIs. The authors identify several complexities in how HSIs may have internal struggles over establishing multiple organizational identities in change processes. They call for more in-depth research in this area, and the chapters in the rest of the volume respond to this call.

In Chapter 3, Anne-Marie Núñez, Gloria Crisp, and Diane Elizondo analyze national quantitative data to examine the structural, demographic, and financial context characteristics of two-year HSIs; in Chapter 4, Núñez and Elizondo do the same for four-year HSIs. These chapters go one step further to examine how these institutional characteristics are related to Hispanic persistence rates (in four-year institutions) and transfer rates (in two-year institutions). Together, they suggest that student characteristics and institutional resources are both significantly related to student outcomes achieved at HSIs, and they lay the groundwork to further understand the relationships between institutional characteristics and student outcomes that are expanded on in later chapters.

Chapter 5, by Gina A. García, encourages us to consider multiple perspectives when exploring HSIs as organizations. This chapter strengthens our understanding of the organizational context of HSIs by examining several organizational theories and analyzing how they shed light on different aspects of HSIs' organizational behavior. Through this exploration, García illustrates the importance of employing several theoretical frameworks to understand the multiple facets of how HSIs enact organizational identity.

Moving more directly to the experiences of critical agents within HSIs, Marcela Cuellar, in Chapter 6, presents findings indicating that, holding background, college experiences, and institutional characteristics constant, Latina/o students in HSIs have better outcomes on academic self-concept and social empowerment than their counterparts at emerging HSIs or non-HSIs. Her research suggests that commonly used outcome measures like graduation rates may not capture the full dimensions of HSI contributions to underserved students and that HSIs perform better than other institutions when we expand our conceptions of meaningful student outcomes related to student success.

In Chapter 7, Leslie D. Gonzales explores how faculty in HSIs develop approaches to research, teaching, and service in ways that are culturally responsive to their communities. Specifically, she argues that HSI faculty have the potential to leverage students' and local communities' "funds of knowledge" (Moll, Amanti, Neff, & González, 1992) to advance postsecondary attainment and to contribute to knowledge creation in unique ways. Similarly, in Chapter 8, Laura J. Cortez explores how faculty and administrators in an HSI located near the U.S.–Mexico border frame the cultural challenges their students face not as deficits, but as untapped assets that they can cultivate. These leaders draw on their community knowledge and familiarity with students' assets to strengthen the institution's capacity to develop culturally relevant responses to the challenges that these students face.

The final chapters, on capacity building and accountability, also suggest that the lenses through which we view HSIs' institutional resources, organizational behavior, and outcomes need to be significantly broadened in scope. In Chapter 9, Noe Ortega, Joanna Frye, Christopher J. Nellum, Aurora Kamimura, and Angela Vidal-Rodríguez examine the financial resources of two-year and four-year HSIs and find significant disparities with those of non-HSIs. For a variety of reasons, HSIs are severely under-resourced relative to other institutions. Ortega and colleagues note that it is difficult for HSIs to meet high expectations on student outcomes when these institutions serve largely low-income, first-generation, and Latina/o students who often require extra academic and financial support. These student characteristics, coupled with limited institutional resources to support students, mean that HSIs' capacity to encourage student persistence and promote other positive outcomes is severely limited in comparison to other institutions in conventional performance funding formulas.

In light of increasing financial constraints in higher education, HSIs may have to draw on alternative resources to foster institutional and student success. In Chapter 10, Sylvia Hurtado, René A. González, and Emily Calderón Galdeano examine organizational learning among HSIs that took part in a unique MSI collaborative designed to encourage institutional capacity-building through a cross-institutional mentoring model. The asset-based approach was based on the primary assumption that models of student success exist in HSIs and that other institutions can learn to adapt similar practices. The authors distill the lessons from this method of collective organizational learning, and this chapter broadens research on organizational learning, using institutional mentoring as a process of bringing together peer institutions to jointly cultivate excellence using their unique institutional qualities and assets.

Given the resource disparities between HSIs and other institutions identified in earlier chapters, Awilda Rodríguez and Emily Calderón Galdeano use propensity score matching in Chapter 11 to compare the graduation rates of HSIs and non-HSIs that have been matched on institutional characteristics other than Hispanic enrollment. They find that accounting for institutional characteristics in effect eliminates the gap in graduation rates between HSIs and non-HSIs. Accordingly, their findings challenge the conventional wisdom that HSIs underperform with reference to other institutions, and reinforce the argument that institutional inputs, including student body composition and financial resources, should be taken into account when measuring HSIs' performance on standard accountability metrics such as graduation rates (Astin, 1985; Núñez, 2014).

Collectively, the chapters in this book lend important insights to critical policy issues. As noted, HSIs serve students that have additional academic and financial needs, and the institutions have fewer institutional resources with which to serve these students. Yet state performance funding formulas typically do not take into account these institutional inputs, and this unfortunately removes critical context for understanding the "underperformance" of public HSIs. With the Obama administration's federal postsecondary ratings system on the horizon for 2015, and the associated proposals to tie funding with institutional performance, the question of how HSIs' institutional performance is evaluated will be even more critical in shaping their access to institutional resources and capacity to serve their students (Núñez, 2014). The empirical research in this book supports the assertion that, for HSIs, notions of institutional performance must be cast in more appropriate and context-specific terms.

Understanding the various organizational contexts of HSIs provides a much more nuanced and textured picture of what it means for an institution to be "Hispanic-Serving." The chapters in this volume suggest that the dichotomy posed in the conventional narrative—that HSIs are either "Hispanic-serving" or "Hispanic-enrolling"—is an artificial one that does not fully reflect the reality of actors' experiences in these institutions. Exploring how faculty and administrators enact the HSI organizational identity in their everyday activities, taking into account HSIs' institutional resources, and examining alternative student outcomes reveals that, while HSIs may struggle to meet conventional student performance outcomes, they may also be supporting students in ways that have not yet been measured.

Scholars, policymakers, and practitioners interested in student and institutional equity and diversity in higher education will find that this book provides unique insights about an understudied group of higher education institutions that serves students from the most diverse racial/ethnic and socioeconomic backgrounds. HSI leaders (both positional and grassroots leaders) and practitioners will find the book useful to gain insights into how to respond to their own institutional contexts and pressures. For instructors in higher education, the book will be useful in a wide range of courses. For example, students exploring the foundations of higher education or issues related to student and institutional diversity in postsecondary settings will find useful insights on diverse topics in these areas. Likewise, students in organizational theory or educational policy will discover new ways of approaching these topics, particularly with respect to understanding broad access institutions, capacity building, and accountability. Most importantly, given the current accountability context and push for higher and multiple levels of performance, policymakers will benefit from a more comprehensive perspective on the contributions and challenges that HSIs face, today and in the future.

This volume is unique in that it simultaneously provides a large-scale overview of HSIs and a more ground level understanding of how actors in HSIs forge organizational identities, build institutional capacity, and develop creative strategies to serve students. Furthermore, this volume provides alternative ways for thinking about how student success is defined in an era of increasing accountability, which has important implications for how the value and contributions of broad access higher education institutions are measured. Using new and innovative data sources to extend research, theory, policy, and practice, the authors of the chapters in this edited volume together paint an especially holistic and nuanced picture of HSIs within the broader landscape of American higher education. More broadly, this book informs scholarship, policy, and practice about how higher education can serve a society that will continue to see substantial demographic transformation. We hope that readers of the volume will be inspired to broaden their ways of understanding HSIs, and to document or conduct additional research about the practices of HSIs, in ways that can be characterized as transformative and inclusive across the teaching, research, and service missions of this important institutional type.

Notes

1 The term Hispanic, originally developed by the Office of Management and Budget to count people of this origin in the U.S. Census, includes people from Mexico, Puerto Rico, Cuba, and Spanish-speaking Caribbean, Central American, and South American countries (Sáenz, 2010). Because the term originated from the U.S. government, some perceive "Hispanic" to be an externally imposed term, and prefer "Latina/o" (which includes both male and female members of this group) because it is more "self-referential" (Oboler, 1995, p. vii). These terms are used interchangeably in this volume to employ the more self-determined connotation of the term Latina/o, while also reflecting the U.S. Census use of the term Hispanic and the federal terminology officially used to designate institutions as "Hispanic-Serving."
2 See Núñez, Hoover, Pickett, Stuart-Carruthers, and Vázquez (2013) for a comprehensive review of studies on Latinas/os in higher education and Hispanic-Serving Institutions.
3 See Calderón Galdeano, Flores, and Moder (2012); Laden (1999); and Santiago (2006) for broader discussions of the agents involved in developing this legislation.
4 National Hispanic University's status has changed since its founding. It became a for-profit institution in 2010 and was no longer eligible to apply for Title V funding. The institution is set to close in 2015.
5 In the absence of this list, two national organizations, HACU and *Excelencia* in Education, have agreed upon a methodology to calculate HSIs, and it is recommended that analysts use this calculation approach. See www.hacu.net and www.edexcelencia.org for more information.

References

Association of American Colleges and Universities. (2014). *Programs: Making excellence inclusive.* Washington, DC: Author. Retrieved from www.aacu.org/compass/inclusive_excellence.cfm.
Astin, A. (1985). *Achieving educational excellence: A critical assessment of priorities and practices in higher education.* San Francisco, CA: Jossey-Bass.
Bastedo, M.N. (2012). Organizing higher education: A manifesto. In M.N. Bastedo (Ed.), *The organization of higher education* (pp. 3–17). Baltimore, MD: Johns Hopkins University Press.
Benítez, M. (1998). Hispanic-Serving Institutions: Challenges and opportunities. In J.P. Merisotis & C.T. O'Brien (Eds.), *Minority-Serving Institutions: Distinct purposes, common goals* (New Directions for Higher Education No. 102, pp. 57–68). San Francisco, CA: Jossey-Bass.
Bensimon, E.M., & Malcom, L. (Eds.). (2012). *Confronting equity issues on campus: Implementing the Equity Scorecard in theory and practice.* Sterling, VA: Stylus.
Birnbaum, R. (1991). Value of different kinds of colleges. In J.L. Bess (Ed.), *Foundations of American higher education: An ASHE Reader* (pp. 111–129). Needham Heights, MA: Simon & Schuster.
Bound, J., Lovenheim, M.F., & Turner, S. (2010). Why have college completion rates declined? An analysis of changing student perception and collegiate resources. *American Economic Journal: Applied Economics, 2*(3), 129–157.
Bowen, H.R. (1977). *Investment in learning: The individual and social value of American higher education.* San Francisco, CA: Jossey-Bass.
Calderón Galdeano, E., Flores, A.R., & Moder, J. (2012). The Hispanic Association of Colleges and Universities and Hispanic-Serving Institutions: Partners in the advancement of Hispanic higher education. *Journal of Latinos and Education, 11*(3), 157–162.

Calderón Galdeano, E., & Santiago, D.A. (2014). *Hispanic-Serving Institutions (HSIs) Fact Sheet: 2012–13.* Washington, DC: *Excelencia* in Education.

Carnevale, A., & Strohl, J. (2013). *Separate and unequal: How higher education reinforces the inter-generational reproduction of White racial privilege.* Washington, DC: Center of Education and the Workforce, Georgetown Public Policy Institute, Georgetown University. Retrieved from http://www9.georgetown.edu/grad/gppi/hpi/cew/pdfs/Separate&Unequal. FR.pdf

Contreras, F.E., Malcom, L.E., & Bensimon, E.M. (2008). Hispanic-Serving Institutions: Closeted identity and the production of equitable outcomes for Latina/o students. In M. Gasman, B. Baez, & C.S.V. Turner (Eds.), *Understanding Minority-Serving Institutions* (pp. 71–90). Albany, NY: State University of New York Press.

Cuellar, M. (2014). The impact of Hispanic-Serving Institutions (HSIs), emerging HSIs, and non-HSIs on Latina/o academic self-concept. *Review of Higher Education, 37*(4), 499–530.

de los Santos, A.G., & Cuamea, K.M. (2010). Challenges facing Hispanic-Serving Institutions in the first decade of the 21st Century. *Journal of Latinos and Education, 9*(2), 190–107.

de los Santos, A.G., & de los Santos, G.E. (2003). Hispanic-serving institutions in the 21st century: Overview, challenges, and opportunities. *Journal of Hispanic Higher Education, 2*(4), 377–391.

Excelencia in Education. (2014). Hispanic-Serving Institutions Center for Policy and Practice (HSI-CP²). Retrieved from http://www.edexcelencia.org/hsi-cp2

Espinosa, L.L., Crandall, J.R., & Tukibayeva, M. (2014). *Rankings, institutional behavior, and college and university choice: Framing the national dialogue on Obama's ratings plan.* Washington, DC: American Council on Education.

Fry, R. (2011). *Hispanic enrollment spikes, narrowing gaps with other groups.* Washington, DC: Pew Hispanic Center.

Gándara, P., & Contreras, F. (2009). *The Latino educational crisis: The consequences of failed social policies.* Cambridge, MA: Harvard University Press.

García, G. (2013). *Challenging the manufactured identity of Hispanic-Serving Institutions: Co-constructing an organizational identity* (Unpublished doctoral dissertation). University of California, Los Angeles, CA.

Goldin, C., & Katz, L.F. (2009). *The race between education and technology.* Cambridge, MA: Belknap Press.

Hamilton, R. (2010, August 19). *Emerging research universities vie for Tier One Status.* Texas Tribune. Retrieved from http://www.texastribune.org/2010/08/19/emerging-research-universities-tier-one-status/

Harmon, N. (2012). *The role of Minority-Serving Institutions in national college completion goals.* Washington, DC: Institute for Higher Education Policy.

Higher Education Act of 1965, 20 U.S.C §§ 1001–1002g (2013).

Higher Education Act of 1965, 20 U.S.C §§ 1103–1103g (2013).

Hispanic Association of Colleges and Universities. (2012). *HACU legislative agenda.* Retrieved from http://www.hacu.net/images/hacu/govrel/2012_Legislative_Agenda.pdf

Hurtado, S. (in press). The transformative paradigm: Principles and challenges. In. A. Alemán, B.P. Pusser, & E. Bensimon (Eds.), *Critical approaches to the study of higher education.* Baltimore, MD: Johns Hopkins University.

Hurtado, S., Álvarez, C.L., Guillermo-Wann, C., Cuellar, M., & Arellano, L. (2012). A model for diverse learning environments: The scholarship on creating and assessing conditions for student success. In J.C. Smart & M.B. Paulsen (Eds.), *Higher education: Handbook of theory and research* (Vol. 27, pp. 41–122). New York, NY: Springer.

Hurtado, S., & Guillermo-Wann, C. (2013). *Diverse learning environments: Assessing and creating conditions for student success. Final report to the Ford Foundation.* Los Angeles, CA: Higher Education Research Institute. Retrieved from http://heri.ucla.edu/dle/Diverse LearningEnvironments.pdf

Kezar, A. (2014). *How colleges change: Understanding, leading and enacting change.* New York, NY: Routledge.

Kirst, M.W., Stevens, M.L., & Proctor, K. (December, 2010). *A report on the conference, "Reform and Innovation in the Changing Ecology of U.S. Higher Education: Inaugural Strategy Session."* Stanford, CA: Stanford University. Retrieved from http://cepa.stanford.edu/ sites/default/files/Research%20Framework%2004–01–11.pdf

Laden, B.V. (1999). Two-year Hispanic-serving colleges. In B.K. Townsend (Ed.), *Two-year colleges for women and minorities: Enabling access to the baccalaureate* (Garland Studies in Higher Education Vol. 16, pp. 151–194). New York, NY: Garland.

Laden, B.V. (2001). Hispanic-Serving Institutions. Myths and realities. *Peabody Journal of Education, 76*(1), 73–92.

Malcom, L., Dowd, A., & Yu, T. (2010). *Tapping HSI-STEM funds to improve Latina and Latino access to STEM professions.* Los Angeles, CA: University of Southern California.

Malcom-Piqueux, L., & Lee, J.M. (2011). *Hispanic-Serving Institutions: Contributions and challenges.* New York, NY: College Board Policy and Advocacy Center. Retrieved from http://advocacy.collegeboard.org/sites/default/files/11b_4853_HSBC_PolicyBrief_ WEB_120110.pdf

Merisotis, J., & McCarthy, K. (2005). Retention and student success at minority-serving institutions. In G.H. Gaither (Ed.), *Minority retention: What works?* (New Directions for Institutional Research No. 125, pp. 45–58). San Francisco, CA: Jossey-Bass.

Mertens, D.M. (2009). *Transformative research and evaluation.* New York, NY: The Guilford Press.

Moll, L.C., Amanti, C., Neff, D., & González, N. (1992). Funds of knowledge for teaching: Using a qualitative approach to connect homes and classrooms. *Theory into Practice, 31*(2), 132–141.

Mulnix, M.W., Bowden, R.G., & López, E.E. (2002). A brief examination of institutional advancement activities at Hispanic-Serving Institutions. *Journal of Hispanic Higher Education, 1*(2), 174–190.

Nora, A., & Crisp, G. (2009). Hispanics and higher education: An overview of research, theory, and practice. In J.C. Smart (Ed.), *Higher education: Handbook of theory and research* (Vol. 24, pp. 317–353). New York, NY: Springer.

Núñez, A.-M. (2014). *Counting what counts for Latinas/os and Hispanic-Serving Institutions: A federal ratings system and postsecondary access, affordability, and success.* Policy brief presented to the President's Advisory Commission on Educational Excellence for Hispanics, New York, NY.

Núñez, A.-M., & Bowers, A.J. (2011). Exploring what leads high school students to enroll in Hispanic-Serving Institutions. A multilevel analysis. *American Educational Research Journal, 48*(6), 1286–1313.

Núñez, A.-M., Crisp, G., & Elizondo, D. (in press). Mapping Hispanic-Serving Institutions: A typology of institutional diversity. *Journal of Higher Education.*

Núñez, A.-M., & Elizondo, D. (2012). *Hispanic-Serving Institutions in the U.S. Mainland and Puerto Rico: Organizational characteristics, institutional financial context, and graduation outcomes* (White paper). San Antonio, TX: Hispanic Association of Colleges and Universities. Retrieved from: http://www.hacu.net/images/hacu/OPAI/

H3ERC/2012_papers/Nuñez%20elizondo%20-%204yr%20hsi%20characteristics%20-%202012.pdf

Núñez, A.-M., Hoover, R., Pickett, K., Stuart-Carruthers, C., & Vázquez, M. (2013). Latinos in higher education: Creating conditions for success. *ASHE monograph 39*(1). San Francisco, CA: Jossey-Bass.

Núñez, A.-M., Murakami, E., & Cuero, K. (2010). Pedagogy for equity: Teaching in a Hispanic-Serving Institution. *Innovative Higher Education, 35*(3), 177–190.

Oakes, R.J., Silver, D., Valladares, S., Terriquez, V., & McDonough, P. (2006). *Removing the roadblocks: Fair college opportunities for all California students.* Los Angeles: UC All Campus Consortium for Research on Diversity and UCLA Institute for Democracy, Education, and Access.

Oboler, L. (1995). *Ethnic labels, Latino lives: Identity and the politics of representation in the United States.* Minneapolis, MN: University of Minnesota Press.

Olivas, M. (1982). Indian, Chicano, and Puerto Rican colleges: Status and issues. *Bilingual Press/Editorial Bilingue, 9*(1), 36–58.

Organisation for Economic Co-operation and Development. (2011). *An overview of growing income inequalities in OECD countries: Main findings.* Paris, France: Author. Retrieved from http://www.oecd.org/els/soc/49499779.pdf

Perna, L.W., Li, C., Walsh, E., & Raible, S. (2010). The status of equity for Hispanics in public higher education in Florida and Texas. *Journal of Hispanic Higher Education, 9*(2), 145–166.

Rendón, L., Dowd, A., & Nora, A. (2012). *Priced out: A close look at postsecondary affordability for Latinos.* Washington, DC: The Higher Education Subcommittee on President Barack Obama's Advisory Commission on Educational Excellence for Hispanics.

Ruiz Alvarado, A. (2014). *Latina/o pathways through college: Characteristics of mobile students and the institutional networks they create* (Unpublished dissertation). University of California, Los Angeles, CA.

Sáenz, R. (2010, December). *Population bulletin update: Latinos in the United States 2010.* Washington, DC: Population Reference Bureau.

Santiago, D.A. (2006). *Inventing Hispanic-Serving Institutions (HSIs): The basics.* Washington, DC: *Excelencia* in Education. Retrieved from http://www.edexcelencia.org/sites/default/files/InventingHSIsFINALRv.pdf

Santiago, D.A. (2007). *Voces (Voices): A profile of today's Latino college students.* Washington, DC: *Excelencia* in Education.

Santiago, D.A., Andrade, S., & Brown, S. (2004). *Latino student success at Hispanic-Serving Institutions (HSIs): Findings from a demonstration project.* Washington, DC: Excelencia in Education. Retrieved from http://www.edexcelencia.org/hsi-cp2/research/latino-student-success-hsi-demonstration-project

Thelin, J. (2013). Success and excess: The contours and character of American higher education since 1960. *Society, 50*, 106–114.

Titus, M. (2006a). The production of bachelor's degrees and financial aspects of state higher education policy: A dynamic analysis. *Journal of Higher Education, 80*(4), 439–468.

Titus, M. (2006b). Understanding the influence of the financial context of institutions on student persistence at four-year colleges and universities. *Journal of Higher Education, 77*(2),

Titus, M.A. (2009). The production of bachelor's degrees and financial aspects of state higher education policy: A dynamic analysis. *Journal of Higher Education, 80*(4), 439–468.

Torres, V., & Zerquera, D. (2012). Hispanic-Serving Institutions: Patterns, predictions, and implication for informing policy discussions. *Journal of Hispanic Higher Education, 11*(3), 259–278.

Toutkoushian, R.K. & Webber, K. (2011). Measuring the research performance of post-secondary institutions. In J.C. Shin, R.K. Toutkoushian, & U. Teichler (Eds.), *University rankings: theoretical basis, methodology and impacts on global higher education* (pp. 123–144). Dordrecht, Netherlands: Springer.

Trow, M. (1970, Winter). Reflections on the transition from elite to mass to universal higher education. *Daedalus 99*, 1–42.

U.S. Census Bureau. (2010). *Population distribution by Hispanic origin*. Retrieved July 24, 2014 from CSPAN_194010.pdf

Valencia, R.R. (2010). *Dismantling contemporary deficit thinking: Educational thought and practice*. New York, NY: Routledge.

Vega, A., & Martínez, R.A. (2012). Latino scorecard for higher Education: A focus on Texas universities. *Journal of Hispanic Higher Education*, 11(1), 41–54.

Villarreal, R.C., & Santiago, D.A. (2012). *From capacity to success: HSIs and Latino student success through Title V*. Washington, DC: *Excelencia* in Education.

Webber, D.A., & Ehrenberg, R.G. (2009). *Do expenditures other than instructional expenditures affect graduation and graduation rates in American higher education?* Ithaca, NY: Cornell Higher Education Research Institute.

PART I

Contextualizing the Culture, Structure, and Identity of Hispanic-Serving Institutions

2

REALIZING THE POTENTIAL OF HISPANIC-SERVING INSTITUTIONS

Multiple Dimensions of Organizational Transformation

Sylvia Hurtado and Adriana Ruiz Alvarado

Unlike Tribal Colleges and Universities (TCUs) and Historically Black Colleges and Universities (HBCUs), which began with the explicit purpose of serving students who have been historically excluded from higher education, the majority of Hispanic-Serving Institutions (HSIs) began as predominantly White institutions and became HSIs because they are located in regions that have experienced significant demographic changes as a result of increases in Hispanic births and immigration. Based on the number of youth in the Latina/o population, we can expect more institutions will become federally designated and plan for "Hispanic-serving" status, necessitating transformations that involve more than simply changes in demographic composition.

The purpose of this chapter is to provide a blueprint for multiple areas that need greater attention as institutions begin to recruit, admit, and ensure the success of Latina/o students—in short, as they become HSIs. Making use of theories of institutional transformation and the Multi-contextual Model for Diverse Learning Environments (MMDLE) (Hurtado, Álvarez, Guillermo-Wann, Cuellar, & Arellano, 2012), we summarize current research on organizational transformation for diversity and propose an agenda for future research on HSIs. In doing so, we seek to identify areas of institutional development that are necessary in order to realize the potential of HSIs in advancing higher education for Latinas/os and other underrepresented groups.

The Potential of HSIs

As a collective, HSIs have the potential to define what it means to be Hispanic-serving in the changing context of an increasingly diverse and global society. They have the potential to span many borders as they draw a local and global Latina/o student population, support faculty research across U.S. and international borders, and create community partnerships to advance the health and economic, social, and political lives of Hispanics in the United States and the Americas. While other colleges and universities may struggle with recruiting and admitting a diverse population, HSIs have already achieved a great deal of compositional diversity at the student level. By all accounts, HSIs can help the nation achieve national education goals, for not only do they educate diverse student bodies, but they are also responsible for more than half of all Hispanic student enrollments and a large share of degree attainments (Calderón Galdeano & Santiago, 2014).

Because most HSIs were not initially intended to serve large numbers of Hispanics, and because their appropriations under Title V require comprehensive five-year plans, most will need to begin to systematically plan for the Hispanic populations they serve—both now and increasingly in the future. Likewise, significant institutional transformation needs to occur, not only to accommodate but also to graduate increasing numbers of Latina/o students (Fry & Taylor, 2013). To date, however, very little has been documented regarding the specific kinds of transcultural changes that will be necessary for these institutions to become truly "Hispanic-serving."

The Process of Becoming "Hispanic-Serving": Multiple Aspects of Institutional Identity and Transformation

Challenges in Understanding HSIs

Perhaps one of the most important questions regarding HSIs is whether these institutions are undergoing considerable transformation in response to changes in their student bodies. There are three primary issues that impede our current knowledge about how institutions enact the true meaning of "Hispanic-serving" in higher education, however. First, there is very little research to draw from that is directly focused on HSIs, and researchers do not always adequately identify HSIs when they are included in studies. Second, the notion of becoming a "Hispanic-serving" institution has evolved in the last 25 years (Laden, 2004; Santiago, 2006), and there is little evidence that institutions have widely adopted a broad agenda focused on serving Hispanic students. A third issue is that the institutions themselves are relatively silent about what it means to become "Hispanic-serving." We focus here on the two latter issues.

Contreras, Malcom, and Bensimon (2008) stated that the "Hispanic-serving" designation is a "manufactured identity" that shifts with enrollment changes, and they questioned the extent to which institutions actually embrace this identity. Laden (2000) noted a great deal of variability among HSIs with respect to whether they identified themselves as such internally (as administrators were more aware of an HSI identity than faculty within the same institution) or externally, through campus publications and public relations materials. Contreras et al. (2008) reviewed the websites of a small percentage of Title V-eligible HSIs to determine whether this institutional identity was reflected in mission statements and other public statements. Although most mentioned diversity in recognition of the student bodies they served, the statements lacked specific reference to serving Hispanics, and a Latina/o agenda was not discernable.

In contrast, in a comprehensive case study of the organizational identity of an HSI, García (2013) found evidence to contest the "manufactured identity" hypothesis. Instead, faculty and staff indicated their core organizational values included a commitment to a regional focus, to the community, and to access and diversity. While the Hispanic-serving identity was latent in people's minds, it was evident in organizational structures reflective of a Latina/o-serving mission, including culturally relevant curricula, pedagogy, and student support services. Moreover, several organizational processes embraced the Latina/o-serving mission, including print and social media, advocacy in supporting Latina/o students, and applications for federal grants that reinforced the critical process and construction of the HSI identity. As a result of García's study, we begin to see how shared values, institutional structures, and organizational processes can change or clash as institutions enact a Hispanic-serving mission.

Regarding the relative silence on the part of HSIs about their transitions, it is possible that institutions in states with growing Latina/o populations may fear that the costs of touting HSI status as an institutional strength outweigh the benefits, as they face challenges such as an anti-affirmative action climate. This relative silence could also indicate that the concept is still new to institutions, or that we simply lack studies that document organizational change as it applies to HSIs. For example, we lack the evidence to understand if transformations are intentional; it is possible that conversion to HSI status has been accidental or evolutionary, rather than strategic and planned.

When enrollment of Black students in higher education was increasing, Peterson et al. (1978) employed case studies and found that institutions that were adaptive and responsive to the enrollment changes were all "marked by supportive external conditions, internal patterns supporting the change, and strong leadership—a combination not found in evolutionary institutions" (p. 301), which are slow and reactive. In the case of proactive change, subsequent case studies on diversification of the faculty (Hyer, 1985) and institutional transformation associated with diversity suggest a similar pattern of external conditions, internal support, and strong leadership at the top as well as the grassroots level (Eckel & Kezar, 2003; Kezar, 2014).

Due to the issues described in this section, the combination of these elements has not been fully explored when it comes to transformation at HSIs. Recent work, however, has documented the long-term struggles of some grassroots leaders as they have advocated for change in support of Latina/o student success, suggesting supportive conditions are not always present (García, 2013; Kezar & Lester, 2011). In spite of these challenges, we can begin to apply theory to understand the potential for organizational change that focuses on how these institutions are serving Hispanic students. Specifically, as we describe in the subsections that follow, we can explore the various ways that an organizational identity is perceived and influenced, and what this may mean for the transformation of HSIs.

The Nature of Institutional Identity

HSIs may have what theorists have called a differentiated organizational identity (Corley, 2004). This occurs when conceptions of "who we are" and sense of purpose in an organization vary according to an individual's position within the organizational hierarchy, when the organizational identity is flexible, and when multiple identities—some of which may be in conflict—co-exist, requiring leaders to manage identity differentiation in the face of turbulent and changing external environments.

Figure 2.1 illustrates the nature of organizational identity derived from a case study of an innovating organization undergoing considerable change (Corley, 2004). This framework indicates that leaders at the top of the hierarchy attempt to strategically redefine the purpose and mission of the organization in order to

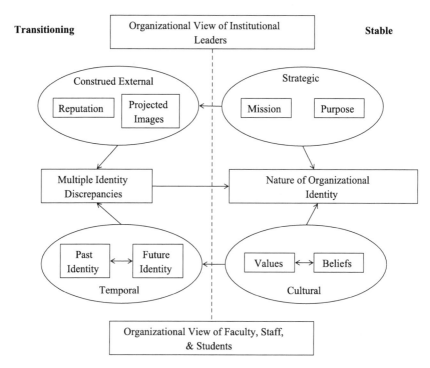

FIGURE 2.1 Differentiated Nature of Organizational Identity (adapted from Corley, 2004)

manage the organizational identity, while those at the bottom view the organizational identity as shaped by the culture of the organization, constituting deeply embedded values and beliefs. This aptly describes academic organizations like HSIs, where faculty are often in the organization for many more years than institutional leaders. Faculty and staff, who work directly with students, may hold different perspectives on the organization's identity. In fact, studies have shown that student peers and practitioners who work directly with students on a diverse campus are more critical of the institution-wide commitment to diversity and skeptical of the commitment of top-level administrators, even though more than 80% of chief academic officers at four-year institutions report that diversity is part of their mission (Hurtado, 1992; Rowley, Hurtado, & Ponjuan, 2002).

To shed light on the process of transformation in higher education, Kezar and Eckel (2005) interviewed 30 college presidents (including some at HSIs) engaged in diversity changes with a significant emphasis on the success of underrepresented students. They found that effective strategies typically included dialogue and discussion. That is, it was not enough simply to declare a new mission; it was important to engage the entire campus in the adoption of new values that included a focus on student success and commitment to diversity. In this regard, the college presidents recognized the need to shape institutional culture in order to begin to make "these values deeply a part of people's consciousness and behavior." They reinforced the values through "the strategic plan, rewarding people for meeting objectives related to diversity, holding people accountable, and providing them with necessary support and resources" (Kezar & Eckel, 2005, p. 29).

Importantly, the basis of the identity change is often articulated by leaders in new language, while faculty, staff, and students look for new meanings that are based in managerial and institution-wide actions (Corley, 2004; Gonzales & Pacheco, 2012). Thus, while it is important for top administrators to articulate new ways of thinking about diversity and institutional priorities, it is just as important to make sure these translate into actions in the daily work of individuals across the institution. Therefore it is arguably not surprising that other effective strategies in Kezar and Eckel's (2005) study included hiring new people and altering the curriculum, which involved more long-term structural change—a topic we further discuss in a later section regarding evidence of transformation versus temporary change.

Institutional Identity of HSIs

So far we have described various aspects of organizational identity in general. But what values are being encouraged and reinforced in HSIs? While these institutions have attempted to form an alliance based on the common goal of educating Latinas/os (Hispanic Association of Colleges and Universities [HACU], 2012), we have to acknowledge that there exist multiple institutional identities *across* and *within* these institutions that determine differences in functions, goals, purposes, and activities. Indeed, HSIs have much more variety in institutional type and function compared to other Minority-Serving Institutions (MSIs). For example, the majority of TCUs are community colleges, and the majority of HBCUs are four-year colleges or universities. In contrast, approximately 53% of HSIs are two-year institutions, 48% offer bachelor's degrees, 38% offer master's degrees, and 18% offer doctoral degrees (Calderón Galdeano & Santiago, 2014). This suggests that while they share service to the Hispanic population, they are also attentive to all the issues and priorities they face within their institutional peer groups. Forging a common HSI identity across institutions may be a much greater challenge than initially anticipated. Regardless, it is important to document how each institutional type is changing in response to increased Latina/o enrollments.

The view within changing organizations is also complex, as members find themselves facing identity discrepancies. For example, community colleges—which comprise more than half of all HSIs—have been referred to as "contradictory colleges" because they sometimes operate in ways that contradict their claims for economic and social mobility (Dougherty, 1994). As Levin (2001) noted, this label has implications for incompatible practices that simultaneously focus on open access and responsiveness to the marketplace (e.g., providing training for workers to build the local economy). In short, a community college possesses multiple identities based on views of what it seems to be, what it ought to be, and what it actually does (Levin, 2001). Leaders must integrate, compartmentalize, aggregate, or delete former institutional identities to incorporate new ones (Corley, 2004). Multiple institutional identities are inevitable because, for a community college, reverting to a single identity would be disastrous and result in an inferior institution (Levin, 2001). These studies highlight the fact that multiple identities exist within a single institutional type whose primary mission is teaching, and it may well be that four-year institutions that incorporate teaching, research, and service missions also possess at least equally complex multiple institutional identities—and colleges and universities that find themselves serving increasingly large Latina/o student populations must now also integrate a Hispanic-serving mission.

These identity discrepancies bring us back to the hierarchy displayed in Figure 2.1. Institutional leaders are arguably most concerned with the reputation of the organization, and they attempt to manage discrepancies in a construed external image (Corley, 2004) that may emerge from media accounts, external assessments of the organization, or interactions with the community in which the organization is located. At the bottom of the hierarchy, among faculty, staff, and students, identity discrepancies are viewed as temporal, depending on changes in the central administration and reflecting a past and a future identity for an institution in transition. Difficulty arises when organizational members view identity discrepancies as conflicting, rather than as part of a multiple institutional identity. For example, many institutions have embarked on planning, spending, and media releases to redefine institutional excellence using a resource and reputation model, basing their excellence on the test scores of entering students rather than on student talent development (Astin & antonio, 2012; Bastedo & Bowman, 2010). Members of these institutions may hold the view that the values of diversity and excellence can co-exist, but are in conflict (Richardson & Skinner, 1991), even though today there are more institutions achieving both as they adopt the concept of inclusive excellence (Association of American Colleges and Universities, 2012).

Because HSIs educate a large number of first-generation college students and students from low-income families (Hurtado, 2003), they are well positioned for building reputations based on student talent development (Cuellar, 2014). But this approach to institutional excellence will require greater attention to assessment of Latina/o students along dimensions beyond raw numbers of degrees and graduation rates. Contreras et al. (2008), for example, indicated that the HSIs in their study did extremely well in attracting and enrolling Latina/o students relative to the population of high school graduates; with a few exceptions, however, Latinas/os were not achieving degrees relative to their representation in the undergraduate enrollment at both two-year and four-year institutions. Most outsiders might assume that HSIs do a much better job of graduating Latinas/os, but insiders are well aware of the retention problems they face (Maestas, Vaquera, & Muñoz Zehr, 2007).

Bringing greater awareness to issues and institutional intentions, acknowledging the past and articulating plans for the future, and focusing on student success are all viable strategies for dealing with discrepant institutional identities. Institutional leaders must manage multiple institutional identities during the process of transformation, however, so that both outsiders and insiders may begin to view the institution as on the move toward becoming truly Hispanic-serving.

Evidence of Institutional Transformation

Beyond knowing what it takes for HSIs to become truly Hispanic-serving—as we have described in the preceding section—it is equally important that we understand what types of changes offer evidence that this transformation has begun. Transformational change in institutions has been defined as the type that affects the institutional culture; is deep, pervasive, and intentional; and occurs over time (Eckel & Kezar, 2003; Kezar, 2014). Though an institution will not develop a completely new culture (as it shares norms with peer institutions), deep change reflects a shift in values and assumptions that underlie daily operations. Eckel and Kezar (2003) distinguished transformation from other types of change, including *adjustments* that continually happen in academia that are neither pervasive nor deep (e.g., the introduction of a diversity course, versus making it a requirement), *isolated change* that may be deep but limited to one unit or program area (e.g., a Hispanic mother/daughter outreach program), or *far reaching change* that affects many across the institution but lacks depth (e.g., use of an affirmative action statement on all hiring and recruitment materials). Institutional responses to changing student enrollments that are proactive and responsive, instead of reactive and resistant, are likely to be characteristic of transformational change (Peterson et al., 1978).

According to Smith (1995), diverse representation at the student level may not necessarily translate to large-scale organizational transformation relative to diversity in other areas of higher education institutions. Rather, it is changes in the structure of the institution that are likely to reflect institutional transformation, including changes to the curriculum, pedagogies, and delivery methods; student learning and assessment practices; alignment of institutional policies with newly articulated goals and values; alignment of budgets with new priorities and values; and the creation of new departments, institutional structures (e.g., a student learning center), and decision-making structures (Eckel & Kezar, 2003). That said, however, compositional diversity—or the representation of diverse people throughout the institution—is key for improving the climate and culture because it influences perceptions about diversity, behaviors, intergroup relations, and interaction patterns across the institution (Hurtado, Milem, Clayton-Pederson, & Allen, 1999). It is important to understand what takes place within institutions to effect improved outcomes for Latinas/os because the result is greater social equity, democratic pluralism, economic stability, and vitality of the nation.

A Model for Diverse Learning Environments: Placing Latina/o Student Identity at the Center

If HSIs adopted the priority of placing Latina/o students' identities at the center, what would they look like? We offer the potential of an adapted Multi-contextual Model for Diverse Learning Environments (MMDLE) (Hurtado, Álvarez et al., 2012) for Latina/o student identity as a lens to understand HSIs' climate, practices, goals for student outcomes, and transformation of the larger society (see Figure 2.2). We then offer a portrait of faculty, staff, and students on key variables in this model in order to illuminate the current status of HSIs with respect to the MMDLE for Latinas/os.

As described in Figure 2.2, multiple policy and sociohistorical contexts inform and create pressures on institutions that inform the climate for teaching and learning. Demographic changes produce institutional changes that result in an HSI designation, but larger societal changes also collide with changing policy and sociohistorical contexts—particularly socioeconomic issues faced by these largely public institutions in key states. For example, institutional budget cuts as a result of reduced state resources have been a top area of stress among more than 83% of faculty at public colleges and universities in the last few years (Hurtado, Eagan, Pryor, Whang, & Tran, 2012). Santos and Sáenz (2014) described the trends coinciding with changing Latina/o demographics, including threats of reduced access and financial aid policy changes, as a "perfect storm." Add to this mix increased accountability demands for degree attainment rates and institutional effectiveness. In this context, HSIs will come under greater scrutiny, but they have the fewest resources to work with their students, who are often first-generation and low-income—a combination that currently leads to relatively low degree

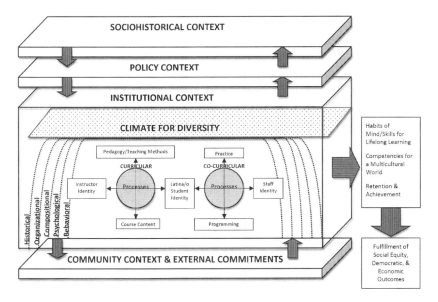

FIGURE 2.2   Multi-contextual Model for Diverse Learning Environments for Latina/o Students (adapted from Hurtado, Álvarez et al., 2012)

attainments (Núñez & Elizondo, Chapter 4, this volume; Ortega et al., Chapter 9, this volume; Rodríguez & Calderón Galdeano, 2014; Titus, 2006).

It is important to note that both the institution and the student also have links with the local, external community, as a relatively high percentage of Latinas/os elect to attend college close to home. More specifically, research has found that Latinas/os are more likely to choose to attend HSIs or emerging HSIs over non-HSIs if being close to home is an important consideration in their college choice process (Cuellar, 2012; Núñez & Bowers, 2011). This selection pattern has resulted in enrollment changes at institutions in areas with growing Latina/o populations. Finances also play an important role, as Latina/o students are more likely to attend HSIs if they prioritize costs in choosing a college (Santiago, 2007a). Likewise, Latina/o freshmen enrolling in HSIs are less likely than Latina/o students enrolling at non-HSIs to rely on parents for financial support or on institutional grants (Cuellar, 2012), suggesting students at these colleges choose the lowest cost option where living at home and working nearby is an option.

There are also important factors that are internal to the institution—specifically, those related to student encounters with faculty and staff in curricular and co-curricular contexts. The MMDLE for Latinas/os posits that various dimensions at the organizational level (including historical legacies; composition of faculty, staff, and students; and organizational structure) and the individual level (psychological and behavioral) affect the overall campus climate for diversity. For example, high achieving Latina/o students have reported lower levels of subtle and overt forms of discrimination at institutions with higher Hispanic enrollments (Hurtado, 1994). Thus, various aspects of the climate, in turn, affect several processes, such as validation in the classroom, community building in the form of sense of belonging to the campus community, and socialization within curricular and co-curricular contexts. With the identity of the student at the center of practice, it is important to understand the special circumstances and unique cultural attributes of Latina/o students at HSIs.

Mapping HSIs to the Adapted MMDLE Model

In order to shed light on the status of HSIs in the context of elements included in the adapted MMDLE model, we drew from recent data from the National Center for Education Statistics and the Higher Education Research Institute. We first compare HSIs to all U.S. colleges and universities on key variables, and then look more broadly at the extant literature to more fully explain some of the trends revealed in this comparison.

Student, Faculty, and Staff Identity

Table 2.1 begins to describe the attributes and identities of the faculty, staff, and students who are at the center of the model where interaction takes place. At the core of the model is Latina/o student identity. Hispanic students are indeed at the center of HSIs, which have an average Hispanic undergraduate FTE (full-time equivalent) of 53.4%. This figure is in stark contrast to the 7.1% Hispanic FTE across all higher education institutions. Another important aspect of student identity in the model is that more than a quarter of students at HSIs (26.9%) are age 25 or older. This supports prior research suggesting that HSIs, especially in the two-year sector, are disproportionately serving students who "do not fit the profile of a traditional college student" (Núñez, Sparks, & Hernández, 2011, p. 34). Further demonstrating this point, an NCES report on MSIs highlighted that 41% of Latinas/os at HSIs work full-time while enrolled, compared to 30% at non-MSIs. Moreover, 43.6% of Latinas/os at four-year public HSIs are low-income, compared to 35.9% of Latinas/os at all higher education institutions (Li & Carroll, 2007). Núñez et al. (2011) also found that Latina/o students who attend HSIs have a higher number of factors that put them at risk for dropping out of college (e.g., delayed enrollment, having dependents) than those attending non-HSIs.

In terms of instructor and staff identities, Latina/o faculty, administrative/managerial, and other professional staff are all alarmingly underrepresented at the national level, especially considering that there were 177 emerging HSIs with Hispanic enrollment between 15% and 24.9% in the year these data were collected (Santiago, 2007b), and the number has only continued to increase. At HSIs in 2006–2007, 31.1% of faculty, 36.9% of administrators/managers, and 43.4% of other professional staff were Latina/o. Though these figures are higher than

TABLE 2.1 *HSI Data Mapped to Adapted Multi-contextual Model for Diverse Learning Environments*

MMDLE Segment	All HSIs (n = 265)	All Institutions (N = 3,293)
Student Identity		
Hispanic Student	53.4%	7.1%
Female Student	60.6%	56.0%
Age 25 or older	26.9%	21.2%
Instructor Identity		
Hispanic Faculty	31.3%	3.1%
Female Faculty	50.3%	46.3%
Non-Tenured Faculty	36.6%	46.5%
Staff Identity		
Hispanics in Executive/Administration and Managerial Positions	36.9%	3.4%
Hispanics in Other Professional Staff Positions	43.4%	4.5%
*Pedagogy/Teaching Methods of Faculty**		
Type of Instruction Included in All Courses:		
Class Discussions	67.2%	64.7%
Group Projects	20.0%	15.7%
Reflective Writing/Journaling	15.9%	9.8%
Course Content		
Type of Content Included in All Courses:		
Community Service as Part of Coursework	4.5%	2.6%
Student-Selected Topics	12.3%	6.8%
Faculty Conduct Research Focused on Racial/Ethnic Minorities	23.1%	20.6%
*Community Context and External Commitments**		
Faculty Collaborate with Local Community in Research/Teaching	45.8%	46.2%

Sources: 2006–2007 Integrated Postsecondary Education Data System (IPEDS) database and 2007 HERI Faculty Survey (indicated with *)
Note: All figures based on FTE counts. HSI list based on institutions included in U.S. Department of Education (2007) and Santiago (2008), selected to match available data on the highest number of HSIs in the HERI Faculty Survey data.

the national average, many still argue that they are not high enough, given the Hispanic-serving identity these institutions have acquired (de los Santos & Vega, 2008; Haro & Lara, 2003). For example, in a qualitative study of eight HSIs, both students and administrators expressed the importance of having staff who reflect the demographics of the student body in order to aid with cultural challenges (Dayton, González-Vásquez, Martínez, & Plum, 2004). Yet, in 2006, only 22 states had at least one institution with a Latina/o chancellor or president, and 94% of those leaders were concentrated at community colleges in 10 states (de los Santos & Vega, 2008).

According to Haro and Lara (2003), more progress has been made in Latina/o appointments to senior administrative positions in student affairs and middle management, but very little progress has been made in the area of academic administration—particularly in four-year research institutions. Using the HACU membership list for institutions in the continental United States, de los Santos and Vega (2008) found that Hispanic presidents led approximately one-third of HSIs, with the majority of increases on this measure in the five-year period captured occurring at two-year institutions. This imbalance is primarily influenced by the limited availability of tenured Latina/o faculty who may be eligible for positions as deans, provosts, and presidents. Most Latina/o faculty are concentrated in public institutions, and the majority are in untenured positions, either as assistant professors or as lecturers and instructors (Ibarra, 2003).

These findings suggest that the leadership and decision-making bodies in postsecondary administration are still predominantly White, raising questions regarding institutional responsiveness to the rapidly changing student population. Because faculty with adequate support may be employed for up to 30 years at a single institution, diversification at all ranks is the single most important long-term structural change in institutional transformation; it is the most effective way to diversify the curriculum, broaden research foci, and increase connections with minority communities (antonio, 2002; Hurtado, 2001) as well as ensure pathways to future academic leadership. Moreover, presidents who brought about significant diversity change in institutions resoundingly agreed that hiring faculty of color was the most important strategy for ensuring the success of students of color (Kezar & Eckel, 2005).

Changes in the structure of the institution must be accompanied by evidence of change in normative attitudes, interactions, and beliefs of members of the organization (Eckel & Kezar, 2003). Evidence of culture change and institutional transformation were found in new patterns of interactions across units, students, and faculty; new language and shared concepts; types of conversations and inclusiveness; the abandonment of old arguments; and new relationships with a variety of stakeholders (Eckel & Kezar, 2003). Although we may be able to document structural changes within HSIs using national data, extensive case studies in the future will continue to provide insight into these elements of culture and the changes in institutional values, structures, and processes that embrace a Hispanic-serving mission (García, 2013).

Instructors' Pedagogy, Content, and Commitments

With regard to the curricular sphere of the MMDLE model, Table 2.1 shows that instructors at HSIs are slightly more likely to incorporate class discussions, group projects, and reflective writing/journaling into all of their courses (2.5%, 4.3%, and 6.1% difference, respectively)—pedagogies that have all been tied to social justice outcomes (Mayhew & Fernández, 2007), communication skills (Colbeck, Campbell, & Bjorklund, 2000), and critical thinking skills (Cooper, 1998). Additionally, these teaching methods reflect a student-centered pedagogy, which research suggests leads to higher levels of student engagement (Umbach & Wawrzynski, 2005). It is important to note that although the percentage of faculty who incorporated these practices into all of their courses was higher at HSIs, there is still room for improvement, since fewer than a quarter of instructors use group projects (20%) or reflective writing (15.9%) in every course.

The content segment of the model reflects that instructors at HSIs are also more likely to provide opportunities for students to engage in community service and to allow them to participate in choosing course topics (1.9% and 5.5% difference, respectively). A slightly larger percentage of faculty at HSIs than at non-HSIs reported conducting research focused on racial or ethnic minorities. The 2.5% difference between the two groups might appear small, but it is notable, given that HSIs are largely institutions that focus on teaching rather than research. A final segment of the model worth noting is community contexts and external commitments, which we discussed at the student level in the previous section. At the instructor level, just under half of all faculty at HSIs (45.8%) and all institutions (46.2%) collaborate with the local community in research and teaching.

Student Outcomes That Result in Societal Transformation

Although there is developing research on a broad set of outcomes for HSIs (see Cuellar, Chapter 6, this volume), here we focus on the three areas in the MMDLE (Figure 2.2): habits of mind for lifelong learning, competencies for a multicultural world, and retention and achievement—all of which lead to improved equity, democratic, and economic outcomes (Hurtado, Álvarez et al., 2012).

As college presidents have acknowledged, in the current accountability context, the success of Latinas/os now determines the success of institutions (Santiago, 2009), but much work has yet to be done to understand how Latina/o college students acquire the skills to become lifelong learners. We do know that along with increased skills comes academic self-confidence in one's writing, mathematics, and general academic ability. Comparing Latinas/os at HSIs with those at emerging HSIs and non-HSIs, Cuellar's (2014) longitudinal study controlled for factors of ability, preparation, and experience, and found increased student academic self-concept at HSIs. This suggests that a great deal of talent development is occurring, at least to the extent that there are improvements in academic self-concept. Indeed, transformative practices exist at HSIs—the Fast Start Program at the Community College of Denver, for example, accelerates students through remedial curricula so that they move more quickly toward credit earning classes and completion (Bragg, Baker, & Puryear, 2010). More research is needed, however, to understand the adaptability and diffusion of innovations in creating self-directed learners and moving students through the curriculum at HSIs to enhance a sense of accomplishment.

Another essential outcome included in the MMDLE is preparation of students for citizenship in a multicultural and global world. For example, increasing students' values toward and commitment to change is important, and we know that diversity on campus plays an important role in advancing many dimensions of students' civic capacities during college (Hurtado, Álvarez et al., 2012: Hurtado, Ruiz, & Whang, 2012). Research in this area specifically related to HSIs is limited. One study found that, by the end of their college years, Latina/o students at HSIs, emerging HSIs, and non-HSIs were relatively similar in their commitment to social agency and change, despite the fact that Latina/o students at non-HSIs began higher on this scale (Cuellar, 2012). This suggests that Latinas/os at HSIs and emerging HSIs experience greater increases in values associated with being agents of social change. But again, replication of these findings is necessary with a broader range of competencies for citizenship in a multicultural world in order to verify the unique role that HSIs play in these outcomes.

Lastly, we address a key accountability outcome—retention and degree attainment rates. Two recent studies using national data have confirmed that, when all other factors are controlled, a more diverse campus results in increased six-year degree attainments for Latina/o students (Arellano, 2011) and students of varying income backgrounds (Franke, 2012). However, Malcom (2010) found that the story of accountability outcomes at HSIs is more complex. Focusing specifically on four-year public institutions in 10 states, she found that HSIs with less than 33% Hispanic enrollment graduated Latinas/os at the highest rates, but they also had a relatively large gap in graduation rates between Latina/o and White students. In contrast, HSIs with a Hispanic enrollment of 33% or higher had the lowest six-year graduation rates for Latinas/os, but they also had the smallest gaps in graduation rates between Latinas/os and Whites. Identifying institutions that are doing better than expected with the first-generation, underrepresented minority, and low-income students they enroll may be a better strategy, particularly given the current emphasis on raising graduation rates (Hurtado, Ruiz Alvarado, Bates, Ramírez, & Stewart, 2014). To further complicate accountability, Rodríguez and Calderón Galdeano (Chapter 11, this volume) showed that relatively few institutions can serve as direct comparisons to HSIs, and that HSIs are doing better than expected once controls for selecting an HSI are accounted for in models predicting completion rates. These complexities demonstrate that HSIs across the spectrum are making strides, but more research on talent development and best practices is needed to bridge the gap between demonstrating commitment to the Hispanic-serving designation and achieving benchmarks along the path toward degree attainment.

Planning for Change: Institutional Awareness and Action

Aspiration for transformative change that is deep and pervasive sets a high bar for institutions seeking to become truly "Hispanic-serving," especially when the majority of these institutions may actually be at different stages of multicultural awareness. These stages have been described as monocultural, nondiscriminatory, and multicultural (Stewart, 1991; Foster, Jackson, Cross, Jackson, & Hardiman, 1988; Richardson & Skinner, 1991). Hurtado and Dey (1997) suggested that these different stages of institutional multicultural awareness are linked with planning, budgeting, and evaluation processes within institutions. Within a monocultural institution, for example, there is a lack of recognition on the part of institutional actors concerning the need to serve new populations of students, and a lack of recognition that the needs of Hispanic students might be different than the needs of other students. Therefore, no special funding is directed at initiatives for these students, nor is evaluation systematically conducted to determine if they have distinct needs.

In the nondiscriminatory stage, there is limited recognition about the need to serve new populations. Planning includes top-down directives and temporary committee structures, budgeting for diversity initiatives that rely on special funding sources rather than reallocation of institutional resources, and evaluation on an ad hoc basis. The orientation is toward making relatively minor adjustments to existing structures and policies as opposed to fundamentally rethinking institutional processes relative to diversity created by increases in Latina/o enrollment. In contrast, in the multicultural stage of awareness, institutions have achieved consensus about the need to serve new populations, and participants throughout the institution see this as a goal, as opposed to something imposed by leaders. There is broad-based participation in diversity planning and investment in the achievement of diversity goals, which become aspects of many operating units on campus, with coordinated oversight at the highest levels of institutional governance. While these models were developed from case studies (Richardson & Skinner, 1991; Stewart, 1991), they are largely hypothetical, because we currently do not know the extent to which HSIs are at various stages of multicultural awareness, nor do we understand how they may implement budget and planning processes to coincide with each stage. Nevertheless, they offer a useful lens for beginning to explore the transformation of institutions to HSI status.

Holland (1999) stated that institutions do not experience transformation uniformly; different units and levels of the organization may be at different stages and move at different paces. She offered a stage process that reflects the idea of "change as an act of scholarship" and suggests a role for administrators in defining key organizational challenges, a role for faculty in developing informed responses and recommendations, and partnerships with like-minded organizations at the regional and national levels. The stages involve *self-assessment* (of an institution's history, culture, assets, and limitations) and the *creation of a distinctive mission* to guide changing priorities, develop broad consensus, and measure organizational performance. In this latter stage, the "Hispanic-serving" institutional identity can be further developed. Then, the *restructuring* stage and subsequent stages require building organizational capacities and realignment of allocations to reflect the mission; building *networks* to promote shared learning; *curricular reform*; and *creating an infrastructure* for new strategies and initiatives. Holland encouraged *redefining scholarship* as one stage in the transformation process, as faculty roles and rewards determine what the institution values. The final stage, *sustaining change*, shifts the organizational culture to match the mission, and ultimately establishes participation in continuous self-assessment (the first stage of the change process).

To initiate self-assessment, the Diversity Scorecard and subsequent Equity Scorecard projects serve as a model for institutional change that begins with developing a deeper awareness within institutions about the magnitude of inequities for underrepresented students—an awareness that can compel campus teams to set goals and develop plans of action to address these inequities (Bensimon, 2004; Bensimon & Malcom, 2012). Each Scorecard addresses equity in educational outcomes in several areas. Examples include the following: (1) *access* to an institution's programs and resources; (2) *retention rates* by academic program, *completion* of basic skill courses, and *degree attainments*; (3) *institutional receptivity* in the form of structural diversity at all levels of the campus; and (4) *excellence* in terms of the racial/ethnic representation of students in courses or majors that lead to advanced study, high levels of student achievement, and the pool of students eligible for graduate study. Approximately eight HSIs have been involved in the Equity Scorecard project to examine the level of equity among their student body, faculty, staff, and administrators. An evidence team on each campus is responsible for selecting the indicators they wish to focus on, analyzing the results, and sharing the results with the president and other decision makers. This evidence-based approach has engaged campus groups in collaborative inquiry and discussions about the state of equity on their campuses and has increased levels of individual commitment to address it.

While the Scorecard projects were designed to encourage institutional change, the related Academic Equity Indicators have also been used across institutions in California to advance policy and provide a framework for accountability focused on racial/ethnic equity of outcomes (Bensimon, Hao, & Bustillos, 2003; USC California Policy Institute, 2005). Findings indicate that Latina/o faculty are severely underrepresented relative to the student enrollment in both the California Community Colleges and on University of California (UC) campuses (the Receptivity Indicator). Latina/o and African American students enroll at lower rates (the Access Indicator) and receive proportionately fewer degrees from UC and California State University (CSU) schools (the Retention Indicator) compared with other racial/ethnic groups and relative to the population of high school graduates and their representation in the state. Contreras et al.'s (2008) subsequent use of

Academic Equity Indicators at 10 HSIs demonstrates that Latina/o students are still not achieving equity in specific majors and degree attainments that result in high-paying/high-skilled jobs relative to their representation in the undergraduate population. These results suggest that the Academic Equity Indicators are one method by which HSIs can monitor their own progress—or researchers can monitor their progress as a group—in order to increase their potential for advancing Latina/o postsecondary success.

Conclusion: Next Steps in Research on HSIs

The goal of this chapter was to stimulate research about what constitutes a "Hispanic-serving" institution, and to move institutions from rhetoric to action in realizing their potential for advancing the education and well-being of a growing Latina/o population. This initial review of the existing literature on "Hispanic-serving" as a distinct institutional identity within higher education revealed large gaps in our knowledge base about how HSIs operate and how they are advancing Hispanic higher education. This is not to say that these institutions are not innovating or embracing their Hispanic-serving role. We simply do not have enough information regarding their distinctiveness as organizations outside of student enrollments. What is certain, however, is that more institutions now find themselves with larger numbers of Latina/o students on campus, and that some degree of institutional change has and will continue to occur. The question that looms is whether this has resulted in minor adjustments that will leave the larger academic culture untouched, or whether institutional responses are indicative of more broad-based transformations that give significant meaning to the "Hispanic-serving" designation.

Several areas may be important for advancing our knowledge about the role HSIs play in American higher education. In general, we need more documentation of the initiatives unique to these institutions, evidence of how these institutions are making a difference in terms of student talent development, and evidence of a culture change that supports the common goal of advancing the education of Hispanics. For example, a collaborative of MSIs funded by the Walmart Foundation was designed to help innovating HSIs work with other HSIs with a strong desire to improve degree attainment rates (see Hurtado, González, & Calderón Galdeano, Chapter 10, this volume). A wide variety of practices and long-term strategies were shared among the campuses, and although the effects may not be known for some time, HSIs need to begin to document practices in relation to student outcomes. Evaluation reports are also needed to spur further development of evidence-based practices that become part of the daily work of faculty and staff. Large-scale databases cannot capture these practices in detail, but they are useful for monitoring changes in student development related to the three key outcomes described in the MMDLE (see Figure 2.2). On a national level, several additional recommendations are offered:

1. **Obtain greater consistency across studies and identify HSIs in research reports.** A general agreement among the research community to obtain consistent reports from federal data on HSIs should be established. At minimum, researchers using similar data sets should provide adequate detail in their reports to understand how HSIs and their students are reflected in their studies. Moreover, at one point, U.S. Department of Education grants indicated the need to include MSIs in funded studies, but not all published studies identify HSIs specifically. Wherever possible, HSIs should engage in partnership with researchers to adequately account for aspects of institutional transformation and to document their contributions to Latina/o student success.

2. **Evaluate the institutional impact of Title V.** Under current Title V provisions, grants are awarded for a five-year period, after which the institution must wait two years before re-applying for a new grant. According to recent studies of institutional transformation involving the success of diverse students, most institutional change takes longer than five years to effectively implement and evaluate (Eckel & Kezar, 2003; Kezar & Eckel, 2005). This suggests that Title V may be encouraging short-term initiatives that can not bring about broad institutional transformation among institutions and programs, and therefore this policy should be reconsidered. Studies of Title V institutions may also provide insight into the use of these funds for distinctive programs, a potentially fruitful area of research for advancing institutional practice.

3. **Study the impact of Hispanic enrollment and institutional change.** To date there is no comprehensive study of the impact of Hispanic enrollment in creating institutional change in the same way that Peterson et al. (1978) monitored changes across postsecondary institutions in response to Black student enrollment increases. Various organizational theory frameworks and general principles derived from case study research on institutional change can be helpful in determining the ways that HSIs (and individuals within them) respond to changes in diverse student enrollments and other aspects of their external environments. Transformation in institutional culture (values and beliefs), organizational structure in terms of policies and curriculum, and processes that reflect inclusive excellence are best analyzed in comprehensive case studies on how institutions integrate a Hispanic-serving identity.

HSIs play a significant role in educating a growing Latina/o population and serving local communities with partnerships and research. There is a growing body of research on these institutions, but it is in a nascent stage relative to many other issues in higher education. As it develops, the research can highlight the contributions of these campuses as well as identify areas for institutional improvement that will advance inclusive excellence and the consequent economic and civic life of Latinas/os in a changing society.

References

antonio, a. l. (2002). Faculty of color reconsidered: Reassessing contributions to scholarship. *Journal of Higher Education*, 73(5), 582–602.

Arellano, L. (2011). *Capitalizing baccalaureate degree attainment: Revealing the path of the Latina/o scholar* (Unpublished doctoral dissertation). University of California, Los Angeles, CA.

Association of American Colleges and Universities. (2012, August 28). *Making excellence inclusive.* Retrieved from www.aacu.org/compass/inclusive_excellence.cfm

Astin, A.W. & antonio, a. l. (2012). *Assessment for excellence* (2nd ed.). Lanham, MD: Rowman & Littlefield.

Bastedo, M.N., & Bowman, N.A. (2010). US News & World Report college rankings: Modeling institutional effects on organizational reputation. *American Journal of Education*, 116(2), 163–183.

Bensimon, E.M. (2004). The diversity scorecard: A learning approach to institutional change. *Change*, 36(1), 45–52.

Bensimon, E.M., Hao, L., & Bustillos, L. (2003). *Measuring the state of equity in public higher education.* Paper presented at the Harvard Civil Rights and UC Conference on Expanding Opportunity in Higher Education: California and the Nation, Sacramento, CA.

Bensimon, E.M., & Malcom, L. (Eds.). (2012). *Confronting equity issues on campus: Implementing the Equity Scorecard in theory and practice.* Sterling, VA: Stylus.

Bragg, D.D., Baker, E.D., & Puryear, M. (2010). *2010 follow-up of Community College of Denver FastStart program.* Champaign, IL: University of Illinois, Office of Community College Research and Leadership. Retrieved from http://occrl.illinois.edu/node/734

Calderón Galdeano, E., & Santiago, D.A. (2014). *Hispanic Serving Institutions (HSIs) fact sheet: 2012–2013.* Washington, DC: *Excelencia* in Education. Retrieved from http://www.edexcelencia.org/research/hsis-fact-sheet-2012–13

Colbeck, C.L., Campbell, S.E., & Bjorklund, S.A. (2000). Grouping in the dark: What college students learn from group projects. *Journal of Higher Education*, 71, 60–83.

Contreras, F.E., Malcom, L.E., & Bensimon, E.M. (2008). Hispanic-Serving Institutions: Closeted identity and the production of equitable outcomes for Latino/a students. In M. Gasman, B. Baez, & C.Turner (Eds.), *Understanding Minority-Serving Institutions: New interdisciplinary perspectives.* Albany, NY: SUNY Press.

Cooper, D. (1998). Reading, writing, and reflection. In R.A. Rhoads & J.P.F. Howard (Eds.), *Academic service learning: A pedagogy of action and reflection* (New Directions for Teaching and Learning No. 73, pp. 47–59). San Francisco, CA: Jossey-Bass.

Corley, K.G. (2004). Defined by our strategy or our culture? Hierarchical differences in perceptions of organizational identity and change. *Human Relations*, 57(9), 1145–1177.

Cuellar, M. (2012). *Latino student success in higher education: Models of empowerment at Hispanic-Serving Institutions (HSIs), emerging-HSIs, and non-HSIs* (Unpublished doctoral dissertation). University of California, Los Angeles, CA.

Cuellar, M. (2014). The impact of Hispanic-Serving Institutions (HSIs), emerging HSIs, and non-HSIs on Latina/o academic self-concept. *Review of Higher Education*, 37(4), 499–530.

Dayton, B., González-Vásquez, N., Martínez, C.R., & Plum, C. (2004). Hispanic-Serving Institutions through the eyes of students and administrators. In A.M. Ortiz (Ed.), *Addressing the unique needs of Latino American students* (New Directions for Student Services No. 105, pp. 29–40). San Francisco, CA: Jossey-Bass.

de los Santos, A.G., & Vega, I.I. (2008). Hispanic presidents and chancellors of institutions of higher education in the United States in 2001 and 2006. *Journal of Hispanic Higher Education*, 7(2), 156–182.

Dougherty, K. (1994). *The contradictory college.* Albany, NY: SUNY Press.

Eckel, P.D., & Kezar, A. (2003). *Taking the reins: Institutional transformation in higher education.* Westport, CT: American Council on Education/Praeger Series in Higher Education.

Foster, B., Jackson, G., Cross, W.E., Jackson, B., & Hardiman, R. (1988). Workforce diversity and business. *Training and Development Journal*, 42(4), 38–41.

Franke, R. (2012). *Towards the education nation: Revisiting the impact of financial aid, college experience, and institutional context on baccalaureate degree attainment using a propensity score matching, multilevel modeling approach* (Unpublished doctoral dissertation). University of California, Los Angeles, CA.

Fry, R., & Taylor, P. (2013). *Hispanic high school graduates pass Whites in rate of college enrollment.* Washington, DC: Pew Hispanic Center.

García, G.A. (2013). *Challenging the "manufactured identity" of Hispanic Serving Institutions (HSIs): Co-constructing an organizational identity* (Unpublished doctoral dissertation). University of California, Los Angeles, CA.

Gonzales, L.D., & Pacheco, A. (2012). Leading change with slogans: Border University in transition. *Journal of Cases in Educational Leadership*, 15(1), 50–65.

Haro, R., & Lara, J.F. (2003). Latinos and administrative positions in American higher education. In J. Castellanos & L. Jones (Eds.), *The majority in the minority: Expanding the representation of Latina/o faculty, administrators, and students in higher education* (pp. 167–175). Sterling, VA: Stylus.

Hispanic Association of Colleges and Universities. (2012). *Hispanic-Serving Institution definitions.* San Antonio, TX: Author. Retrieved August 24, 2012 from www.hacu.net/hacu/HSI_Definition1.asp

Holland, B.A. (1999). From murky to meaningful: The role of mission in institutional change. In R.G. Bringle, R. Games, & E.A. Malloy (Eds.), *Colleges and universities as citizens* (pp. 48–73). Boston, MA: Allyn and Bacon.

Hurtado, S. (1992). Campus racial climates: Contexts for conflict. *Journal of Higher Education, 5*, 539–569.

Hurtado, S. (1994). The institutional climate for talented Latino students. *Research in Higher Education*, 35(1), 21–41.

Hurtado, S. (2001). Linking diversity with educational purpose: How the diversity impacts the classroom environment and student development. In G. Orfield (Ed.), *Diversity challenged: Legal crisis and new evidence* (pp. 187–203). Cambridge, MA: Harvard Publishing Group.

Hurtado, S. (2003). Institutional diversity in American higher education. In S. Komives & D. Woodard (Eds.), *Student services: A handbook for the profession* (pp. 23–44). San Francisco, CA: Jossey-Bass.

Hurtado, S., Álvarez, C.L., Guillermo-Wann, C., Cuellar, M., & Arellano, L. (2012). A model for diverse learning environments: The scholarship on creating and assessing conditions for student success. In J.C. Smart & M.B. Paulsen (Eds.), *Higher education: Handbook of theory and research* (Vol. 27, pp. 41–122). New York, NY: Springer.

Hurtado, S., & Dey, E.L. (1997). Achieving the goals of multiculturalism and diversity. In M.W. Peterson, D.D. Dill, & L.A. Metz (Eds.), *Planning and management for a changing environment: A handbook on redesigning postsecondary institutions* (pp. 405–431). San Francisco, CA: Jossey-Bass.

Hurtado, S., Eagan, M.K., Pryor, J.H., Whang, H., & Tran, S. (2012). *The American college teacher, 2010–2011.* Los Angeles, CA: Higher Education Research Institute.

Hurtado, S., Milem, J.F., Clayton-Pederson, A., & Allen, W.A. (1999). *Enacting diverse learning environments: Improving the campus climate for racial/ethnic diversity in higher education* (ASHE-ERIC Series). San Francisco, CA: Jossey-Bass.

Hurtado, S., Ruiz Alvarado, A., Bates, A., Ramírez, J.J., & Stewart, T.J. (2014). *Closing the gap for first generation, underrepresented minority students.* Paper presented at the meeting of the Association for Institutional Research, Orlando, FL.

Hurtado, S., Ruiz, A., & Whang, H. (2012). Advancing and assessing civic learning: New results from the Diverse Learning Environments Survey. *Diversity & Democracy: Civic learning for Shared Futures,* 15(3), 10–12.

Hyer, P.B. (1985). Affirmative action for women faculty: Case studies of three successful institutions. *Journal of Higher Education,* 56(3), 282–299.

Ibarra, R.A. (2003). Latina/o faculty and the tenure process in cultural context. In J. Castellanos & L. Jones (Eds.), *The majority in the minority: Expanding the representation of Latina/o faculty, administrators, and students in higher education* (pp. 207–219). Sterling, VA: Stylus.

Kezar, A. (2014). *How colleges change: Understanding, leading and enacting change.* New York, NY: Routledge.

Kezar, A.J., & Eckel, P.D. (2005). *Leadership strategies for advancing campus diversity: Advice from experienced presidents.* Washington, DC: American Council on Education.

Kezar, A.J., & Lester, J. (2011). *Enhancing campus capacity for leadership: An examination of grassroots leaders in higher education.* Redwood City, CA: Stanford University Press.

Laden, B.V. (2000). *Hispanic serving two-year institutions: What accounts for their high transfer rates?* Paper presented at the meeting of the Association for the Study of Higher Education, Sacramento, CA.

Laden, B.V. (2004). Hispanic-Serving Institutions: What are they? Where are they? *Community College Journal of Research and Practice, 28,* 181–198.

Levin, J.S. (2001). *Globalizing the community college: Strategies for change in the twenty-first century.* New York, NY: Palgrave Macmillan.

Li, X., & Carroll, C.D. (2007). *Characteristics of Minority-Serving Institutions and minority undergraduates enrolled in these institutions* (NCES 2008–156). Washington, DC: National Center for Education Statistics.

Maestas, R., Vaquera, G.S., & Muñoz Zehr, L. (2007). Factors impacting sense of belonging at a Hispanic-Serving Institution. *Journal of Hispanic Higher Education,* 6(3), 237–256.

Malcom, L.E. (2010). *Hispanic-serving or Hispanic-enrolling? Assessing the institutional performance of public 4-Year HSIs and emerging HSIs.* Paper presented at the meeting of the American Educational Research Association, Denver, CO.

Mayhew, M.J., & Fernández, S.D. (2007). Pedagogical practices that contribute to social justice outcomes. *Review of Higher Education, 31,* 55–80.

Núñez, A.-M., & Bowers, A.J. (2011). Exploring what leads high school students to enroll in Hispanic-Serving Institutions: A multilevel analysis. *American Educational Research Journal,* 48(6), 1286–1313.

Núñez, A.-M., Sparks, P.J., & Hernández, E.A. (2011). Latino access to community colleges and Hispanic-Serving Institutions: A national study. *Journal of Hispanic Higher Education,* 10(1), 18–40.

Peterson, M., Blackburn, R.T., Gamson, Z.F., Arce, C.H., Davenport, R.W., & Mingle, J.R. (1978). *Black students on White campuses: The impacts of increased Black enrollments.* Ann Arbor, MI: Institute for Social Research.

Richardson, R.C., & Skinner, E.F. (1991). *Achieving quality and diversity: Universities in a multicultural society.* New York, NY: American Council on Education/MacMillan.

Rodríguez, A., & Calderón Galdeano, E. (2014). *What is working for Latinos? Understanding Latinos' postsecondary outcomes at HSIs versus non-HSIs.* Paper presented at the meeting of the American Educational Research Association, Philadelphia, PA.

Rowley, L., Hurtado, S., & Ponjuan, L. (2002). *Organizational rhetoric or reality? The disparities between avowed commitments to diversity and formal programs and initiatives in higher education.* Paper presented at the meeting of the American Educational Research Association, New Orleans, LA. Retrieved from http://www.umich.edu/~divdemo/2002%20aera%20institutional%20survey%20paper.pdf

Santiago, D.A. (2006). *Inventing Hispanic-Serving Institutions (HSIs): The basics.* Washington, DC: *Excelencia* in Education. Retrieved from http://www.edexcelencia.org/pdf/InventingHSIsFINAL.pdf

Santiago, D.A. (2007a). *Choosing Hispanic-Serving Institutions: A closer look at Latino students' college choices.* Washington, DC: *Excelencia* in Education.

Santiago, D.A. (2007b). *Emerging Hispanic-Serving Institutions: 2006–2007.* Washington, DC: *Excelencia* in Education. Retrieved from www.edexcelencia.org/sites/default/files/EmergingHSIList-2006–07.pdf

Santiago, D.A. (2008). *Hispanic-Serving Institution list: 2006–2007.* Washington, DC: *Excelencia* in Education.

Santiago, D.A. (2009). *Leading in a changing America: Presidential perspectives from Hispanic-Serving Institutions.* Washington, DC: *Excelencia* in Education.

Santos, J.L., & Sáenz, V.B. (2014). In the eye of the perfect storm: The convergence of policy and Latina/o trends in access and financial concerns, 1975–2008. *Educational Policy,* 28(3), 393–424.

Smith, D.G. (1995). Organizational implications of diversity. In M.M. Chemers, S.O. Oskamp, & M.A. Constanzo (Eds.), *Diversity in organizations: New perspectives for a changing workplace.* Thousand Oaks, CA: SAGE.

Stewart, J.B. (1991). Planning for cultural diversity: A case study. In H. Cheatham (Ed.), *Cultural pluralism on campus* (pp. 161–191). Washington, DC: American College Personnel Association.

Titus, M.A. (2006). Understanding the influence of the financial context of institutions on student persistence at four-year colleges and universities. *The Journal of Higher Education,* 77(2), 353–375.

Umbach, P.D., & Wawrzynski, M.R. (2005). Faculty do matter: The role of college faculty in student learning and engagement. *Research in Higher Education,* 46(2), 153–184.

USC California Policy Institute. (2005). Measuring equity in higher education: An accountability framework for California colleges and universities. *Research Update: Education,* 2. Retrieved from http://cue.usc.edu/research/CPI_Seder_Measuring_Equity_in_Higher_Education_2005.pdf

U.S. Department of Education. (2007). *Accredited postsecondary minority institutions: Institutions with high Hispanic enrollment from IPEDS spring 2007 survey (fall 2006 enrollment).* Retrieved from http://www2.ed.gov/about/offices/list/ocr/edlite-minorityinst-list-hisp-tab.html

3

HISPANIC-SERVING COMMUNITY COLLEGES AND THEIR ROLE IN HISPANIC TRANSFER

Anne-Marie Núñez, Gloria Crisp, and Diane Elizondo

Community colleges serve nearly 40% of all students attending postsecondary education in the United States (McIntosh & Rouse, 2009), including a disproportionate number of Hispanic students and students from other historically underrepresented minority groups (Cohen & Brawer, 2008). Like other community colleges, those that are Hispanic-serving are tasked with four main functions: (1) academic preparation for transfer to four-year institutions, (2) vocational education to prepare students to enter the workforce directly, (3) developmental education to prepare students for college-level work, and (4) community and multicultural education to serve regional residents (Cohen & Brawer, 2008).

Hispanic-serving community colleges (also referred to in this chapter as two-year Hispanic-Serving Institutions) comprised just more than half (54%) of Hispanic-Serving Institutions (HSIs) in the 2008–2009 academic year (Núñez, Crisp, & Elizondo, 2014), and more community colleges are becoming Hispanic-serving (Torres & Zerquera, 2012). These institutions play a critical role in offering Hispanic students access to postsecondary education, including bachelor's degrees through the transfer function (Núñez, Sparks, & Hernández, 2011; Perna, Li, Walsh, & Raible, 2010). A recent national longitudinal study found that 39% of Hispanic community college students who began in the 2003–2004 academic year began at Hispanic-serving community colleges, and that half (51%) of all students enrolled at Hispanic-serving community colleges were from Hispanic backgrounds (Núñez et al., 2011).

In this chapter we first briefly describe the characteristics of Hispanic-serving two-year institutions, using data from a full census of these institutions (Núñez et al., 2014). We then draw on the Beginning Postsecondary Students Longitudinal Study to examine the student characteristics, institutional characteristics, and transfer patterns of Hispanic students in Hispanic-serving community colleges over six academic years (2003–2004 to 2008–2009). First, we use data from the Beginning Postsecondary Students (BPS) Longitudinal Study to compare the characteristics of students at two-year HSIs and two-year non-HSIs (Núñez et al., 2011). We then review the general literature about student and institutional factors related to Hispanic student transfer. We continue by presenting findings from the BPS that track these factors in relation to Hispanic transfer at two-year HSIs. In particular, we examine the individual characteristics of the total sample of Hispanic students who began in Hispanic-serving community colleges, and then compare these characteristics to those of the subset of Hispanic students who eventually transferred to four-year institutions (an outcome known as vertical transfer) within six years. We conclude with implications for research, policy, and practice.

A Profile of Two-Year Hispanic-Serving Institutions

The proportion of Hispanic enrollment in two-year HSIs across the United States and Puerto Rico averages 44%, but it varies widely, from 25% to 100% (Núñez et al., 2011; Núñez, Crisp, & Elizondo, 2014). Table 3.1, which includes information on two-year HSIs in 2008–2009 from the Integrated Postsecondary Education Data System (IPEDS), illustrates other dimensions of variability among two-year HSIs. For instance, enrollments averaged 6,383 students and ran as high as 25,500 students. On average, just more than one-third (36%) of students in these institutions were enrolled full time, and the majority (58%) were female. More than one-quarter (28%) of the students received Pell Grants, but the proportion ranged as high as 97%. Table 3.1 also reveals that financial context variables, such as the total amount institutions spent in this time frame on instruction, academic support, and student services, varied quite widely. Two-year HSIs are also situated in quite diverse local and geographical conditions, which can affect the revenues they receive from sources like tuition and fees. In fact, Núñez and colleagues (in press) conducted a cluster analysis to examine the extent to which HSIs formed groups on common characteristics, and identified two distinctive groups of two-year HSIs: "Urban Enclave Community Colleges" and "Rural Dispersed Community Colleges". In short, two-year HSIs overall serve disproportionately high proportions of students who historically have not had access to higher education, but the student characteristics and resources in these institutions still vary widely. Therefore, as we seek to understand the transfer function at two-year HSIs, we must also recognize that these institutions are quite heterogeneous.

TABLE 3.1 *Variation among Two-Year Hispanic-Serving Institutions*

Characteristic	Mean or %	Minimum	Maximum	Std. Dev.
Enrollment size	6,383	100	25,500	5,255
Faculty Characteristics				
% Hispanic	14%	0%	76%	12.1
% Full time	35%	13%	98%	15.5
Student Characteristics				
% Hispanic	44%	25%	100%	19.3
% Female	58%	23%	97%	8.7
% Full time	36%	2%	98%	23.5
% on Pell Grants	28%	4%	97%	18.4
Financial Context[a]				
Instruction	$4,702.12	$160.45	$4,026.95	$626.10
Academic support	$265.28	$34.51	$2,231.86	$209.60
Student services	$388.15	$39.37	$5,259.06	$459.60
Tuition and fees	$496.00	$61.93	$12,239.08	$1,170.20
Community Context				
Region of country				
West	42%	—	—	—
Central	8%	—	—	—
South	37%	—	—	—
East	6%	—	—	—
Rocky Mountains	2%	—	—	—
Puerto Rico	5%	—	—	—
Urbanicity				
City	52%	—	—	—
Suburb	23%	—	—	—
Town	14%	—	—	—
Rural	16%	—	—	—

Source: 2008–2009 Integrated Postsecondary Education Data System (IPEDS) database.

Note: N = 145. Percentages may not sum to 100% due to rounding.

[a]*Instruction,* academic support, and student services reflect the amount spent per full-time equivalent (FTE) student on respective institutional functions. Tuition and fees reflects the amount received per FTE student.

Characteristics of Students Who Enroll at Two-Year HSIs

One study employing BPS data indicated that, in the 2003–2004 academic year, Hispanic-serving community colleges enrolled 39% of Hispanic students, compared with 7%, 10%, and 21% of White, Black, and Asian American community college students, respectively (Núñez et al., 2011). This same study indicated that about half (51%) of students enrolled in two-year HSIs were Hispanic, compared with 27% White, 11% Black, and 6% Asian American, with the remainder from other ethnic groups. This was very different from the racial/ethnic enrollment patterns at community colleges that were not designated as Hispanic-serving, where just 13% of Latina/o, 62% of White, 16% of Black, and 4% of Asian American students in the sample were enrolled (Núñez et al., 2011). Therefore, Hispanics were about four times as likely to be enrolled in two-year HSIs than in two-year non-HSIs, while far fewer (roughly half as many) Whites and slightly more Blacks were enrolled in two-year HSIs. In addition, two-year HSIs enrolled a population comprising just more than one-quarter (28%) first-generation immigrant students—about twice as many as two-year colleges that were not Hispanic-serving (13%) (Núñez et al., 2011).

Multivariate research from the Núñez et al. (2011) study also indicates that, holding other demographic, academic background, and college choice factors constant, students from non-White backgrounds (Hispanic, Black, or Asian American) are more likely to enroll in two-year HSIs than in community colleges that are not Hispanic-serving, and students enrolled in two-year HSIs are far more likely to report a higher number of factors associated with being at risk for dropping out of college, such as having children, working full time, and/or enrolling part time. Such factors constitute "environmental pull" characteristics (Bean, 1990; Nora, 2004) that can draw students away from their studies and into handling other responsibilities, making it harder to focus on college. Despite these conditions, Núñez and her colleagues (2011) found that Latinas/os in Hispanic-serving community colleges were more than twice as likely as Latinas/os who enrolled in other community colleges to report an intention to transfer.

Finally, little is known regarding Hispanic students' academic and social experiences at Hispanic-serving community colleges. Qualitative research does indicate that Hispanics who choose to attend two-year HSIs are influenced by their social networks—including family, friends, and sometimes faculty members—in their choice of institution (Cejda, Casparis, Rhodes, & Seal-Nyman, 2008). Compared with those who attend community colleges that are not Hispanic-serving, Hispanic students who attend two-year HSIs are also more likely to be the first in their families to attend college (Núñez et al., 2011). These students may be less familiar with how to navigate the college environment than their counterparts whose parents have more education, and therefore may rely more on institutional agents (e.g., staff, faculty) within the community college to educate them about the transfer process (Bensimon & Dowd, 2009).

Next, to provide further context for our analysis, we turn to a review of a full range of factors that can influence Latina/o students' likelihood of transferring from two-year to four-year institutions.

Individual and Institutional Factors Related to Hispanic Transfer

Although all community colleges can offer students from historically underrepresented groups a critical gateway to bachelor's degrees, two-year institutions have lower retention and graduation rates when compared to universities (Schuetz, 2005) and low transfer rates to four-year institutions (Melguizo, Kienzl, & Alfonso, 2011).

For instance, among a recent national cohort representing all first-time beginning community college students who initially intended to transfer to four-year institutions, only 15% had successfully done so within three years of beginning college (Horn, 2009). A study of beginning Hispanic students at a community college indicated that six semesters later, just 9% had a full set of criteria (including academic course requirements) to be ready to transfer to four-year institutions (Hagedorn & Lester, 2006).

Holding other demographic, academic preparation, and college choice factors constant, research suggests that Hispanic students who enroll at Hispanic-serving community colleges are more likely than their counterparts who attend other community colleges to intend to transfer to four-year institutions (Núñez et al., 2011). Further, some research suggests that Hispanic students who attend Hispanic-serving community colleges actually do transfer to four-year institutions at higher rates (Hagedorn, Chi, Cepeda, & McLain, 2007; Laden, Hagedorn, & Perrakis, 2008). Unfortunately, however, very little empirical or theoretical work exists to identify individual and institutional factors that may be related to the transfer rates of Hispanic students who attend Hispanic-serving community colleges.

Although not specific to HSIs, one framework often used to explore influences on outcomes, such as transfer, among Hispanic and/or community college students is Nora's (2004) student/institution engagement model (e.g., Arbona & Nora, 2007; Cabrera & Nora, 1994; Cabrera, Nora, & Castañeda, 1993; Crisp & Nora, 2010; Crisp & Núñez, 2014; Nora, 2004; Nora & Cabrera, 1996). This framework emphasizes that the nature of interactions between a community college student and an institution has a critical influence on transfer and related outcomes. More specifically, the theory postulates that, at the individual level, a student's sociodemographic characteristics, pre-college preparation, environmental pull characteristics, educational plans, and academic and social experiences collectively influence his or her likelihood of transferring.

On the whole, current research supports the relevance of Nora's model in identifying factors influencing transfer among Hispanic students. For instance, gender and ethnicity have consistently been found to be associated with transfer to four-year institutions (Grubb, 1991; Lee & Frank, 1990; Surette, 2001; Vélez & Javalgi, 1987). Among Hispanic community college students, being female has been shown to be positively related to transfer to four-year institutions (Arbona & Nora, 2007). In general, a student's age also appears salient, as older students transfer at lower rates (e.g., Dougherty & Kienzl, 2006; Porchea, Allen, Robbins, & Phelps, 2010).

Among Hispanic community college students, those at HSIs are more likely than their counterparts at non-HSIs to be the first in their families to go to college (Núñez et al., 2011). Yet, for Hispanic community college students as well as community college students in general, coming from a family with lower parental education can be related to lower transfer rates, in part because students may not understand how to navigate transfer pathways (Alexander, García, González,

Grimes, & O'Brien, 2007; Crisp & Nora, 2010; Crisp & Núñez, 2014; Porchea et al., 2010; Rendón & Valadez, 1993). Linguistic minority status—i.e., having limited English language skills—can also be a hindrance to transfer to a four-year college for Hispanic students, particularly when community college transfer policies and articulation policies are not clearly communicated (Alexander et al., 2007; Bunch & Endris, 2012; Perrakis & Hagedorn, 2010). Immigration status, which is linked with language skills, also merits consideration in understanding Hispanic community college transfer experiences because Hispanic community college students are more likely than others to be first-generation immigrants (Núñez et al., 2011).

Community college students with higher academic preparation—as measured by high school grade point average (GPA) (Lee & Frank, 1990; Vélez & Javalgi, 1987) and math scores or course-taking (Dougherty & Kienzl, 2006; Lee & Frank, 1990)—are more likely to transfer to four-year institutions. This is true in general and, in particular, for Hispanic students (Arbona & Nora, 2007; Crisp & Nora, 2010; Suárez, 2003). Conversely, a lack of academic preparation for college has been shown to hinder Hispanic students' likelihood of transferring (Alexander et al., 2007). Future educational plans also appear to be related to transfer: Higher educational aspirations or expectations are related to a higher likelihood of transfer for community college students in general (Dougherty & Kienzl, 2006; Grubb, 1991; McCormick & Carroll, 1997; Porchea et al., 2010), and for Hispanic students in particular (Arbona & Nora, 2007).

Environmental factors that may pull students away from campus and their studies, such as family responsibilities and working off-campus (Nora, 2004), have been shown to be related to the likelihood of transfer for community college students. Also, as noted previously, Hispanic students in Hispanic-serving community colleges are more likely than those in non-HSIs to have these environmental pull factors (Núñez et al., 2011). Among a national sample of Hispanic community college students, an increased number of hours worked per week was shown to be negatively related to transfer (Crisp & Nora, 2010). However, enrolling in community college full time as opposed to part time may positively predict transfer to four-year institutions for community college students in general (Dougherty & Kienzl, 2006; Doyle, 2009; Lee & Frank, 1990; McCormick & Carroll, 1997; Porchea et al., 2010), and for Hispanic community college students in particular (Crisp & Nora, 2010). Moreover, limited access to financial resources can hinder transfer for Hispanic students (Alexander et al., 2007), whereas increased access to income and financial aid is positively related to transfer for these students (Cejda & Rhodes, 2004; Crisp & Nora, 2010).

Although many community college students do not necessarily receive personal guidance in the process of transferring to four-year institutions (Bensimon & Dowd, 2009; Yoshimi & Núñez, 2011), there is evidence that this type of assistance is particularly important for Latina/o students (Bensimon & Dowd, 2009).

Bensimon and Dowd (2009) used the term *transfer agents* to refer to institutional personnel who personally support students in the transfer process. More generally, positive and attentive faculty–student interactions can facilitate academic engagement for Hispanic community college students (Cejda & Rhodes, 2004; Cejda et al., 2008; Cejda & Hoover, 2010–2011). Participation in academic activities like study groups can also promote transfer to four-year institutions among community college students in general (Dougherty & Kienzl, 2006).

In addition to academic support, social support for Hispanic community college students can promote positive outcomes. Such support may include culturally relevant programming (Perrakis & Hagedorn, 2010). In addition, academic and social affirmation and encouragement of community college students, sometimes known as academic and interpersonal validation (Rendón, 1994), may be positively related to academic engagement and persistence. Further, validation has been shown to be especially important for Hispanic community college students in feeling a sense of belonging (Barnett, 2011a, 2011b; Suárez, 2003).

The type of academic pathway a community college student pursues is also related to the likelihood of transfer, with vocational (in comparison to transfer-oriented) pathways being negatively related to transfer for all students (Alfonso, Bailey, & Scott, 2005; Dougherty & Kienzl, 2006; Grubb, 1991). Crisp and Núñez (2014) found that, for a national sample of Hispanic and Black students, holding a battery of critical student and institutional factors constant, being enrolled in a vocational program was a negative predictor of transfer.

Hispanic students are overrepresented in developmental (also known as remedial) courses in college (Bettinger & Long, 2005; Sparks & Malkus, 2013). Data from the BPS would also suggest that Hispanic students who attend community colleges are, on the whole, less academically prepared in terms of math courses taken during high school and high school GPAs when compared to Hispanic students who enroll in developmental coursework at four-year institutions (Nora & Crisp, 2012).

The influence of developmental education on academic outcomes (including transfer) for community college and/or Hispanic students remains somewhat unclear. For instance, enrolling in developmental courses has been shown to decrease community college students' odds of transfer to four-year institutions, in particular for students enrolled in English and mathematics developmental courses (Crisp & Delgado, 2014). Findings specific to Hispanic community college students, however, would suggest that enrolling in one or more developmental education courses during the first year of college may serve to increase the odds of persisting to the end of the second year (Crisp & Nora, 2010). At the same time, it is notable that Hispanic students who require higher amounts of remediation are less likely than students who enroll in one or two courses to be academically successful. For instance, recent findings from a national study of Hispanic students by Crisp, Reyes, and Doran (2014) suggest that students who only enroll in one remedial mathematics course are more likely to pass the developmental course and subsequently enroll in and pass college-level math than are students who enroll in two or more developmental courses.

Although less examined in the research literature, institutional characteristics and factors may also be related to transfer for both community college students in general and Hispanic students more specifically (Bensimon & Dowd, 2009; Bensimon & Malcom, 2012). Institutional characteristics such as higher enrollment size or higher percentage of part-time, underrepresented minority, and female students on campus have been found to be negatively related to transfer among community college students (Bailey, Calcagno, Jenkins, Kienzl, & Leinbach, 2005; Bailey, Calcagno, Jenkins, Leinbach, & Kienzl, 2006). In addition, larger proportions of part-time faculty have been shown to be related to lower transfer rates (Bailey et al., 2005; Porchea et al., 2010). Other research has found that community colleges with higher proportions of traditional-aged students, lower proportions of underrepresented minority students, higher levels of student socioeconomic status (SES) and academic preparation, and greater emphasis on transfer programs have higher six-year transfer rates (Wassmer, Moore, & Shulock, 2004). There is also evidence that greater in-state tuition may be positively related to individual community college transfer rates, even after controlling for entering student characteristics such as high school performance and parental income and educational levels (Porchea et al., 2010). Further, there is some evidence to suggest that community college students, regardless of race, may benefit from being taught by instructors who are the same race/ethnicity (Fairlie, Hoffman, & Oreopoulos, 2011).

Some research suggests that institutional characteristics may not influence Hispanic transfer rates in the same way as for community college students in general (Gándara et al., 2012; Hagedorn et al., 2007). Notably, however, with the exception of a few studies focusing on Hispanics at high Hispanic-enrolling community colleges (e.g., Hagedorn et al., 2007; Laden et al., 2008), most studies that have examined the relationship between community college institutional characteristics and transfer have not focused specifically on Hispanic students. Indeed, most research has not disaggregated transfer outcomes by race/ethnicity (Chase, Dowd, Pazich, & Bensimon, 2012). Hagedorn and colleagues (2007) did find that an increased percentage of Hispanic students at a community college was actually positively associated with transfer rates for Hispanic students, which is consistent with Laden and colleagues' (2008) finding that Hispanic-serving community colleges see higher transfer rates for Hispanics than do other HSIs. These findings could be related to an increased presence of role models through Hispanic faculty and other Hispanic students, as well as more culturally sensitive curricula and programs targeting Hispanics (Hagedorn et al., 2007; Hagedorn, 2010; Laden, 2001). Therefore, the individual and institutional factors that are related to Hispanic transfer at Hispanic-serving community colleges merit attention.

Description of Transfer Among Hispanic Students Attending Two-Year HSIs

The following section provides a national profile of Hispanic students who participated in the Beginning Postsecondary Students Longitudinal Study that collected data specific to transfer patterns, enrollment, persistence, and degree attainment over six academic years (2003–2004 to 2008–2009). Our relevant subsample of Hispanic students was limited to the 310 students who were less than 24 years of age and who first enrolled in one of 95 institutions that were classified as two-year Hispanic-Serving Institutions during the 2003–2004 academic year. The sample excluded non-traditional aged students because certain data elements thought to be critical to account for transfer outcomes (such as high school GPA) were not available in the dataset for students age 24 or older. BPS data were merged with data from the IPEDS fall 2003–2004 surveys to provide information regarding institutional characteristics. Various individual and institutional characteristics of Hispanic students at Hispanic-serving community colleges were examined in the analysis and are displayed in the following tables.

Table 3.2 describes characteristics of Hispanic students who began at two-year Hispanic-Serving Institutions. Characteristics were selected for inclusion based on the preceding research literature review. Comparative data are shown for students who successfully transferred to four-year institutions within six academic years. Among the national sample of Hispanic students who began college at Hispanic-serving community colleges in the 2003–2004 academic year, the majority were female (59%). Only 14% of students had a parent who had earned a bachelor's degree or higher, and the majority (59%) had parents who had never attended any postsecondary education. Additionally, more than half (53%) of the students who began their postsecondary education at two-year HSIs had incomes in the lowest quartile. Forty percent of the sample did not grow up speaking English as the primary language in their homes; more than three-fourths (78%) of the students were classified as second or third generation citizens.

In terms of high school experiences, nearly half (44%) of the Hispanic students who attended two-year HSIs earned cumulative grade point averages (GPAs) lower than 3.0 during high school. Moreover, only 17% of the sample took a pre-calculus or calculus course during high school, and nearly half (46%) had not taken a course higher than Algebra II prior to attending college. Notably, 30% of the sample did not immediately enroll in college after high school.

This sample of traditional-aged Hispanic students who began college at two-year HSIs had several outside factors serving to "pull" them away from campus and their studies. Roughly one-third (29%) did not receive any form of financial aid support during the first year of college, and another half (48%) received less than $5,000. Sixty-one percent of the students were employed off-campus; 51% worked 20 or more hours per week. It is not surprising, then, that nearly half

TABLE 3.2 *Comparison of Characteristics of All Hispanic Students Who Began at HSIs and Hispanic Students Who Began at HSIs and Successfully Transferred to Four-Year Institutions*

	All who began at 2-year HSIs (N = 310)	Those who transferred (n = 70)	Sig.[a]
Sociodemographic Variables			
Female	59%	64%	
Parental Education			
Did not attend college	59%	51%	
Less than a 4-year degree	27%	29%	
4-year degree	8%	13%	
More than a 4-year degree	6%	7%	
Income Quartile			
Low	53%	49%	
Low middle	29%	26%	
High middle	13%	17%	
High	6%	9%	
English was primary language spoken in home	60%	56%	
Immigration status (time in U.S.)			
Non-citizen or student w/visa	14%	14%	
First-generation citizen	8%	6%	
Second-generation citizen	40%	47%	
Third-generation or later citizen	38%	33%	
Pre-college Factors			
High school GPA			*
2.4 or less	21%	18%	
2.5 to 2.9	23%	14%	
3.0 to 3.4	48%	50%	
3.5 to 4.0	9%	17%	
Highest math course taken			**
Algebra II	46%	40%	
Trigonometry and Algebra II	15%	14%	
Precalculus	11%	19%	
Calculus	6%	14%	
Other	22%	13%	
Earned non-language college credit	11%	14%	
Delayed enrollment into college	30%	26%	
Environmental Pull Factors			
Did not have children	88%	93%	
Hours worked off-campus			
20 or more hours per week	51%	44%	
Less than 20 hours per week	10%	16%	
Did not work	38%	40%	

	All who began at 2-year HSIs (N = 310)	Those who transferred (n = 70)	Sig.[a]
Financial aid amount received			*
Did not receive aid	29%	36%	
Less than $2,500	23%	14%	
Between $2,500 and $4,999	25%	30%	
Between $5,000 and $9,999	13%	16%	
More than $10,000	11%	4%	
Did not exclusively attend full-time	47%	44%	
Left college	33%	23%	*
Educational Plans/Expectations			
Planned to transfer to a 4-year institution	60%	70%	*
Highest degree expected			*
Less than a bachelor's degree	15%	9%	
Bachelor's degree	37%	30%	
Master's degree or certificate	34%	39%	
Doctoral or professional degree	15%	23%	
Academic and Social Experiences			
Frequency of support from "transfer agent"[b]	.698	.828	
Frequency of faculty–student interaction[c]	.535	.692	*
Frequency of social support[d]	.281	.414	*
Program type (transfer)			**
Vocational/technical program	31%	14%	
Transfer program	69%	86%	
Took developmental math course	33%	34%	
First-year GPA	2.74	2.92	*
Took distance education course	8%	14%	*

$*p < .05, **p < .01, ***p < .001$

Source: 2008–2009 Integrated Postsecondary Education Data System (IPEDS) database.

Note. Percentages may not add to 100% due to rounding. Data are rounded to the nearest 10th per IES guidelines.

[a]Results of chi square or *t* tests identifying significant relationship between the student-level variable and student transfer.

[b]Average frequency with which students met with an advisor concerning academic plans in 2003–2004 (0=never, 1=sometimes, 2=often).

[c]Composite of two items reflecting the frequency with which students had informal or social contact with faculty or talked with faculty about academic matters outside of class in 2003–2004 (0=never, 1=sometimes, 2=often).

[d]Composite of three items reflecting the frequency with which students participated in school clubs, school sports, and study groups in 2003–2004 (0=never, 1=sometimes, 2=often).

(47%) of the students did not attend college exclusively on a full-time basis and 33% left college for at least one semester.

One-third (33%) of Hispanic students who began their college education at Hispanic-serving community colleges enrolled in a developmental mathematics coursework during the first year of college. Although 86% of students expected to earn bachelor's degrees or higher, only 60% reported plans to transfer to four-year institutions. At the same time, a slightly higher percentage (69%) of Hispanic students who first enrolled at two-year HSIs were formally enrolled in academic transfer programs. Despite their expectations and plans, only 23% successfully transferred to four-year institutions within six academic years.

Table 3.3 represents the institutional characteristics of the two-year HSIs that all Hispanic students attended, compared with the institutional characteristics of the institutions attended by those who successfully transferred to four-year institutions. Among all students who began college at two-year HSIs, the average enrollment of the colleges attended was 12,389. On average, 20% of the full-time faculty were Hispanic. In this national sample, the Hispanic students at two-year HSIs attended institutions where less than half (47%) of the instructional staff were employed full-time. The mean tuition and fee revenues per full-time student were just more than $2,000 per year. Further, the average student attended a community college that awarded substantially more associate's degrees than other degrees or certificates (68%). The average percentage of students who transferred to other institutions within three years among Hispanic students enrolled at two-year HSIs was only 16%. Given the location of HSIs, it is not surprising that the large majority of students attended two-year HSIs that were located in the West or Rocky Mountain area or in the Southern states (87%). These are all geographic areas that serve the largest percentages of Hispanic postsecondary students in the country.

Relationship Between Student and Institutional Variables and Transfer

The right hand columns of Tables 3.2 and 3.3 identify student and institutional variables that were found using chi-square and t tests to be significantly related to student transfer. Overall, the data suggest that the relatively small percentage of Hispanic students who successfully transferred to four-year institutions from two-year HSIs were in many respects representative of the broader sample of Hispanic students who began college at institutions of this type. Similarly, few statistically significant relationships were found between institutional characteristics and individual students' transfer behavior. There were, however, a few notable relationships. On the whole, Hispanic students who successfully transferred from two-year HSIs to four-year institutions within six years were more likely to

TABLE 3.3 *Comparison of Institutional Characteristics of All Hispanic Students Who Began at HSIs and Hispanic Students Who Transferred to Four-Year Institutions*

	All who began at 2-year HSIs (N = 310)	Those who transferred (n = 70)	Sig.[a]
Academic and Social Environment			
Average total enrollment at the institution	12,389	14,816	*
Average % of full-time faculty who are Hispanic	20%	19%	
Average % of instructional staff who are classified as full-time	47%	50%	
Average tuition and fee revenues per FTE	$2,117	$1,636	
Average academic support expenses per FTE	$574	$575	
Average instruction expenses per FTE	$2,928	$2,990	
Average student services expenses per FTE	$708	$740	
Average state and local government appropriation revenues per FTE	$3,886	$4,175	
Average % of total awards that are associate's degrees	68%	71%	
Average institutional transfer rate[b]	16%	18%	
Location			
West or Rocky Mountains	40%	30%	
Central	4%	4%	
South	47%	49%	
East	10%	16%	
Aggregate Sociodemographics			
Average % Hispanic students	54%	50%	
Average % female students	58%	57%	
Average % students received federal aid	48%	38%	*

* $p < .05$, ** $p < .01$, *** $p < .001$

Note. Percentages may not add to 100% due to rounding. Data are rounded to the nearest 10th per IES guidelines.

[a]Results of chi square or *t*-tests identifying significant relationship between the institutional variable and student transfer.

[b]Average percentage of students who transferred to other institutions within three years of beginning college.

- Be more academically prepared (i.e., in terms of high school GPA and level of math preparation)
- Receive higher amounts of financial support
- Remain continuously enrolled

- Have plans to transfer to a four-year institution
- Hold higher degree expectations
- Have informal or social contact with faculty or talk with faculty about academic matters outside of class
- Participate in school clubs, school sports, and/or study groups
- Enroll in an academic transfer program
- Earn a higher GPA during the first year of college
- Enroll in one or more distance education classes
- Attend a large community college
- Attend a community college with a relatively lower percentage of students receiving financial aid

Implications

This analysis compared student and institutional characteristics of a general sample of Hispanic students enrolled in two-year HSIs with the characteristics of the subset who eventually transferred to four-year institutions. Future research on students in Hispanic-serving community colleges can employ multivariate techniques, such as logistic regression, propensity score matching, and hierarchical linear modeling, to hold other factors constant when examining the association between a factor of interest and the outcome of transfer for Hispanic community college students (Crisp & Núñez, 2014; Núñez et al., 2011). For example, Rodríguez and Calderón Galdeano (Chapter 11, this volume) use propensity score matching to examine graduation rates of students in four-year HSIs and comparable four-year non-HSIs. They also examine the extent to which two-year non-HSIs have other institutional characteristics that are comparable to those of two-year HSIs. This methodological approach could also be applied to the predictors of student transfer from two-year HSIs to compare them with predictors of transfer at two-year non-HSIs that constitute an appropriate comparison group.

Surprisingly, our study found a discrepancy in the number of students who expressed an intention to transfer and those who expressed an intention to earn bachelor's degrees. This interesting finding suggests that Hispanic community college students' ambitions may not align exactly with their knowledge of the process of attaining a bachelor's degree. Therefore, more research is warranted to examine how students at Hispanic-serving community colleges make sense of transfer and of the process of attaining higher postsecondary degrees. Notably, Gándara and colleagues (2012) found that California colleges that transferred high proportions of Latina/o students to four-year institutions were not necessarily well known for having high transfer rates of students in general. However, many of them offered culturally relevant curricula, programming, and outreach to Hispanic communities. Further research on the experiences of Hispanic students who successfully transfer from two-year HSIs to four-year institutions would be instructive in understanding the kinds of supports that they need (Bensimon & Dowd, 2009).

Furthermore, we found that few institutional characteristics distinguished students who transferred from those who did not. Exploring in more depth the organizational culture at Hispanic-serving community colleges would provide further insight into what these institutions can do to support Hispanic transfer. Specifically, understanding their organizational behavior could inform how administrators, faculty, and staff might develop a "transfer culture"—an organizational culture that is oriented toward supporting students in the transfer function (Bensimon & Dowd, 2009; Gándara et al., 2012; Pérez & Ceja, 2010; Wassmer et al., 2004; Wolf-Wendel, Twombly, Morphew, & Sopcich, 2004).

This chapter advances our knowledge on Hispanic students' experiences and outcomes in Hispanic-serving community colleges. However, it is only a first step in developing a better understanding of the experiences of the significant proportion of Hispanic students who begin their postsecondary careers in these institutions. We hope that this chapter offers researchers, policymakers, and practitioners ideas about what directions to pursue in serving this critical population of students.

References

Alexander, B.C., García, V., González, L., Grimes, G., & O'Brien, D. (2007). Barriers in the transfer process for Hispanic and Hispanic immigrant students. *Journal of Hispanic Higher Education, 6*(2), 174–184.

Alfonso, M., Bailey, T.R., & Scott, M. (2005). The educational outcomes of occupational sub-baccalaureate students: Evidence from the 1990s. *Economics of Education Review, 24*, 197–212.

Arbona, C., & Nora, A. (2007). The influence of academic and environmental factors on Hispanic college degree attainment. *The Review of Higher Education, 30*(3), 247–270.

Bailey, T., Calcagno, J.C., Jenkins, D., Kienzl, G., & Leinbach, T. (2005). *Community college student success: What institutional characteristics make a difference?* New York, NY: Community College Research Center.

Bailey, T., Calcagno, J.C., Jenkins, D., Leinbach, T., & Kienzl, G. (2006). Is student-right-to-know all you should know? An analysis of community college graduation rates. *Research in Higher Education, 47*(5), 491–519. doi: 10.1007/s11162-005-9005-0

Barnett, E. (2011a). Faculty validation and persistence among nontraditional community college students. *Enrollment Management Journal, 5*(2), 97–117.

Barnett, E. (2011b). Validation experiences and persistence among nontraditional community college students. *Review of Higher Education, 34*(2), 193–220.

Bean, J. (1990). Why students leave: Insights from research. In D. Hossler, J.P. Bean, & associates (Eds.), *The strategic management of college enrollments* (pp. 147–169). San Francisco, CA: Jossey-Bass.

Bensimon, E.M., & Dowd, A. (2009). Dimensions of the transfer choice gap: Experiences of Latina and Latino students who navigated transfer pathways. *Harvard Educational Review, 79*(4), 632–658.

Bensimon, E.M., & Malcom, L. (2012). *Confronting equity issues on campus: Implementing the equity scorecard in theory and in practice.* Sterling, VA: Stylus.

Bettinger, E.P., & Long, B.T. (2005). Remediation at the community college: Student participation and outcomes. In C. Kozeracki (Ed.), *Responding to the challenges of developmental education* (New Directions for Community Colleges No. 129, pp. 17–26). San Francisco, CA: Jossey-Bass.

Bunch, G.C., & Endris, A. (2012). Navigating "open access" community colleges: Matriculation policies and practices for U.S.-educated language minority students. In Y. Kanno & L. Harklau (Eds.), *Linguistic minority students go to college: Preparation, access, and persistence* (pp. 165–183). New York, NY: Routledge.

Cabrera, A.F., & Nora, A. (1994). College students' perceptions of prejudice and discrimination and their feelings of alienation: A construct validation approach. *The Review of Education/Pedagogy/Cultural Studies, 16*(3–4), 387–409.

Cabrera, A.F., Nora, A., & Castañeda, M.B. (1993). College persistence: Structural equation modeling test of an integrated model of student retention. *Journal of Higher Education, 64*(2), 123–137.

Cejda, B.D., Casparis, C., Rhodes, J., & Seal-Nyman, I. (2008). The role of social capital in the educational decisions of Hispanic students attending Hispanic-serving community colleges. *Enrollment Management Journal, 2*(1), 32–59.

Cejda, B.D., & Hoover, R.E. (2010–2011). Strategies for faculty-student engagement: How community college faculty engage Latino students. *Journal of College Student Retention: Research, Theory and Practice, 12*, 135–153.

Cejda, B.D., & Rhodes, J.H. (2004). Through the pipeline: The role of faculty in promoting associate degree completion among Hispanic students. *Community College Journal of Research and Practice, 28*(3), 249–262.

Chase, M.M., Dowd, A.C., Pazich, L.B., & Bensimon, E.M. (2012). Transfer equity for "minoritized" students: A critical policy analysis of seven states. *Educational Policy.* Retrieved from: http://epx.sagepub.com/content/early/2012/12/06/0895904812468227

Cohen, A.M., & Brawer, F.B. (2008). *The American community college.* San Francisco, CA: Jossey-Bass.

Crisp, G., & Delgado, C. (2014). The impact of developmental education on community college student success. *Community College Review, 42*(2), 99–117. doi: 10.1177/0091552113516488

Crisp, G., & Mina, L. (2012). The community college: Retention trends and issues. In A. Seidman (Ed.), *College student retention: Formula for student success* (2nd ed., pp. 147–166). Lanham, MD: Rowman & Littlefield.

Crisp, G., & Nora, A. (2010). Hispanic student success: Factors influencing the persistence and transfer decisions of Latino community college students enrolled in developmental education. *Research in Higher Education, 51*(2), 175–194. doi: 10.1007/s11162-009-9151-x

Crisp, G., & Núñez, A. (2014). Modeling transfer among minority and non-minority community college students who intend to transfer and earn a 4-year degree. *The Review of Higher Education, 37*(3), 291–320. doi: 10.1353/rhe.2014.0017

Crisp, G., Reyes, N., & Doran, E. (2014). *Predicting successful remediation among Latina/o students.* Paper presented at the meeting of the American Educational Research Association, Philadelphia, PA.

Dougherty, K.J., & Kienzl, G.S. (2006). It's not enough to get through the open door: Inequalities by social background in transfer from community colleges to four-year colleges. *Teachers College Record, 108*(3), 452–487.

Doyle, W.R. (2009). Impact of increased academic intensity on transfer rates: An application of matching estimators to student-unit record data. *Research in Higher Education, 50*(1), 52–72.

Fairlie, R., Hoffman, F., & Oreopoulos, P. (2011). *A community college instructor like me: Race and ethnicity interactions in the classroom.* Cambridge, MA: National Bureau of Economic Research.

Gándara, P., Alvarado, E., Driscoll, A., & Orfield, G. (2012). *Building pathways to transfer: Community colleges that break the chain of failure for students of color.* Los Angeles, CA: The Civil Rights Project.

Grubb, W.N. (1991). The decline of community college transfer rates: Evidence from national longitudinal surveys. *Journal of Higher Education, 62*(2), 194–222.

Hagedorn, L.S. (2010). The pursuit of student success: The directions and challenges facing community colleges. In J.C. Smart (Ed.), *Higher education: Handbook of theory and research* (Vol. 25, pp. 181–218). Netherlands: Springer.

Hagedorn, L.S., Chi, W., Cepeda, R.M., & McLain, M. (2007). An investigation of critical mass: The role of Latino representation in the success of urban community college students. *Research in Higher Education, 48*(1), 73–91. doi: 10.1007/s11162-006-9024-5

Hagedorn, L.S., & Lester, J. (2006). Hispanic community college students and the transfer game: Strikes, misses, and grant experiences. *Community College Journal of Research and Practice, 30*(10), 827–853.

Horn, L. (2009). *On track to complete? A taxonomy of beginning community college students and their outcomes 3 years after enrolling: 2003–04 through 2006.* Washington, DC: National Center for Education Statistics.

Laden, B.V. (2001). Hispanic Serving Institutions: Myths and realities. *Peabody Journal of Education, 76*(1), 73–92.

Laden, B.V., Hagedorn, L.S., & Perrakis, A. (2008). Donde estan los hombres?: Examining success of Latino male students at Hispanic serving community colleges. In B.B.M. Gasman & C.S.V. Turner (Eds.), *Understanding minority-serving institutions* (pp. 127–140). Albany, NY: SUNY Press.

Lee, V.E., & Frank, K.A. (1990). Student characteristics that facilitate the transfer from 2-year to 4-year colleges. *Sociology of Education, 63*(3), 178–193.

McCormick, A.C., & Carroll, C.D. (1997). *Transfer behavior among beginning postsecondary students: 1989–94. Postsecondary education descriptive analysis reports. Statistical analysis report* (NCES 97–266). Washington, DC: National Center for Education Statistics. Retrieved from http://nces.ed.gov/pubs97/97266.pdf

McIntosh, M.F., & Rouse, C.E. (2009). *The other college: Retention and completion rates among two-year college students.* Washington, DC: Center for American Progress. Retrieved from: www.americanprogress.org/issues/2009/02/pdf/two_year_colleges.pdf

Melguizo, T., Kienzl, G., & Alfonso, M. (2011). Comparing the educational attainment of community college students and four-year college rising juniors using propensity score matching methods. *Journal of Higher Education, 82*(3), 265–291.

Nora, A. (2004). The role of habitus and cultural capital in choosing a college, transitioning from high school to higher education, and persisting in college among minority and non-minority students. *Journal of Hispanic Higher Education, 3*(2), 180–208.

Nora, A., & Cabrera, A.F. (1996). The role of perceptions of prejudice and discrimination on the adjustment of minority students to college. *Journal of Higher Education, 67*(2), 120–148.

Nora, A., & Crisp, G. (2012). *Hispanic student participation and success in developmental education* (White paper). San Antonio, TX: Hispanic Association of Colleges and Universities.

Núñez, A.-M., & Bowers, A.J. (2011). Exploring what leads high school students to enroll in Hispanic-Serving Institutions. *American Educational Research Journal, 48*(6), 1286–1313. doi: 10.3102/0002831211408061

Núñez, A.-M., Crisp, G., & Elizondo, D. (in press). Mapping Hispanic-Serving Institutions: A typology of institutional diversity. *Journal of Higher Education.*

Núñez, A.-M., Sparks, P.J., & Hernández, E.A. (2011). Latino access to community colleges and Hispanic-Serving Institutions: A national study. *Journal of Hispanic Higher Education, 10*(1), 18–40.

Pérez, P.A., & Ceja, M. (2010). Building a Latina/o student transfer culture: Best practices and outcomes in transfer to universities. *Journal of Hispanic Higher Education, 9*(1), 6–21. doi: 10.1177/1538192709350073

Perna, L.W., Li, C., Walsh, E., & Raible, S. (2010). The status of equity for Hispanics in public higher education in Florida and Texas. *Journal of Hispanic Higher Education, 9*(2), 145–166.

Perrakis, A.H., & Hagedorn, L.S. (2010). Latino/a student success in community colleges and Hispanic-Serving Institution status. *Community College Journal of Research and Practice, 34*(10), 797–813.

Porchea, S.F., Allen, J., Robbins, S., & Phelps, R.P. (2010). Predictors of long-term enrollment and degree outcomes for community college students: Integrating academic, psychosocial, socio-demographic and situational factors. *Journal of Higher Education, 81*(6), 750–778.

Rendón, L.I. (1994). Validating culturally diverse students: Toward a new model of learning and student development. *Innovative Higher Education, 19*(1), 33–51.

Rendón, L.I., & Valadez, J.R. (1993). Qualitative indicators of Hispanic student transfer. *Community College Review, 20*, 27–37. doi: 10.1177/009155219302000404

Schuetz, P. (2005). Campus environment: A missing link in studies of community college attrition. *Community College Review, 32*(4), 60–82.

Sparks, D., & Malkus, N. (2013). *Statistics in brief: First-year remedial coursetaking: 1999–2000, 2003–04, 2007–08.* Washington, DC: National Center for Education Statistics.

Suárez, A.L. (2003). Forward transfer: Strengthening the educational pipeline for Latino community college students. *Community College Journal of Research and Practice, 27*(2), 95–117. doi: 10.1080/713838110

Surette, B.J. (2001). Transfer from 2-year to 4-year college: An analysis of gender differences. *Economics of Education Review, 20*(2), 151–163.

Torres, V., & Zerquera, D. (2012). Hispanic-Serving Institutions: Patterns, predictions, and implications for informing policy discussions. *Journal of Hispanic Higher Education, 11*(3), 259–278.

Vélez, W., & Javalgi, R.G. (1987). Two-year college to four-year college: The likelihood of transfer. *American Journal of Education, 96*(1), 81–94.

Wassmer, R., Moore, C., & Shulock, N. (2004). Effect of racial/ethnic composition on transfer rates in community colleges: Implications for policy and practice. *Research in Higher Education, 45*(6), 651–672.

Wolf-Wendel, L., Twombly, S., & Morphew, C., Sopcich, J. (2004). From the barrio to the bucolic: The student transfer experience from HSIs to Smith College. *Community College Journal of Research and Practice, 28*(3), 213–231. doi: 10.1080/10668920490256408

Yoshimi, J., & Núñez, A.-M. (2011). *A phenomenology of transfer.* Paper presented at the meeting of the Association for the Study of Higher Education, Charlotte, NC.

4

INSTITUTIONAL DIVERSITY AMONG FOUR-YEAR HISPANIC-SERVING INSTITUTIONS

Anne-Marie Núñez and Diane Elizondo

Four-year Hispanic-Serving Institutions (HSIs) constituted just under half (46%) of all HSIs in the 2008–2009 academic year (Núñez, Crisp, & Elizondo, in press). According to recent reports, these institutions award 40% of the baccalaureate degrees earned by Latinas/os (Malcom-Piqueux & Lee, 2011) and an even a greater share (54%) in science, technology, engineering, and mathematics (STEM) fields (Harmon, 2012). And although a minimal proportion (12%) of four-year HSIs were classified as research or doctorate-granting institutions in the Carnegie Classification system (McCormick & Zhao, 2005) during the 2008–2009 academic year (Núñez & Elizondo, 2012), recent data also indicate that 25% of Latina/o doctorates receive their doctoral degrees from HSIs (Malcom-Piqueux & Lee, 2011).

Despite their critical role in producing Latina/o postsecondary degree holders, HSIs are often criticized for seemingly low graduation rates. Some observers argue that the extent to which HSIs are intentionally serving Hispanic students could be called into question, in part because most do not foreground their identities as HSIs in their mission statements (e.g., Contreras, Malcom, & Bensimon, 2008). Furthermore, studies show mixed results with respect to whether faculty attitudes and Hispanic student experiences and outcomes differ between HSIs and non-HSIs (e.g., Bridges, Kinzie, Nelson Laird, & Kuh, 2008; Cuellar, Chapter 6, this volume; Hubbard & Stage, 2009; Nelson Laird, Bridges, Morelon-Quainoo, Williams, & Holmes, 2007).

One reason for these inconclusive findings could be the heterogeneity among four-year HSIs, which vary markedly by sector, Carnegie type, enrollment size, percentage of Hispanic students, amount of financial resources, and regional considerations (Núñez & Elizondo, 2012). Yet, with some exceptions (Cole, 2011; Cuellar, Chapter 6, this volume; Hubbard & Stage, 2009; Núñez & Elizondo,

2012; Rodríguez & Calderón Galdeano, Chapter 11, this volume), most analyses that compare HSIs with non-HSIs treat four-year HSIs as one category, without controlling for these important characteristics.

To address this gap in the literature, this chapter explores in depth the institutional diversity among four-year HSIs. First, we discuss existing research on four-year HSIs' institutional contexts and student outcomes. Second, because of the concern about the extent to which HSIs are fostering positive outcomes for students (e.g., Contreras, Malcom, & Bensimon, 2008), we describe a conceptual lens that addresses the relationship between institutional contexts and student outcomes. Third, we apply that lens to present findings illustrating the diverse characteristics of a national census of four-year HSIs (Núñez, Crisp, & Elizondo, 2014) and a sub-group of four-year HSIs with general undergraduate missions, rather than missions primarily focused on sub-baccalaureate degrees or on specialized fields of study (e.g., medicine, religion, or art) (Núñez & Elizondo, 2012). Finally, we discuss the implications of this institutional diversity for future research, policy, and practice concerning four-year HSIs.

Faculty and Students in Four-Year HSIs

Four-year HSIs undoubtedly produce a large proportion and number of Latina/o baccalaureate and post-baccalaureate degree holders in the United States (Harmon, 2012; Malcom-Piqueux & Lee, 2011), yet these institutions are frequently criticized for graduation rates that are comparatively lower than at non-HSIs, particularly for Latina/o students. This criticism raises questions about the extent to which HSIs are actually *serving* versus merely *enrolling* Latina/o students (e.g., Contreras et al., 2008; Malcom-Piqueux & Lee, 2011).

Findings in studies comparing faculty attitudes and student experiences and outcomes at four-year HSIs and non-HSIs have been mixed. In their exploration of faculty attitudes toward academic responsibilities, for example, Hubbard and Stage (2009) found that faculty in four-year HSIs do not differ from faculty at predominantly White institutions (PWIs) in reporting a focus on supporting and teaching students. They also found, however, that these attitudes and perceptions vary by Carnegie type, and they recommended that future research address these variations to better understand faculty experiences. In contrast, other researchers have found that HSI faculty members are more likely than their counterparts at non-HSIs to report using instructional strategies such as class discussion, collaborative learning, reflective thinking, and student choice in assignments (Hurtado & Ruiz Alvarado, Chapter 2, this volume).

Notably, compared with four-year non-HSIs, four-year HSIs serve more students from lower socioeconomic (SES) backgrounds and students with less academic preparation (Núñez & Bowers, 2011; Núñez & Elizondo, 2012). Likewise, they have fewer institutional resources to spend per student than non-HSIs (Hispanic

Association of Colleges and Universities [HACU], 2012; Merisotis & McCarthy, 2005; Ortega et al., this volume; Santiago, 2006). Holding other factors constant, postsecondary institutions with lower SES students, less academically prepared students, and fewer institutional resources to spend per student see lower graduation rates (Bound, Lovenheim, & Turner, 2010; Titus, 2006a, 2006b, 2009; Webber & Ehrenberg, 2009). In keeping with this broader pattern, these factors are also negatively related to four-year HSIs' graduation rates (García, 2013; Núñez & Elizondo, 2012). Therefore, criticisms of HSIs' lower graduation rates can overlook the possibility that, rather than inhibiting student success, HSIs are actually doing "more with less" (Malcom, Dowd, & Yu, 2010, p. 12), particularly when equity, diversity, access, and resource measures are taken into account (Vega & Martínez, 2012).

In response to questions about the extent to which HSIs truly serve and support the success of Hispanic students, the research has yielded contradictory results concerning Latina/o students' college experiences. For example, Nelson Laird and colleagues (2007) found that Latinas/os in four-year HSIs do not differ from their Latina/o counterparts in four-year PWIs in perceiving a supportive campus environment, experiencing high-quality student–faculty interactions, or being satisfied with their college experiences. In contrast, however, Bridges and colleagues (2008) found that Hispanics in four-year HSIs are more likely than their counterparts in four-year non-HSIs to live on campus and to participate in co-curricular activities. Furthermore, consistent with Hurtado and Ruiz Alvarado's findings that HSI faculty are more likely to report using collaborative learning techniques (see Chapter 2, this volume), Nelson Laird and colleagues (2007) found that Latina/o students in four-year HSIs are more likely than their counterparts in non-HSIs to report participating in collaborative learning activities. In addition, Nelson Laird and colleagues (2007) found that Latina/o students in four-year HSIs, compared with their counterparts in non-HSIs, reported greater gains in overall academic development, and Cuellar (2014, and Chapter 6, this volume) found that Latina/o students in four-year HSIs are more likely than Latina/o students in other institutions to report community engagement and high academic self-concept.

Although it is clear that four-year HSIs produce a large number of Latina/o STEM baccalaureate holders (Harmon, 2012), the evidence on the extent to which this results from distinctive organizational qualities in HSIs is inconclusive. Figueroa, Hurtado, and Eagan (2013) found, for example, that attending an HSI does not have an independent effect on whether underrepresented minority students complete STEM degrees. In contrast, Stanton-Sálazar and et al.'s (2010) qualitative research indicated that certain faculty and administrators in four-year HSIs provide unique opportunities to Hispanic undergraduate students by encouraging them to pursue STEM degrees and by linking them with research opportunities and internships, which can provide them with financial support that offsets the need to pursue employment outside of the university (Godoy, 2010; Stanton-Sálazar, Macías, Bensimon, & Dowd, 2010). This kind of support is critical for Latina/o students, who face significant financial challenges in paying for college and also work more often during college than students from other racial/ethnic groups (Dowd & Malcom, 2012; Núñez, Hoover, Pickett, Stuart-Carruthers, & Vázquez, 2013; Rendón, Dowd, & Nora, 2012). This can have potentially negative implications for Latina/o students' success, because working longer hours has been found to be negatively related to engagement in college, as well as to outcomes including grade point average and college persistence (Bozick, 2007; Darolia, 2014; DeSimone, 2008; Pascarella, Edison, Nora, Hagedorn, & Terenzini, 1998; Pike, Kuh, & Massa-McKinley, 2008).

One reason for these mixed and inconclusive results concerning faculty attitudes in HSIs and the effect of attending an HSI on student engagement and graduation is that few studies have disaggregated the different types of HSIs. Furthermore, with some exceptions (e.g., Cole, 2011; Godoy, 2010), they typically have not addressed the question of whether the effect of attending an HSI in Puerto Rico is different from the effect of attending an HSI on the U.S. mainland. For example, there is some evidence that HSIs in Puerto Rico—compared with HSIs on the U.S. mainland—have an increased likelihood of offering ethnic studies classes on Latina/o issues (Cole, 2011). Beyond isolated findings such as this, however, we know little about the differences between HSIs in the two distinct settings, particularly with regard to institutional characteristics and student outcomes.

Collectively, this research raises the question of whether significant variation among four-year HSIs may contribute to the mixed results in studies that seek to understand student experiences and outcomes at HSIs, particularly for Latina/o students. It also points to the importance of comparing Puerto Rican HSIs with those on the U.S. mainland. Thus, our goal in this chapter is to provide an overview of institutional variation among four-year HSIs according to certain student and institutional factors known to affect student outcomes.

Conceptual Lens on HSIs' Institutional Diversity and Student Outcomes

To guide our selection of variables to examine institutional diversity among four-year HSIs, we employed a conceptual lens that addresses the relationship between institutional characteristics and student outcomes. Specifically, we drew on Berger and Milem's (2000) framework, which accounts for the relationship between organizational behavior and student outcomes and Titus's (2006a, 2006b) application of resource dependency theory to this framework. Resource dependency theory postulates that the behavior of organizations striving toward organizational autonomy may be constrained by external factors such as limited financial resources (Pfeffer & Salancik, 1978). As also noted elsewhere in this volume—by García (Chapter 5), Rodríguez and Calderón Galdeano (Chapter 11), and especially

Ortega et al. (Chapter 9)—resource dependency theory is particularly salient to understanding HSIs because of their vulnerability to external forces, including limited institutional resources.

Berger and Milem's (2000) conceptual model stipulates that, together, students' entering characteristics (e.g., demographic and high school background) and organizational characteristics shape an institution's peer group characteristics and student experiences. Organizational characteristics include structural demographic features (e.g., size, control, selectivity, Carnegie type, and location) and organizational behavior (i.e., the norms and shared culture of institutional personnel and systems). Peer group characteristics include psychological, behavioral, and structural (demographic) characteristics. Student experiences comprise formal and informal behaviors in the academic, social, and functional (bureaucratic) realms, as well as student perceptions of the institutional environment in these realms (Berger & Milem, 2000). Together, these factors influence a range of student outcomes, including degree completion. Titus's (2006b) adaptation of Berger and Milem's (2000) framework emphasizes the systemic dimension—more specifically, the institutional financial context of organizational behavior, which includes factors such as where the organization spends its resources and how it gains revenue. The systemic dimension focuses on how external forces, such as state and federal law, technology, and market dynamics, influence organizational behavior. Together, these factors affect the availability of resources that an institution can draw upon in its operations.

Employing Titus's (2006b) extension of Berger and Milem's framework enabled us to focus in the structural demographic and peer contexts, and to explore institutional financial context factors, location (or community context), and outcomes (as measured by six-year graduation rates). Our results portray the full landscape of four-year HSIs based on a census of these institutions in a single academic year. In addition, we found that a significant minority of four-year HSIs had very specialized missions (e.g., only focusing on one field of study, such as medicine, art, or religion) or missions not focused on baccalaureate degrees (according to Carnegie classifications). Therefore, we examined and compared these characteristics for a subset of four-year HSIs on the U.S. mainland and in Puerto Rico that had general undergraduate missions.

Method

To develop a profile of four-year HSIs, we drew data from the Integrated Postsecondary Education Data System (IPEDS) for 2008–2009, as well as from the 2005–2009 American Community Survey of the U.S. Census and the USDA Economic Research Service 2003 Rural–Urban Continuum Codes. Although more recent IPEDS data were available, items from the 2008–2009 academic year had the fewest pieces of missing data for critical elements. The data included the entire population of accredited, not-for-profit Hispanic-Serving Institutions (HSIs) in 2008–2009 (N = 123).

Variables

In our examination of the full census of four-year HSIs, we included several variables to capture structural demographic characteristics of HSIs, including the highest degree awarded, control (i.e., public or private), emphasis on graduate education (measured by the percentage of students who were enrolled in graduate programs), and full-time enrollment. We also included the percentage of Hispanic faculty and percentage of full-time faculty. And together, the percentages of Hispanic undergraduate students, full-time students, students receiving Pell Grant aid, and women, as well as a selectivity measure based on the percentage of applicants admitted to the institution, addressed student characteristics at HSIs.

Several expense variables were used to capture each institution's financial context, including the total sum spent on instruction, academic support, and student services divided by the number of full-time equivalent (FTEs) students. Additionally, the total dollar amounts received in revenue from the state government and from tuition and fees per FTE were included as measures of institutional revenue. Categorical measures of institutional region (e.g., West, South) and whether the institution was located in a city, suburb, town, or rural area provided information on location. Additional community context variables included the percentage of persons in the county who (1) held bachelor's degrees or higher, (2) were unemployed, and (3) self-classified as Hispanic. Finally, we compared each institution's six-year graduation rate to graduation rates among the full census of four-year HSIs.

As previously noted, this chapter also presents the results of a related analysis focused on a subset of institutions that we refer to as four-year general mission HSIs because of their focus on undergraduate education in a wide range of fields (Núñez & Elizondo, 2012). The decision to focus on four-year general mission HSIs was guided by initial findings that about 15% of colleges and universities in the full census were classified by the Carnegie system as special focus institutions, offering specialized fields of study, such as medicine, religion, aeronautics, or arts. Another 15% were primarily or substantially associate's degree schools— i.e., among the growing number of community colleges that offer baccalaureate degrees, but whose primary function is not to offer such degrees (Cohen & Brawer, 2008). Because this analysis focused on institutional characteristics in relation to graduation rates, we felt it was important to exclude institutions whose missions were not primarily focused on baccalaureate education in a wide array of fields. This analysis compared the institutional characteristics of U.S. mainland and Puerto Rican four-year general mission HSIs. (See Núñez & Elizondo, 2012, for additional information on variables.)

Analysis

Descriptive statistics were used to identify institutional and community context characteristics that distinguished institutions in the full census of HSIs. Subsequently, in our analysis of four-year general mission HSIs, we used chi-square and *t* tests to compare institutions on the U.S. mainland and in Puerto Rico on the various institutional characteristics described previously.

Findings

Close to one-half (47%) of all four-year HSIs were public institutions. These institutions averaged just under 6,000 students in enrollment, ranging from 23 to 36,075 students. Most four-year HSIs emphasized undergraduate education. About one in five students in these institutions (21%) was a graduate student, though graduate enrollment ranged from 0% to 87%. Just under half of faculty members were Hispanic or full-time (45% and 47%, respectively), and again, there was a good deal of variation in these figures—for example, the percentage of faculty who were Hispanic ranged from 2% to 100%.

On average, two-thirds (65%) of students in four-year HSIs were Hispanic, ranging from 25% to 100%. Similarly, 67% of students were enrolled full-time, varying from 6% to 97% of the total proportion of students enrolled. Mirroring trends across U.S. higher education more generally, about 6 in 10 students (61%) in HSIs were women. Four-year HSIs appeared to be relatively open access, admitting, on average, 60% of their students. Just more than half (53%) of students in four-year HSIs were receiving Pell Grants. Table 4.1 shows also that there was significant variation on each of these characteristics.

With respect to financial context characteristics, four-year HSIs spent an average of $8,888 on instructional expenses per student, and an additional $1,951 on academic support. These institutions spent about three-quarters the amount ($1,393) on student services as on academic support per student. On average, four-year HSIs received similar amounts in revenue per student from state appropriations ($6,194) and tuition and fees ($6,418). However, as Table 4.1 shows, there was again tremendous variation in the amounts for each of these factors.

More than one-third of the four-year HSIs (37%) were located in Puerto Rico, and slightly fewer (33%) were in the U.S. mainland South (which included Texas). An additional one-fifth (21%) were located in the West. Fewer than 10% of HSIs were located in the Central (Midwest), Eastern, or Rocky Mountain region. The majority of four-year HSIs were located in cities (56%) or suburbs (29%). Among all four-year HSIs, the average six-year graduation rate was 36%.

Table 4.2 shows how the subset of four-year general mission institutions on the U.S. mainland and in Puerto Rico compared on select characteristics. In general, this table illustrates that Puerto Rican institutions differed significantly from U.S. mainland institutions on many institutional characteristics. The majority of U.S. mainland

TABLE 4.1 *Variation within a Census of Four-Year Hispanic-Serving Institutions*

Characteristic	Mean or %	Minimum	Maximum	Std. Dev.
Structural				
Control (Public)	47%	—	—	—
% Graduate student enrollment	21%	0%	87%	20.0
Enrollment size	5,925	23	36,075	7517.3
Faculty Characteristics				
% Hispanic	45%	2%	100%	41.7
% Full-time faculty	47%	12.1%	95%	20.2
Student Characteristics				
% Hispanic	65%	25%	100%	30.6
% Full-time	67%	6%	97%	17.5
% Students on Pell Grants	53%	10%	96%	22.7
% Female	61%	13%	91%	12.2
% Admitted	60%	12%	100%	20.8
Financial Context (Expenditures)[a]				
Instruction	$8,888.11	$378.02	$278,587.80	$30,208.80
Academic support[b]	$1,950.75	$134.20	$38,862.90	$4,526.73
Student services	$1,393.27	$127.41	$7,430.80	$1,284.21
Financial Context (Revenues)[c]				
State appropriations	$6,194.04	$0.00	$276,282.17	$28,477.09
Tuition and fees	$6,418.20	$283.93	$50,284.64	$8,482.52
Community Context				
Region of country				
West	21%	—	—	—
Central	2%	—	—	—
South	33%	—	—	—
East	7%	—	—	—
Rocky Mountains	1%	—	—	—
Puerto Rico	37%	—	—	—
Urbanicity				
City	56%	—	—	—
Suburb	29%	—	—	—
Town	9%	—	—	—
Rural	7%	—	—	—
Student Outcomes				
Six-year graduation rate	36%	3%	100%	19.0

Source: 2008–2009 Integrated Postsecondary Education Data System (IPEDS) database.

Note. N = 123. Figures may not sum to 100% due to rounding.

[a]Expenditures per full-time enrolled student.

[b]Expenditures on activities and services that support the institution's primary missions of instruction, research, and public service, per full-time enrolled student.

[c]Revenues per full-time enrolled student.

TABLE 4.2 *Descriptive Profile of Institutional Characteristics of General Mission HSIs and Differences between U.S. Mainland and Puerto Rican Institutions*

Characteristic	Total HSIs (N = 86)		U.S. Mainland (n = 56)	Puerto Rican (n = 30)	t or Chi-Square Value
	Mean or %	SD	Mean or %	Mean or %	
Structural					
Control					
Public	51%	—	61%	33%	5.86*
Private	49%	—	39%	67%	
Enrollment size	5,491	5,764	6,288	3,999	2.16*
Carnegie classification					
Baccalaureate	33%		11%	73%	35.10***
Master's	56%		75%	20%	
Research/doctoral	12%		14%	7%	
Student characteristics					
% Hispanic	63%	30.7	43%	100%	22.93***
% Students on Pell Grants	52%	22.0	41%	73%	7.49***
Financial Context (Expenditures)[a]					
Academic and social support[b]	$14,784	$8,057	$19,005	$6,905	11.132***
Financial support[c]	$1,328	$1,496	$1,555	$906	1.95†
Administration	$5,743	$4,812	$7,494	$2,475	6.58***
Financial Context (Revenues)[d]					
State appropriations	$5,480	$6,314	$6,333	$3,886	1.73†
Tuition and fees	$9,816	$9,175	$12,641	$4,542	5.42***
Grants and contracts	$3,949	$4,134	$5,073	$1,853	4.65***
Student Outcomes					
Six-year graduation rate	35%	15.4	39%	26%	3.98***

†$p < .1$, *$p < .05$, **$p < .01$, ***$p < .001$.

Source: 2008–2009 Integrated Postsecondary Education Data System (IPEDS) database.

Note. Figures may not sum to 100% due to rounding.

[a] Expenditures per full-time equivalent (FTE) student.

[b] Academic and social support includes expenditures on four functions: instruction, academic support, auxiliary services, and student services.

[c] Financial support is the amount of expenditures per FTE on grants and scholarships.

[d] Revenues per FTE student.

institutions in this sample (61%) were public, almost twice as many as the proportion of public HSIs in Puerto Rico (33%). On average, U.S. mainland HSIs also enrolled more students than HSIs in Puerto Rico (6,288 versus 3,999, respectively).

Overall, just more than one-half (56%) of general mission HSIs across the U.S. mainland and Puerto Rico were master's institutions, one-third (33%) were baccalaureate institutions, and the remaining 12% were research or doctoral institutions. However, the Carnegie classifications of HSIs on the U.S. mainland and in Puerto Rico were very different. Three-quarters (75%) on the U.S. mainland were master's institutions, while nearly three-quarters (73%) in Puerto Rico were baccalaureate institutions. Overall, very few HSIs (12%) were research institutions; these were twice as likely to be located on the U.S. mainland as in Puerto Rico (14% versus 7%, respectively).

On average, Puerto Rican HSIs enrolled 100% Latina/o students—not a surprising figure, given the demographics of Puerto Rico more broadly. Meanwhile, U.S. mainland four-year general mission HSIs, on average, enrolled a student body consisting of 43% Hispanic students. About half of the students in four-year general mission HSIs (52%) received Pell Grants; however, students in Puerto Rico were much more likely (73%) than their U.S. counterparts (41%) to receive Pell Grants.

Reflecting differences in control, enrollment size, and Carnegie classification, HSIs on the U.S. mainland and in Puerto Rico differed markedly along institutional financial context variables. HSIs in the United States spent significantly more ($19,005) than those in Puerto Rico ($6,905) on academic and social support per student and on administration per student ($7,494 versus $2,475, respectively). In both of these arenas, U.S. mainland HSIs spent nearly three times as much per student as Puerto Rican HSIs.

With respect to revenue, HSIs in the United States received significantly more in tuition per student ($12,641), nearly three times as much as Puerto Rican HSIs ($4,542). Mainland HSIs also received significantly more revenue from grants and contracts per student ($5,073)—again, nearly three times as much as Puerto Rican HSIs ($1,853). Similar to all four-year HSIs, the average graduation rate in these general mission institutions was 35%, but the rate was 39% on the U.S. mainland and 26% in the Puerto Rican HSIs, a significant difference. Collectively, the descriptive results illustrate the diversity among HSIs in structural demographic and peer characteristics as well as institutional financial contexts, both within and between HSIs on the U.S. mainland and in Puerto Rico.

Implications of Institutional Variation for Understanding Student Outcomes

This research suggests that the very diverse institutional characteristics of four-year HSIs have significant implications for the extent to which they are actually serving and supporting the success of Latina/o students. Differences in student body composition, institutional resources, and community context characteristics are all important, particularly when we compare U.S. mainland and Puerto Rican general mission four-year HSIs. Four-year HSIs also vary markedly in terms of six-year student graduation rates. Any attempt to explore the extent to which four-year HSIs truly serve Latina/o students must take into account this institutional variation.

The metrics upon which four-year HSIs are typically measured for institutional performance (including for state performance funding formulas) may not be the most salient to their students' population characteristics and pathways through postsecondary education (Cook & Pullaro, 2010; Espinosa, Crandall, & Tukibayeva, 2014; Núñez & Elizondo, 2012). Student graduation rates are a contested measure of student outcomes because the way that they are currently measured in IPEDS only takes into account students who begin at an institution for the first time in a given fall semester and who complete a degree at that same institution within six years (Cook & Pullaro, 2010). Students who transfer out of HSIs are classified as non-completers, and transfer students and students who take longer than six years to complete a bachelor's degree are not included in the graduation rates. These latter qualities happen to characterize many Latina/o college students and students who begin at HSIs (Núñez, 2014).

While HSIs are frequently criticized for lower persistence and graduation rates for Latinas/os (e.g., Contreras et al., 2008), our findings indicate that the 35% six-year graduation rate among all four-year HSIs does not significantly differ from the 36% graduation rate for Latinas/os among *all* U.S. four-year postsecondary institutions (Radford, Berkner, Wheeless, & Shepherd, 2010). Considering that, compared with other postsecondary institutions, HSIs (1) receive far less federal funding per student (HACU, 2012), (2) spend considerably less on instruction and other institutional functions because of limited funding (Merisotis & McCarthy, 2005), and (3) enroll students with far less access to academic, financial, cultural, and social capital (Núñez & Bowers, 2011), HSIs' graduation rates begin to look far less negative than is typically portrayed. In other words, given that the conditions of lower institutional peer SES (Titus, 2006b) and lower levels of institutional funding (Bound et al., 2010; Webber & Ehrenberg, 2009) are each negatively and independently related to student persistence, HSIs on the whole may in fact be doing more with less in terms of advancing Hispanics' educational attainment (Malcom et al., 2010; Vega & Martínez, 2012).

Other research bolsters this assertion. Similar to our findings for all institutions, researchers have found that, among four-year HSIs, a higher percentage of students on Pell Grants, fewer institutional resources, and lower institutional selectivity are each independently associated with lower six-year Latina/o student graduation rates (García, 2013; Núñez & Elizondo, 2012). Therefore, when we consider the Latina/o student outcomes of HSIs, we must recognize that four-year HSIs vary considerably along dimensions that have significant implications for graduation rates.

Furthermore, comparing four-year HSIs' student outcomes with student outcomes at non-HSIs can be particularly problematic because four-year HSIs vary so much internally and have such different student body and institutional characteristics. In fact, Rodríguez and Calderón Galdeano (Chapter 11, this volume) found that, on the basis of institutional characteristics *besides* percentage of Hispanic enrollment, it was impossible to identify a full set of non-HSI four-year institutions that would be appropriate to compare to HSI four-year institutions. When they compared graduation rates of the subset of HSIs that could be matched with an appropriate comparison group of non-HSIs, they found that differences in graduation rates of all students, as well of Latina/o students, vanished (see also Rodríguez & Calderón Galdeano, 2014).

Collectively, this emerging research on student outcomes indicates that it is primarily student body characteristics (e.g., higher percentages of students on Pell Grants) and lower institutional resources—rather than four-year HSIs' specific organizational behaviors and practices with students—that account for significant gaps between graduation rates of four-year HSIs and non-HSIs. Therefore, to hold HSIs accountable for graduation rates without taking into account their different student characteristics and institutional resources can create an unfair playing field in understanding institutional performance, especially if graduation rates or other typical student outcome measures are the only ones considered in performance funding.

Comparing Puerto Rican and U.S. Mainland HSIs

The concerns described in the previous section are exacerbated for Puerto Rican four-year HSIs, which have lower graduation rates, enroll higher proportions of students on Pell Grants, and have fewer institutional resources than HSIs on the U.S. mainland. In addition to these characteristics, Puerto Rican four-year HSIs' graduation rates should be viewed in light of their historical, economic, and social contexts, which differ from those on the U.S. mainland. For example, the labor participation rate in Puerto Rico is one of the lowest in the world, making it more difficult for residents of the island to fund their postsecondary educations. This trend corresponds with an economic trend in which, since 1997, government funding for the University of Puerto Rico (UPR) system (the main four-year public education institution system on the island) has been cut substantially. Consequently, the UPR system has faced budget deficits and implemented tuition increases of up to 50% (Rodríguez, 2011). Because student and institutional access to financial capital is critical in promoting Latinas/os' graduation rates, these challenging economic and higher education conditions make sustaining Latina/o graduation rates in Puerto Rico even more difficult.

Implications for Research

Confirming that there is significant institutional diversity among HSIs, recent research has identified a typology of six distinctive types of HSIs, including: (1) Urban Enclave Community Colleges, (2) Rural Dispersed Community Colleges, (3) Big Systems 4-Year Institutions, (4) Small Communities 4-Year Institutions, (5) Puerto Rican Institutions, and (6) Health Science Schools (Núñez et al., in press).

Future research should account for variations among four-year HSIs and employ caution in comparing their student outcomes to outcomes in non-HSIs. This consideration is especially germane to historically underrepresented populations in four-year HSIs. Specifically, with respect to graduation outcomes, students from low-SES backgrounds benefit even more from increased institutional expenditures on academic and social support than do their higher-SES counterparts (Webber & Ehrenberg, 2009).

Considering the regional concentrations of four-year HSIs on the U.S. mainland, future research should address variations in state policy environments that influence the amount of state appropriations in four-year HSIs, since these appropriations have an independent and positive effect on graduation rates in general (Titus, 2009). Furthermore, as Latinas/os continue to settle in states where they have not historically resided—a phenomenon some have termed the "New Latino Diaspora" (Wortham, Clonan-Roy, Link, & Martínez, 2013)—researchers should address how local community characteristics may influence the missions and functioning of institutions that are in the process of becoming four-year HSIs (Torres & Zerquera, 2012).

Implications for Policy and Practice

The increased popularity of performance funding (Dougherty & Reddy, 2013) and the Obama administration's recent proposal to institute a federal ratings system of postsecondary institutions for consumer information and accountability purposes (Espinosa, Crandall, & Tukibayeva, 2014) only intensifies the importance of accounting for how institutional variation among higher education institutions—including four-year HSIs—influences differences in institutions' student outcomes (Núñez, 2014). A reliance on narrow measures of institutional success (like graduation rates) without attention to inputs and environments that shape those outcomes will disadvantage the evaluation of four-year HSIs and other institutions that serve large proportions of low-income and historically underrepresented racial/ethnic minority students (Astin, 1985; Astin & antonio, 2012). Research tells us that if negative evaluations are tied to decreases in funding for four-year HSIs, these institutions and their historically and disproportionally underserved students will suffer (e.g., Espinosa et al., 2014; Núñez, 2014).

To sustain federal and state support of four-year HSIs, it will be important to better document the contributions that four-year HSIs make to advance the educational attainment of historically underrepresented students, including baccalaureate and postgraduate degree production and the production of STEM degrees among these populations (e.g., Harmon, 2012). Furthermore, it is important to broaden our conception of what constitutes successful outcomes and benefits of higher education. Although higher education has increasingly been positioned as a private good, it also offers many social benefits to individuals and society (Bowen, 1977; McMahon, 2009). Cuellar's research (2014, and Chapter 6, this volume) takes a step in this direction, as it illustrates that Latina/o students at HSIs experience benefits in academic self-confidence and community engagement to a greater degree than at other institutions. Raising the postsecondary educational attainment of U.S. residents will be impossible without raising the postsecondary attainment of Latinas/os and other historically underserved students, and four-year HSIs will continue to play a vital role in this endeavor.

References

Astin, A. (1985). *Achieving educational excellence: A critical assessment of priorities and practices in higher education.* San Francisco, CA: Jossey-Bass.

Astin, A., & antonio, a. (2012). *Assessment for excellence* (2nd ed.). Lanham, MD: Rowman & Littlefield.

Berger, J.B., & Milem, J.F. (2000). Organizational behavior in higher education and student outcomes. In J.C. Smart (Ed.), *Higher education: Handbook of theory and research* (Vol. 25, pp. 268–338). New York, NY: Agathon Press.

Bound, J., Lovenheim, M.F., & Turner, S. (2010). Why have college completion rates declined? An analysis of changing student perception and collegiate resources. *American Economic Journal: Applied Economics, 2*(3), 129–157.

Bowen, H.R. (1977). *Investment in learning: The individual and social value of American higher education.* San Francisco, CA: Jossey-Bass.

Bozick, R. (2007). Making it through the first year of college: The role of students' economic resources, employment, and living arrangements. *Sociology of Education, 80*(3), 261–285.

Bridges, B.K., Kinzie, J., Nelson Laird, T., & Kuh, G.D. (2008). Student engagement and student success at Historically Black and Hispanic-Serving Institutions. In M. Gasman, B. Baez, & C.S.V. Turner (Eds.), *Understanding minority-serving institutions* (pp. 217–236). Albany, NY: SUNY Press.

Cohen, A., & Brawer, F. (2008). *The American community college* (5th ed.). San Francisco, CA: Jossey-Bass.

Cole, W.M. (2011). Minority politics and group-differentiated curricula at minority-serving colleges. *Review of Higher Education, 34*(3), 381–422.

Contreras, F.E., Malcom, L.E., & Bensimon, E.M. (2008). Hispanic-Serving Institutions: Closeted identity and the production of equitable outcomes for Latina/o students. In M. Gasman, B. Baez, & C.S.V. Turner (Eds.), *Understanding minority-serving institutions* (pp. 71–90). Albany, NY: SUNY Press.

Cook, B., & Pullaro, N. (2010). *College graduation rates: Behind the numbers.* Washington, DC: American Council on Education.

Cuellar, M. (2014). The impact of Hispanic-Serving Institutions (HSIs), emerging HSIs, and non-HSIs on Latina/o academic self-concept. *Review of Higher Education, 37*(4), 499–530.

Darolia, R. (2014). Working (and studying) day and night: Heterogeneous effects of working on the academic performance of full-time and part-time students. *Economics of Education Review, 38,* 38–50.

DeSimone, J.S. (2008). *The impact of employment during school on college student academic performance* (NBER Working Paper No. 14006). Cambridge, MA: National Bureau of Economic Research.

Dougherty, K., & Reddy, V. (2013). Performance funding for higher education: What are the mechanisms? What are the impacts? *ASHE Monograph, 39*(2).

Dowd, A.C., & Malcom, L.E. (2012). *Reducing undergraduate debt to increase Latina and Latino participation in STEM professions.* Los Angeles, CA: University of Southern California.

Espinosa, L.L., Crandall, J.R., & Tukibayeva, M. (2014). *Rankings, institutional behavior, and college and university choice: Framing the national dialogue on Obama's ratings plan.* Washington, DC: American Council on Education.

Figueroa, T., Hurtado, S., & Eagan, K. (2013). *Making it! . . . or Not: Institutional contexts and biomedical degree attainment.* Paper presented at the meeting of the Association for Institutional Research, Long Beach, CA.

García, G. (2013). Does percentage of Latinas/os affect graduation rates at 4-year Hispanic-Serving Institutions (HSIs), Emerging HSIs, and non-HSIs? *Journal of Hispanic Higher Education,* 12(3), 256–268.

Godoy, C. (2010). *The contribution of HSIs to the preparation of Hispanics for STEM careers: A multiple case study* (Unpublished doctoral dissertation). University of Pennsylvania, Philadelphia, PA.

Harmon, N. (2012). *The Role of Minority-Serving Institutions in national college completion goals.* Washington, DC: Institute for Higher Education Policy.

Hispanic Association of Colleges and Universities. (2012). *Hispanic Association of Colleges and Universities (HACU) Hispanic Higher Education Research Collective (H3ERC) research agenda: Impacting education and changing lives through understanding.* San Antonio, TX: Author.

Hubbard, S.M., & Stage, F.K. (2009). Attitudes, perceptions, and preferences of faculty at Hispanic Serving and Predominantly Black Institutions. *Journal of Higher Education, 80*(3), 270–289.

Malcom, L., Dowd, A., & Yu, T. (2010). *Tapping HSI-STEM funds to improve Latina and Latino access to STEM professions.* Los Angeles, CA: University of Southern California.

Malcom-Piqueux, L., & Lee, J.M. (2011). *Hispanic-Serving Institutions: Contributions and challenges.* New York, NY: College Board Policy and Advocacy Center. Retrieved from http://advocacy.collegeboard.org/sites/default/files/11b_4853_HSBC_PolicyBrief_WEB_120110.pdf

McCormick, A.C., & Zhao, C.-M. (2005). Rethinking and reframing the Carnegie Classification. *Change,* 37(5). 51–57.

McMahon, W. (2009). *Higher learning, greater good.* Baltimore, MD: Johns Hopkins University Press.

Merisotis, J., & McCarthy, K. (2005). Retention and student success at Minority-Serving Institutions. In G.H. Gaither (Ed.), *Minority retention: What works?* (New Directions for Institutional Research No. 125, pp. 45–58). San Francisco, CA: Jossey-Bass.

Nelson Laird, T.F., Bridges, B.K., Morelon-Quainoo, C.L., Williams, J.M., & Holmes, M.S. (2007). African American and Hispanic student engagement at Minority Serving and Predominantly White Institutions. *Journal of College Student Development*, 48(1), 39–56.

Núñez, A.-M. (2014). *Counting what counts for Latinas/os and Hispanic-Serving Institutions: A federal ratings system and postsecondary access, affordability, and success.* Policy brief presented to the President's Advisory Commission on Educational Excellence for Hispanics, New York, NY.

Núñez, A.-M., & Bowers, A.J. (2011). Exploring what leads high school students to enroll in Hispanic-Serving Institutions: A multilevel analysis. *American Educational Research Journal, 48*(6), 1286–1313.

Núñez, A.-M., Crisp, G., & Elizondo, D. (in press). Mapping Hispanic-Serving Institutions: A typology of institutional diversity. *Journal of Higher Education.*

Núñez, A.-M., & Elizondo, D. (2012). *Hispanic-Serving Institutions in the U.S. mainland and Puerto Rico: Organizational characteristics, institutional financial context, and graduation outcomes* (White paper). San Antonio, TX: Hispanic Association of Colleges and Universities.

Núñez, A.-M., Hoover, R., Pickett, K., Stuart-Carruthers, C., & Vázquez, M. (2013). Latinos in higher education: Creating conditions for success. *ASHE Monograph, 39*(1). San Francisco, CA: Jossey-Bass.

Pascarella, E.T., Edison, M.I., Nora, A., Hagedorn, L.S., & Terenzini, P.T. (1998). Does work inhibit cognitive development during college? *Educational Evaluation and Policy Analysis*, 20(2), 75–93.

Pfeffer, J., & Salancik, G. (1978). *The external control of organizations: A resource dependence perspective.* New York, NY: Harper and Row.

Pike, G.R., Kuh, G.D., & Massa-McKinley, R. (2008). First-year students' employment, engagement, and academic achievement: Untangling the relationship between work and grades. *NASPA Journal*, 45(4), 560–582.

Radford, A.W., Berkner, L., Wheeless, B., & Shepherd, B. (2010). *Persistence and attainment of 2003–4 Beginning Postsecondary Students: After 6 years* (NCES 2011-151). Washington, DC: National Center for Education Statistics.

Rendón, L., Dowd, A., & Nora, A. (2012). *Priced out: A close look at postsecondary affordability for Latinos.* Washington, DC: The Higher Education Subcommittee on President Barack Obama's Advisory Commission on Educational Excellence for Hispanics.

Rodríguez, A., & Calderón Galdeano, E. (2014). *What is working for Latinos? Understanding Latinos' postsecondary outcomes at HSIs versus non-HSIs.* Paper presented at the meeting of the American Educational Research Association, Philadelphia, PA.

Rodríguez, V.M. (2011). Social protest and the future of Puerto Rico. *Academe, 97*(4).

Santiago, D.A. (2006). *Inventing Hispanic-Serving Institutions (HSIs): The basics.* Washington, DC: *Excelencia* in Education.

Stanton-Salazar, R.D., Macías, R.M., Bensimon, E.M., & Dowd, A.C. (2010). *The role of institutional agents in providing institutional support to Latino students in STEM.* Annual Meeting of the Association for the Study of Higher Education, Indianapolis, IN.

Titus, M.A. (2006a). Understanding college degree completion of students with low socio-economic status: The influence of the institutional financial context. *Research in Higher Education, 47*(4), 371–398.

Titus, M.A. (2006b). Understanding the influence of the financial context of institutions on student persistence at four-year colleges and universities. *Journal of Higher Education,* 77(2), 353–375.

Titus, M.A. (2009). The production of bachelor's degrees and financial aspects of state higher education policy: A dynamic analysis. *The Journal of Higher Education, 80*(4), 439–468.

Torres, V., & Zerquera, D. (2012). Hispanic-Serving Institutions: Patterns, predictions, and implications for informing policy discussions. *Journal of Hispanic Higher Education, 11*(3), 259–278.

Vega, A., & Martínez, R.A. (2012). Latino scorecard for higher Education: A focus on Texas universities. *Journal of Hispanic Higher Education*, 11(1), 41–54.

Webber, D.A., & Ehrenberg, R.G. (2009). *Do expenditures other than instructional expenditures affect graduation and graduation rates in American higher education?* Ithaca, NY: Cornell Higher Education Research Institute.

Wortham, S., Clonan-Roy, K., Link, H., & Martínez, C. (2013). Scattered challenges, singular solutions: The new Latino diaspora. *Phi Delta Kappan, 94*(6), 14–19.

5

USING ORGANIZATIONAL THEORY TO STUDY HISPANIC-SERVING INSTITUTIONS

An Imperative Research Agenda

Gina A. García

In the last forty years, we have witnessed the burgeoning of the Latina/o student population in both two- and four-year colleges and universities. This proliferation has led to the development of a new organizational label, Hispanic-Serving Institutions (HSIs), for postsecondary institutions enrolling 25% or more Latina/o students. Although HSIs have struggled for organizational recognition since 1984, when Senator Paul Simon introduced H.R. 5240, they were not formally acknowledged by the federal government until the signing of the Higher Education Act (HEA) of 1992 (Calderón Galdeano, Flores, & Moder, 2012; MacDonald, Botti, & Clark, 2007; Santiago, 2006). This signing not only ensured federal appropriations for these institutions, it also provided them with legitimacy as an emerging form within the organizational field of postsecondary institutions. Beyond the 25% enrollment requirement, however, there are no clear indicators of what a federally designated HSI is, what it should do, or how it ought to "serve" Latina/o students, bringing to the forefront the most pervasive argument amongst HSI scholars, that they are merely "Hispanic-enrolling" as opposed to "Hispanic-serving."

Using conventional metrics, it appears that HSIs are not serving Latinas/os any better than non-HSIs. At the same time, many of the traditional outcomes that we use to determine success are narrowly defined and dictated by a hegemonic ideology of education. They ignore the insidious effects of structural and cultural racism that have contributed to the achievement gap between Latina/o and White students throughout the P–20 educational pipeline. To expect HSIs to mend the unrelenting effects of oppression and discrimination faced by Latinas/os falls just short of waiting for a miracle. Instead, the federal government, advocacy organizations such as the Hispanic Association of Colleges and Universities (HACU), HSI administrators, and, most importantly, HSI scholars need to find ways to challenge the dominate paradigm for viewing HSIs. Like the scholars who argue that we must reframe research focused on Latina/o students, which is often conducted through a deficit lens (Valencia & Solórzano, 1997), I propose that we find ways to study HSIs using a strengths-based approach.

One way to do this is to study HSIs using an organizational lens. By pulling from interdisciplinary theories that stem from sociology, management, organizational behavior, and higher education, we can begin to examine the ways in which HSIs are transforming as we analyze the challenges facing these institutions and focus on the strengths inherent within them. Although I agree that HSIs need to embrace their identity as Latina/o-serving in order to effectively transform from historically White institutions and dismantle the pervasive effects of racism and oppression, we as scholars must assist them in this immense task by conducting research that is focused on the potential that these organizations have to change and excel.

By using theories that highlight the role of the external environment in shaping HSIs, the unique organizational culture within HSIs, the changing nature of the organizational identity of HSIs, and the role of forces within these organizations that are transforming them, we can offer suggestions for advancing the effectiveness of HSIs while highlighting best practices for leading them. This chapter discusses some of the most prominent organizational theories that can be used to advance the research on HSIs, with an emphasis on theories that focus on organizational change. Additionally, it highlights current research on HSIs that uses an organizational lens to illuminate how organizations that were not founded as Latina/o-serving may in fact be transforming in order to embrace a more Latina/o-serving mission.

Why Use Organizational Theory?

Organizational theory has long been used in research as a way to view change within postsecondary institutions. Despite the enduring assumption that change is slow and inertial in colleges and universities, it is an inevitable part of organizational life (Kezar, 2012). The establishment of HSIs is confirmation that the postsecondary landscape does adapt to changes in the environment. As Latina/o students began to enter postsecondary education in higher numbers, campus administrators responded with a push for federal legislation to recognize the needs of Latina/o students and the institutions that serve them. Although it took time and several failed attempts to amend the HEA in order to recognize HSIs as a legitimate organizational form, this change eventually took place. The increase in the number of HSIs each year and the growing interest in applying for HSI grants offered by the federal government is evidence that this change will continue.

Organizational theory that looks at change is imperative for studying HSIs and can help to reframe the dichotomous approach to understanding the way they serve Latinas/os. Rather than asking, "Do HSIs adequately serve Latinas/os or just enroll them?" we can begin to ask broader questions that look at the complex and systemic nature of higher education. Perhaps we should more thoroughly examine the nature of the political and sociohistorical environments that are shaping the way HSIs serve students. Or perhaps it is important to understand that HSIs are undergoing a temporal process of becoming institutions that serve Latina/o students, rather than dismissing them as historically White institutions that are structurally racist and discriminatory in nature. Using an organizational lens will help to reframe the research in hopes of finding ways in which HSIs are in fact changing, albeit slowly, into organizations that embrace their newfound role to serve Latina/o students. Although there is an abundance of organizational theory that offers different vantage points from which to view HSIs, this chapter reviews four major bodies of literature that focus on the organizational environment, organizational culture, organizational identity, and social movements. Each of these should be considered important for understanding the way institutions that were not originally founded with the purpose of serving Latina/o students can, in fact, change.

Environmental Theories

It is essential to understand the relationship between an organization and its environment since the environment often affects the activities and structures of the organization, who it serves, and whether or not it will survive and thrive. There are a number of theories that focus on how the environment fosters change within an organization, with each theory varying in the proposed degree of control that the environment has over the organization and, likewise, the organization's perceived degree of freedom to control its environment (Bess & Dee, 2008). These theories are important in studying HSIs in particular since the environment has a significant level of control, making the institutions vulnerable to changes in state and federal legislation regarding issues of enrollment, affirmative action, financial aid, and competitive grant funding. As a political construct (Santiago, 2012), the very nature of the HSI label is susceptible to changes in the federal legislation that define them. This section discusses three environmental theories that are well established and have the potential to address some of the major concerns that HSI scholars have articulated.

Resource Dependence Theory

Resource dependence theory was originally developed in the 1970s with the underlying premise that all organizations strive to ensure their survival and enhance their autonomy (Davis & Cobb, 2010). The theory has three main themes laid out by Pfeffer and Salancik (2003) in their largely cited book, *The External Control of Organizations: A Resource Dependence Perspective*: (1) social context matters for understanding what decisions are made, (2) organizations have the ability to obtain more autonomy and pursue organizational interests through a variety of strategies, and (3) power matters for understanding intraorganizational and inter-organizational behavior. As suggested by the theory, organizations must interact with their social environments and acquire resources that will support the activities that lead to desired outcomes (Pfeffer & Salancik, 2003). In resource dependence, there is an emphasis on the actions of individuals within an organization in an attempt to manage relationships with other organizations. Understanding the level of dependence that individual organizations have on external entities is important, with three critical factors that determine the level of dependence, including the importance of the resource for survival, the extent to which the interest group has control over the resource, and the availability of alternatives (Pfeffer & Salancik, 2003).

There are a number of external entities that attempt to control the actions of institutions of higher education, including the federal government, state and local governments, accrediting organizations, donors, regulatory boards, and other colleges and universities (Gladieux, King, & Corrigan, 2005; Harcleroad & Eaton, 2005). In studying environmental effects on postsecondary institutions, resource dependence theory dictates that these entities be considered. Tolbert (1985) tested the effects of resource dependence (as measured by revenue generated from the state and federal government, private gifts, and self-generated funds) on administrative differentiation (as measured by the number of public and private funding offices on campus) and found that increasing dependence does not lead to greater differentiation, unless dependency relations are not institutionalized. Santos (2007) used a resource dependence perspective to analyze the internal allocation of resources at public research institutions and found that undergraduate teaching activities had a greater return in the social sciences than in engineering and the physical sciences, and teaching is often used to cross-subsidize research activities in these areas. In two different studies, Titus (2006a, 2006b) combined a number of persistence theories with resource dependence theory and found that, after accounting for student-level predictors of persistence, the institution's reliance on tuition dollars as a source of revenue also significantly predicted student persistence. A number of scholars have used resource dependence theory to better understand institutions of higher education, and have often combined it with other theories, suggesting that it has significant value to higher education research.

For example, Núñez and Elizondo (2012) built off the work of Titus (2006a, 2006b) in order to illuminate the degree to which academic, social, and financial resources could explain six-year institutional graduation rates of Latina/o students attending four-year HSIs. Like Titus, they found a significant relationship between tuition dollars and graduation rates; however, they noted significant differences between U.S. mainland and Puerto Rican HSIs in the amount of revenue received per student from tuition, grants, and contracts. This environmental effect is important to note, as resources are clearly not distributed equally across all HSIs. Institutional resources are, however, important indicators of six-year graduation rates for Latina/o students at HSIs (García, 2013b; Núñez & Elizondo, 2012) and therefore have a contextual effect, with HSIs in Puerto Rico having lower graduation rates (Núñez & Elizondo, 2012).

In Chapter 9 in this volume, Ortega, Frye, Nellum, Kamimura, and Vidal-Rodríguez also use a resource dependence framework to analyze the financial resources of HSIs. In Chapter 11, Rodríguez and Calderón Galdeano build on Nuñéz and Elizondo's (2012; Chapter 4, this volume) work to compare institutional characteristics and student outcomes in HSIs and non-HSIs. As evidenced by its surge in popularity in examining HSIs, resource dependence theory can clearly help us understand how the environment affects the survival of HSIs while allowing us to critically examine how they may interact with their environment in order to survive.

Population Ecology

The population ecology of organizations was conceived by Hannan and Freeman (1977) as an alternative to the dominant adaptation perspective of the 1970s. The theory takes into consideration the role of the environment in determining the distribution and limitation of organizations within the environment. Hannan and Freeman proposed that the unit of analysis should be the population of organizations, which includes the aggregate of organizations, suppliers, and members served by the population. By looking at the entire population of organizations, the focus shifts from individual decision making and strategy formulation within the organization to a systemic level of action and determinism. In developing a theory about population ecology of organizations, Hannan and Freeman expanded on basic human ecology theories and incorporated notions of competition and niche markets. Competition ensues as organizations within the population compete for limited resources while becoming either specialists or generalists, depending on the stability of the environment (Hannan & Freeman, 1977).

Numerous studies have used a population ecology perspective to determine the likelihood that an organization will survive within a population (i.e., Baum & Singh, 1994; Carroll, 1985), but relatively few have used it to study postsecondary institutions. Birnbaum (1983) and Morphew (2009) are exceptions. Both used a population ecology perspective to look at institutional diversity in colleges and universities in the United States and found that, despite growth in the number of institutions (over two different time periods), there continued to be less diversity among postsecondary institutions. This may be the result of the tendency of organizations to mimic other organizations rather than developing new specializations (DiMaggio & Powell, 1983).

Analyzing HSIs at the population level is an important way to study them, particularly as we begin to think of HSIs as their own organizational form. Thus, we can use population ecology to frame the research on HSIs, posing a number of questions that look at the entire population of these institutions. As suggested by current reports produced by *Excelencia* in Education, HSIs are increasing in number at a tremendous rate (Calderón Galdeano & Santiago, 2014). With this increase, there is a need to understand these institutions as a population rather than as individual units. More specifically, I suggest we use population ecology to understand the diversity of HSIs since they are quite heterogeneous in nature, ranging from public to private, two-year to four-year, and small to large. As noted by Núñez and Elizondo (2012; Chapter 4, this volume), there are also significant differences in the revenue and outcomes of U.S. mainland and Puerto Rican HSIs. Their findings suggest that we must account for their diversity, considering them as unique institutions within a larger population.

Institutional Theory

Like population ecology theory, institutional theory is based on the principle that the environment is largely deterministic, exerting a high level of control over organizations (Bess & Dee, 2008). According to Bess and Dee (2008), institutional theory emphasizes the normative and ideological aspects of the environment that shape the way organizations behave, and when institutions conform to the expectations set forth by the environment, they are viewed as legitimate or "acting in accordance with well-established and accepted patterns of behavior" (p. 142). Legitimacy, therefore, is an important foundation of institutional theory because it shapes the way organizations attempt to align themselves with similar organizations while conforming to societal expectations.

Meyer and Rowan (1977) were early institutional theorists, arguing that rationalization in post-industrial organizations is more influenced by social norms and behaviors than by formal structures and rules. They asserted that organizations strive for legitimacy through isomorphic behaviors, acting in ways that establish their image and prestige in light of public opinion (Meyer & Rowan, 1977). DiMaggio and Powell (1983) drew on this early work and developed a testable theory of institutional isomorphism while suggesting that there is an enormous amount of homogeneity among organizations. They proposed that an organizational field emerges as a result of three types of isomorphic behavior, including coercive, mimetic, and normative (DiMaggio & Powell, 1983). Coercive pressures are exerted by other organizations within the field and often include governmental forces and legislation; mimetic pressures are caused by uncertainty, forcing organizations to imitate or copy one another; and normative pressures are often dictated by professionalization and widespread industry-specific standards to which organizations attempt to adapt (DiMaggio & Powell, 1983).

These concepts have been tested by a number of scholars using the postsecondary landscape as the population. Lounsbury and Pollack (2001) provided support for the theory of institutionalism by tracking the emergence of service learning within higher education, arguing that it became legitimated and institutionalized as the result of the changing nature of field logic from an unarticulated closed-system logic (knowledge is universal) to an open-system logic (knowledge is subjective). Kraatz and Zajac (1996) argued that neoinstitutionalism is limited, using quantitative data to show that when faced with powerful market-based pressures in the 1970s, liberal arts colleges rarely mimicked their more prestigious counterparts, instead incorporating illegitimate curricula contrary to normative practices. This led to the field becoming less homogenous.

Institutional theory can be powerful for studying the population of postsecondary institutions, and it is relevant for studying HSIs. Beyond the internal context for change, HSIs are forced to negotiate the external context, including social, political, and financial demands. Understanding the effects of coercive pressures that come from other organizations, including state and federal governments, is an important endeavor for HSI research. Since HSIs are eligible for federal funding, they are more susceptible to pressures from the federal government. Recent requests for proposals issued by the U.S. Department of Education (2013) for HSI capacity building grants call for institutions to focus on science, technology, engineering, and mathematics (STEM) and articulation. Institutions interested in receiving these monies, therefore, are being pressured to focus on these two issues, whether or not they believe they are the most pertinent issues facing the Latina/o students in their institutions.

It may also be worthwhile to study the effects of mimetic and normative pressures on HSIs. This may include a deeper analysis of the ways in which the Hispanic Association of Colleges and Universities (HACU), a professionalization organization, has influenced how HSIs operate. Additionally, it is important to understand how HSIs are mimicking each other by sharing best practices. Some states with a large number of HSIs, such as California, are developing their own collaborative consortiums to coordinate the efforts of local HSIs. Understanding the ways that these consortiums have a mimetic effect on the organizational identity of HSIs is a noteworthy research agenda. Institutional theory, therefore, can help us to better understand the entire population of HSIs, rather than only individual institutions.

Organizational Culture

Organizational culture is a complex notion that has been studied by anthropologists and borrowed by organizational theorists as a way of understanding and explaining behavior within organizations (Bess & Dee, 2008). Specifically defined, culture "incorporate[s] the idea of a shared philosophy or ideology, or a set of values, beliefs, expectations, and assumptions that guide behavior in a social system" (Bess & Dee, 2008, pp. 362–363). Understanding organizational culture can help decision makers problem solve by identifying patterns of performance and effectiveness as well as conflicts within the organization (Tierney, 1988). Higher education scholars have tested theories focused on organizational culture more extensively than environmental theories. Several researchers have also developed frameworks specifically for studying organizational culture within postsecondary institutions.

Tierney (1988) argued that there are six essential concepts to be considered in an organizational analysis of culture, including environment, mission, socialization, information, strategy, and leadership. His model was an early attempt to develop a framework to be used to study culture specifically within a college or university setting. Kuh and Whitt (1988) identified four main layers in their framework, including the external environment, the institution itself, subcultures, and individual actors.

In recognizing the need to focus on race within organizational studies of higher education, Chesler, Lewis, and Crowfoot (2005) proposed a framework that could be used to study the culture of institutions striving to become more multicultural, including eight distinct dimensions that should be examined: mission, culture, power, membership, climate, technology, resources, and boundary management. Similarly, Hurtado, Álvarez, Guillermo-Wann, Cuellar, and Arellano (2012) built off of models that emphasized the organizational nature of the campus climate for diversity (Milem, Chang, & antonio, 2005; Williams, Berger, & McClendon, 2005) and proposed a model that places social identities at the center while including the broader context for establishing policies and practices. Hurtado et al. (2012) defined several organizational structures that should be considered in analyzing the culture and climate for diversity, including those related to tenure processes, decision-making processes, faculty and staff recruitment, and hiring and budget allocations. These frameworks offer a unique perspective for studying organizational culture and climate since they allow researchers to examine racism, sexism, and other forms of oppression within institutions of higher education.

In many ways, current research on HSIs is largely focused on organizational culture. Although a majority of studies have used individuals as the unit of analysis and few authors have constructed studies using an organizational lens, empirical research suggests that the organizational culture of each HSI is unique and enhances a number of outcomes. Scholars portend that the cultural identity of Latina/o students is largely intertwined with the culture of the institution, which may foster their connections with the campus and enhance their chances of persisting to degree (Arana, Castañeda-Sound, Blanchard, & Aguilar, 2011; Dayton, González-Vásquez, Martínez, & Plum, 2004). For Latina/o students attending HSIs, having a cultural connection with Latina/o faculty and administrators who can serve as mentors and advocates is a unique experience and is of utmost importance to their success (Dayton et al., 2004; Medina & Posadas, 2012; Stanton-Sálazar, Macias, Bensimon, & Dowd, 2010). The culture of HSIs has also been found to foster students' ethnic identity development (González, 2010; Guardia & Evans, 2008), linguistic connections with other students and staff on campus (Sebanc, Hernández, & Alvarado, 2009), sense of belonging (Maestas, Vaquera, & Muñoz Zehr, 2007), and diversity awareness (Kiser & Scobey, 2010).

These findings suggest that studying the organizational culture of HSIs is an important endeavor because the culture is in fact unique and transformative. A majority of studies, however, have only focused on one aspect of the culture, such as individual actors, climate, or membership. Future research should use the organization as the unit of analysis in order to provide evidence for the ways that the organizational culture affects both individual- and organizational-level outcomes. The technology of organizations, for example, or the ways in which inputs are transformed into outputs (Chesler et al., 2005), should be studied more closely using a cultural lens. Specifically, we should determine whether the curriculum, pedagogy, and programming at HSIs is transforming in order to adapt to the changing needs of students and also explore the ways in which these variables influence the culture of the institutions.

Some empirical research at the classroom level has begun to reveal the distinct characteristics of organizational elements of HSIs that may affect the culture. For example, Cole (2011) conducted an extensive investigation of the curriculum at HSIs and found that, on average, only 3% of all courses offered at HSIs were ethnocentric, meaning they specifically focused on the history, experiences, and perspectives of one group. This suggests that the curriculum at HSIs has not yet been transformed with the purpose of actually serving Latina/o students and may not have an influence on the organizational culture. A few single-site examples, however, reveal that faculty at HSIs have in fact incorporated successful pedagogical techniques to adapt to the changing needs of students at HSIs. Kiasatpour and Lasley (2008) found that political science faculty at HSIs in Texas incorporated student-centered assignments—such as service-learning, group work, and free writing activities—more often than faculty at non-HSIs as a way to increase the engagement and learning of Latina/o students. Bridges, Kinzie, Nelson Laird, and Kuh (2008) similarly reported that faculty at HSIs in California were using culturally relevant approaches to connect students' strengths to course-based learning objectives. García (2013a) found that the Chicana/o Studies curriculum at one HSI has had a transformative effect on the way members construct their organizational identity as an HSI. Future research should further scrutinize the relationship between the distinct elements of the organizational structures and culture, with an emphasis on enhancing individual and organizational outcomes at HSIs.

Organizational Identity

The field of organizational identity has evolved over the past 25 years as researchers have begun to recognize its importance in research, practice, and policy. Early scholarship has found that having a strong sense of organizational identity is important for strategic management (Gioia & Thomas, 1996; Stimpert, Gustafson, & Sarason, 1998), for sustaining a competitive advantage (Stimpert et al., 1998), for interpreting and responding to current issues (Gioia & Thomas, 1996), for adapting to instability and changes in the environment (Gioia, Schultz, & Corley, 2000; Hsu & Hannan, 2005; Ran & Golden, 2011; Ravasi & Schultz, 2006), and for guiding the organization when transforming its core functions (Nag, Corley, & Gioia, 2007).

Although not always labeled as "organizational identity," Weerts, Freed, and Morphew (2014) mapped out four distinct narratives used in higher education scholarship that can be considered part of the organizational identity body of literature. Scholars in other fields, particularly organizational behavior, have also largely used higher education institutions as sites for studying the theoretical notion of organizational identities. Gioia and Thomas (1996), for example, found that when postsecondary administrators attempt to change the core mission of an institution, they use sensemaking processes to project a desired future image or identity. Meanwhile, Humphreys and Brown (2002) discovered that simply changing labels is not enough to change the identity of a postsecondary organization because various members construct their identities based on their own perceptions of the organization. Together these findings suggest that college and university administrators have the ability to influence how members see the organization, but, ultimately, the members define the organizational identity based on their own experiences.

There is an abundance of literature that outlines the theoretical development of an organizational identity. Albert and Whetten (1985) claimed that organizational identity is best understood by asking members to respond to the question, "Who are we as an organization?" They argued that there are three necessary and sufficient criteria for organizational identity, including central, distinctive, and enduring characteristics. Clegg, Rhodes, and Kornberger (2007) contended that organizational identity is located within the belief system of organizations. Notably, the best way to study organizational identity is to ask various institutional members, including mangers, employees, and external constituents, to construct their assumptions about the realities present within their organization (Albert, 1998; Clegg et al., 2007; Scott & Lane, 2000). In conducting research on the changing nature of organizational identities, some have argued that it is important to understand how members attach meaning to identity labels as opposed to the actual labels (Humphreys & Brown, 2002).

With the widespread argument that HSIs are simply "Hispanic-enrolling," studying the organizational identity of the institutions is crucial. Despite the fact that most HSIs were not originally founded with the intention to enroll, serve, and graduate Latina/o students, an HSI organizational identity can in fact become salient and may be intertwined with institutional missions and values (García, 2013c). Using a case study design, García (2013c) found that although various institutional members (including administrators, faculty, and staff) did not immediately label their institution as being an HSI, through sensemaking processes they constructed their identity as being regionally focused, committed to community, dedicated to access, and diverse-serving. These characteristics were largely intertwined with their conceptions of being Latina/o-serving, providing evidence that organizational identity is held deep within the shared assumptions and belief systems of an organization (Clegg et al., 2007; Gioia et al., 2000). Similarly, Perrakis and Hagedorn (2010) found that although students may not be aware of an institution's status as an HSI, there is a level of salience and recognition of the critical mass of Latina/o students on campus and of the importance of services and support programs that cater to Latina/o students. HSI organizational identity, therefore, may not be connected to awareness, but rather attached to meaning making that organizational members use to define their experiences (García, 2013a). Future studies should continue to analyze the fluidity of organizational identity within HSIs and determine its relationship to various student-level outcomes such as engagement and graduation.

Social Movement Theory

Social movement theory has historical roots dating back to the 1970s when social activism was particularly vibrant. Early scholarship sought to explain the emergence of social movements (McAdam, McCarthy, & Zald, 1996), while the last decade has witnessed a proliferation in scholarship that analyzes the political consequences of social movements (Amenta, Caren, Chiarello, & Su, 2010) and the role of social movements in altering markets (King & Pearce, 2010).

As a framework, there are a number of ways that social movement theory has been used to frame progress in higher education. Rojas (2006) found that non-disruptive tactics, such as demonstrations and rallies, had a positive effect on the creation of African American Studies programs at 1,423 colleges and universities. Lounsbury (2001) also discovered that the activities of a national social movement organization that supports environmental activism on college and university campuses predicted organizational practices and staffing related to recycling. And Slaughter (1997) used social movement theory to analyze the expansion of higher education curriculum that centers on race, class, and gender.

Several models and theoretical paradigms have been developed as a way to understand the rise of social movements, including resource mobilization (McCarthy & Zald, 1977), political process models (Tilly, 1978), and identity-oriented paradigms (Cohen, 1985). Although the paradigms vary, the basic tenets are similar across models. As proposed by McAdam et al. (1996), there are three basic theoretical concepts in social movement theory, including political opportunities, mobilizing structures, and framing processes. The opportunity structure refers to external opportunities that emerge due to the political environment (Morris, 2000). Mobilizing structures include formal and informal networks, preexisting structures, and organizations that actors use to mobilize for collective action (Morris, 2000). Framing includes the meaning-making processes that allow individuals to situate themselves within the movement, which are often based on culture, emotions, and deeply held beliefs (Benford & Snow, 2000). The framing component was largely missing from early social movement scholarship until Snow and colleagues (as cited in McAdam et al., 1996) stressed the importance of understanding cognitive ideas and ideational sentiments in the shaping of social movements.

Studying HSIs from an organizational perspective presents a unique opportunity to utilize social movement theory. In particular, there is a dearth of research that focuses on the ways in which social movements have led to structural change (Amenta et al., 2010), which is a vital research imperative for HSIs. Guided by social movement theory, García and Okhidoi (2013) used a case study to determine the relationship between the Chicano Movement of the late 1960s and the construction of an organizational identity for serving Latina/o students at one HSI.[1] They found that the Chicano Movement provided a ripe opportunity structure for the establishment of Chicana/o Studies programs at colleges and universities across the Southwest. Although the movement was short-lived, García and Okhidoi (2013) argued that it had a long-term impact on the organizational structures of the institution they studied. In particular, participants identified the Chicana/o Studies department as a primary way in which the institution reflected its ability to serve Latina/o students, by offering culturally relevant curriculum and pedagogy. Using historical data, García and Okhidoi (2013) highlighted the ways that the institution had removed the Chicana/o Studies program from the margins and placed it at the core of the institution, causing a transformational effect on the way organizational members constructed their identity as an HSI. Future research should continue to look at the ways that social movements have influenced the founding and development of HSIs.

Conclusion

Among higher education scholars, organizational theory has been extensively utilized in order to frame and analyze a number of issues. As a well-accepted framework, it is a logical choice for approaching some of the most pressing research concerns for HSI scholars. At the same time, organizational theory has been losing popularity within higher education research, which Bastedo (2012) suggested is related to its seeming lack of relevance in analyzing issues of social justice in postsecondary institutions. I contend that organizational theory can be quite powerful in framing issues related to diversity, equity, and social justice in higher education and particularly in HSIs. Rather than focusing on individual experiences and outcomes for students, faculty, and administrators at HSIs, an organizational lens forces us to think about how organizations that are arguably among the most diverse in the country are adjusting their policies, programs, and practices in order to adequately serve Latinas/os and other students of color. This is vital to understanding how an entire organization can take social action in order to dismantle racist structures and discriminatory policies that continue to plague students of color in the postsecondary pipeline.

Although there are numerous organizational theories that can be used to study HSIs, this chapter has focused on four types of theories that offer the most fruitful perspectives from which to study them. Environmental theories will help us take a more global approach to studying HSIs from a systemic level. With HSIs continuing to increase in number, there is a greater need for researchers to study these organizational forms within broader social, cultural, economic, and political contexts. Studying HSIs from a population perspective will give us a better understanding of the heterogeneous nature of these organizations in order for us to more closely scrutinize how individual HSIs can become specialists based on characteristics such as size, institutional type, control, and regional location.

Empirical research tells us that HSIs have unique cultures. These environments should be studied more closely using the organization as the unit of analysis. Theories that look specifically at the organizational culture can help us to understand the relationship between culture and a number of important outcomes, such as student adjustment, sense of belonging, persistence, graduation, and ultimate success. Moving beyond culture, HSIs must also understand their organizational identity as HSIs, which may affect how they make decisions, interact with the environment, and ultimately serve Latina/o students. Finally, we must determine how internal conflicts and contentious behaviors have ultimately transformed HSIs. Considering these theories individually and in conjunction with one another is imperative as we move forward with the study of Hispanic-Serving Institutions.

Note

1 "Chicano" is used to refer to the formal movement, which was largely exclusive of women.

References

Albert, S. (1998). The definition and metadefinition of identity. *Identity in organizations: Building theory through conversations.* Thousand Oaks, CA: SAGE.

Albert, S., & Whetten, D.A. (1985). Organizational identity. In L.L. Cummings & B.M. Staw (Eds.), *Research in organizational behavior* (Vol. 7, pp. 263–295). Greenwich, CT: JAI Press.

Amenta, E., Caren, N., Chiarello, E., & Su, Y. (2010). The political consequences of social movements. *Annual Review of Sociology, 36,* 287–307.

Arana, R., Castañeda-Sound, C., Blanchard, S., & Aguilar, T.E. (2011). Indicators of persistence for Hispanic undergraduate achievement: Toward an ecological model. *Journal of Hispanic Higher Education, 10*(3), 237–251.

Bastedo, M.N. (2012). Organizing higher education: A manifesto. In M.N. Bastedo (Ed.), *The organization of higher education: Managing colleges for a new era.* Baltimore, MD: Johns Hopkins University.

Baum, J.A.C., & Singh, J.V. (1994). Organizational niches and the dynamics of organizational mortality. *American Journal of Sociology, 100*(2), 346–380.

Benford, R.D., & Snow, D.A. (2000). Framing processes and social movements: An overview and assessment. *Annual Review of Sociology, 26,* 611–639.

Bess, J.L., & Dee, J.R. (2008). *Understanding college and university organizations: Theories for effective policy and practice* (Vol. 1–2). Sterling, VA: Stylus.

Birnbaum, R. (1983). *Maintaining diversity in higher education.* San Francisco, CA: Jossey-Bass.

Bridges, B.K., Kinzie, J., Nelson Laird, T.F., & Kuh, G.D. (2008). Student engagement and student success at historically Black and Hispanic-Serving Institutions. In M. Gasman, B. Baez, & C.S.V. Turner (Eds.), *Understanding minority-serving institutions* (pp. 217–236). Albany, NY: SUNY Press.

Calderón Galdeano, E., Flores, A.R., & Moder, J. (2012). The Hispanic Association of Colleges and Universities and Hispanic-Serving Institutions: Partners in the advancement of Hispanic higher education. *Journal of Latinos and Education, 11*(3), 157–162.

Calderón Galdeano, E., & Santiago, D.A. (2014). Hispanic-Serving Institutions (HSIs): 2012–2013 fact sheet. Washington, DC: *Excelencia* in Education. [Electronic source]. Retrieved from http://www.edexcelencia.org/research/2012-2013-hsi-lists

Carroll, G.R. (1985). Concentration and specialization: Dynamics of niche width in populations of organizations. *American Journal of Sociology, 90*(6), 1262–1283.

Chesler, M., Lewis, A., & Crowfoot, J. (2005). *Challenging racism in higher education: Promoting justice.* Boulder, CO: Rowman & Littlefield.

Clegg, S.R., Rhodes, C., & Kornberger, M. (2007). Desperately seeking legitimacy: Organizational identity and emerging industries. *Organization Studies, 28*(4), 495–513.

Cohen, J.L. (1985). Strategy or identity: New theoretical paradigms and contemporary social movements. *Social Research, 52*(4), 663–716.

Cole, W.M. (2011). Minority politics and group-differentiated curricula at minority-serving colleges. *The Review of Higher Education, 34*(3), 381–422.

Davis, G.F., & Cobb, J.A. (2010). Resource dependence theory: Past and future. *Research in the Sociology of Organizations, 28*, 21–42.

Dayton, B., González-Vásquez, N., Martínez, C.R., & Plum, C. (2004). Hispanic-Serving Institutions through the eyes of students and administrators. In A.M. Ortiz (Ed.), *Addressing the unique needs of Latino American students* (New Directions for Student Services No. 105, pp. 29–40). San Francisco, CA: Jossey-Bass.

DiMaggio, P.J., & Powell, W.W. (1983). The iron cage revisited: Institutional isomorphism and collective rationality in organizational fields. *American Sociological Review, 48*(2), 147–160.

García, G.A. (2013a). *Challenging the manufactured identity of Hispanic Serving Institutions: Co-constructing an organizational identity* (Unpublished doctoral dissertation). University of California, Los Angeles, CA.

García, G.A. (2013b). Does the percentage of Latina/os affect graduation rates at four-year Hispanic Serving Institutions (HSIs), emerging HSIs, and non-HSIs? *Journal of Hispanic Higher Education, 12*(3), 256–268.

García, G.A. (2013c). *It's more than just a label: Exploring the construction of an organizational identity for Hispanic Serving Institutions (HSIs).* Paper presented at the meeting of the Association for the Study of Higher Education, St. Louis, MO.

García, G.A., & Okhidoi, O. (2013). *Connecting social movements, historical legacies, and the organizational identity of a Hispanic Serving Institution (HSI).* Paper presented at the meeting of the Association for the Study of Higher Education, St. Louis, MO.

Gioia, D.A., Schultz, M., & Corley, K.G. (2000). Organizational identity, image, and adaptive instability. *The Academy of Management Review, 25*(1), 63–81.

Gioia, D.A., & Thomas, J.B. (1996). Identity, image, and issue interpretation: Sensemaking during strategic change in academia. *Administrative Science Quarterly, 41*(3), 370–403.

Gladieux, L.E., King, J.E., & Corrigan, M.E. (2005). The federal government and higher education. In P.G. Altbach, R.O. Berdahl, & P.J. Gumport (Eds.), *American higher education in the twenty-first century: Social, political, and economic challenges* (pp. 272–303). Baltimore, MD: Johns Hopkins University.

González, R.G. (2010). Ethnic identity at a majority Hispanic-Serving Institution. *Journal of Latinos and Education, 9*(4), 284–302.

Guardia, J.R., & Evans, N.J. (2008). Factors influencing the ethnic identity development of Latino fraternity members at a Hispanic Serving Institution. *Journal of College Student Development, 49*(3), 163–181.

Hannan, M.T., & Freeman, J. (1977). The population ecology of organizations. *American Journal of Sociology, 82*(5), 929–964.

Harcleroad, F.F., & Eaton, J.S. (2005). The hidden hand: External constituencies and their impact. In P.G. Altbach, R.O. Berdahl, & P.J. Gumport (Eds.), *American higher education in the twenty-first century: Social, political, and economic challenges* (2nd ed., pp. 253–283). Baltimore, MD: Johns Hopkins University.

Hsu, G., & Hannan, M. (2005). Identities, genres, and organizational forms. *Organization Science, 16*(5), 474–490.

Humphreys, M., & Brown, A.D. (2002). Narratives of organizational identity and identification: A case study of hegemony and resistance. *Organization Studies, 23*(3), 421–447.

Hurtado, S., Álvarez, C., Guillermo-Wann, C., Cuellar, M., & Arellano, L. (2012). A model for diverse learning environments: The scholarship on creating and assessing conditions for student success. In J.C. Smart & M.B. Paulson (Eds.), *Higher education: Handbook of theory and research* (Vol. 27, pp. 41–122). New York, NY: Springer.

Kezar, A. (2012). Organizational change in a global, postmodern world. In M.N. Bastedo (Ed.), *The organization of higher education: Managing college for a new era* (pp. 181–221). Baltimore, MD: Johns Hopkins University.

Kiasatpour, S., & Lasley, S. (2008). Overcoming the challenges of teaching political science in the Hispanic-serving classroom: A survey of institutions of higher education in Texas. *Journal of Political Science Education, 4*(2), 151–168.

King, B.G., & Pearce, N.A. (2010). The contentiousness of markets: Politics, social movements, and institutional change in markets *Annual Review of Sociology, 36,* 249–267.

Kiser, A.I.T., & Scobey, B. (2010). Assessing diversity awareness in university business students at a Hispanic serving liberal arts institution. *Journal of Hispanic Higher Education, 9*(4), 294–303.

Kraatz, M.S., & Zajac, E.J. (1996). Exploring the limits of the new institutionalism: The causes and consequences of illegitimate organizational change. *American Sociological Review, 61*(5), 812–836.

Kuh, G.D., & Whitt, E.J. (1988). *The invisible tapestry: Culture in American colleges and universities* (ASHE-ERIC Higher Education Report, Vol. 17). Washington, DC: The George Washington University, Graduate School of Education and Human Development.

Lounsbury, M. (2001). Institutional sources of practice variation: Staffing college and university recycling programs. *Administrative Science Quarterly, 46,* 29–56.

Lounsbury, M., & Pollock, S. (2001). Institutionalizing civic engagement: Shifting logics and the cultural repackaging of service-learning in U.S. higher education. *Organization, 8*(2), 319–339.

MacDonald, V.M., Botti, J.M., & Clark, L.H. (2007). From visibility to autonomy: Latinos and higher education in the U.S., 1965–2005. *Harvard Educational Review, 77*(4), 474–504.

Maestas, R., Vaquera, G.S., & Muñoz Zehr, L. (2007). Factors impacting sense of belonging at a Hispanic-Serving Institution. *Journal of Hispanic Higher Education, 6*(3), 237–256.

McAdam, D., McCarthy, J.D., & Zald, M.N. (1996). Introduction: Opportunities, mobilizing structures, and framing processes-toward a synthetic, comparative perspective on social movements. In D. McAdam, J.D. McCarthy, & M.N. Zald (Eds.), *Comparative perspectives on social movements: Political opportunities, mobilizing structures, and cultural framings* (pp. 1–20). New York, NY: Cambridge University Press.

McCarthy, J.D., & Zald, M.N. (1977). Resource mobilization and social movements: A partial theory. *American Journal of Sociology, 82*(6), 1212–1241.

Medina, C.A., & Posadas, C.E. (2012). Hispanic student experiences at a Hispanic-Serving Institution: Strong voices, key message. *Journal of Latinos and Education, 11*(3), 182–188.

Meyer, J.W., & Rowan, B. (1977). Institutionalized organizations: Formal structures as myth and ceremony. *American Journal of Sociology, 83*(2), 340–363.

Milem, J.F., Chang, M.J., & antonio, a.l. (2005). *Making diversity work on campus: A research-based perspective.* Washington, DC: Association of American Colleges and Universities.

Morphew, C.C. (2009). Conceptualizing change in the institutional diversity of U.S. colleges and universities. *Journal of Higher Education, 80*(3), 243–269.

Morris, A. (2000). Reflections on social movement theory: Criticisms and proposals. *Contemporary Sociology, 29*(3), 445–454.

Nag, R., Corley, K.G., & Gioia, D.A. (2007). The intersection of organization identity, knowledge, and practice: Attempting strategic change via knowledge grafting. *Academy of Management Journal, 50*(4), 821–847.

Núñez, A.-M., & Elizondo, D. (2012). *Hispanic-Serving Institutions in the U.S. mainland and Puerto Rico: Organizational characteristics, institutional financial context, and graduation outcomes.* San Antonio, TX: Hispanic Association of Colleges and Universities.

Perrakis, A., & Hagedorn, L.S. (2010). Latino/a student success in community colleges and Hispanic-Serving Institution status. *Community College Journal of Research and Practice, 34*(10), 797–813.

Pfeffer, J., & Salancik, G.R. (2003). *The external control of organizations: A resource dependence perspective.* Stanford, CA: Stanford University.

Ran, B., & Golden, T.J. (2011). Who are we? The social construction of organizational identity through sense-exchanging. *Administration & Society, 43*(4), 417–445.

Ravasi, D., & Schultz, M. (2006). Responding to organizational identity threats: Exploring the role of organizational culture. *Academy of Management Journal, 49*(3), 433–458.

Rojas, F. (2006). Social movement tactics, organizational change and the spread of African-American studies. *Social Forces, 84*(4), 2147–2166.

Santiago, D.A. (2006). *Inventing Hispanic-Serving Institutions (HSIs): The basics.* Washington, DC: *Excelencia* in Education.

Santiago, D.A. (2012). Public policy and the Hispanic-Serving Institutions: From invention to accountability. *Journal of Latinos and Education, 11*(3), 163–167.

Santos, J.L. (2007). Resource allocation in public research universities. *The Review of Higher Education, 30*(2), 125–144.

Scott, S.G., & Lane, V.R. (2000). A stakeholder approach to organizational identity. *The Academy of Management Journal, 25*(1), 43–62.

Sebanc, A.M., Hernández, M.D., & Alvarado, M. (2009). Understanding, connection, and identification: Friendship features of bilingual Spanish-English speaking undergraduates. *Journal of Adolescent Research, 24*(2), 194–217.

Slaughter, S. (1997). Class, race and gender and the construction of postsecondary curricula in the United States: Social movement, professionalization and political economic theories of curricular change. *Journal of Curriculum Studies, 29*(1), 1–30.

Stanton-Sálazar, R.D., Macias, R.M., Bensimon, E.M., & Dowd, A.C. (2010). *The role of institutional agents in providing institutional support to Latino students in STEM.* Paper presented at the meeting of the Association for the Study of Higher Education, Indianapolis, IN.

Stimpert, J.L.L., Gustafson, L.T., & Sarason, Y. (1998). Organizational identity within the strategic management conversation: Contributions and assumptions. In D.A. Whetten & P.C. Godfrey (Eds.), *Identity in organizations: Building theory through conversations.* Thousand Oaks, CA: SAGE.

Tierney, W.G. (1988). Organizational culture in higher education: Defining the essentials. *Journal of Higher Education, 59*(1), 2–21.

Tilly, C. (1978). *From mobilization to revolution.* Reading, MA: Addison-Wesley.

Titus, M.A. (2006a). Understanding college degree completion of students with low socioeconomic status: The influence of the institutional financial context. *Research in Higher Education, 47*(4), 371–398.

Titus, M.A. (2006b). Understanding the influence of the financial context of institutions on student persistence at four-year colleges and universities. *Journal of Higher Education, 77*(2), 353–375.

Tolbert, P.S. (1985). Institutional environments and resource dependence: Sources of administrative structure in institutions of higher education. *Administrative Science Quarterly, 30*(1), 1–13.

U.S. Department of Education. (2013). *Developing Hispanic-Serving Institutions program—Title V.* Washington, DC: Author. Retrieved from http://www2.ed.gov/programs/idueshsi/index.html

Valencia, R.R., & Solórzano, D.G. (1997). Contemporary deficit thinking. In R.R. Valencia (Ed.), *The evolution of deficit thinking: Educational thought and practice* (pp. 160–210). Washington, DC: Falmer Press.

Weerts, D.J., Freed, G.H., & Morphew, C.C. (2014). Organizational identity in higher education: Conceptual and empirical perspectives. In M.B. Paulsen (Ed.), *Higher education: Handbook of theory and research* (Vol. 29, pp. 229–278). New York: Springer.

Williams, D.A., Berger, J.B., & McClendon, S.A. (2005). *Toward a model of inclusive excellence and change in postsecondary institutions.* Washington, DC: Association of American Colleges and Universities.

PART II

Framing Institutional Actors and Experiences Within Hispanic-Serving Institutions

6

LATINA/O STUDENT CHARACTERISTICS AND OUTCOMES AT FOUR-YEAR HISPANIC-SERVING INSTITUTIONS (HSIs), EMERGING HSIs, AND NON-HSIs

Marcela Cuellar

Latinas/os now comprise the largest racial/ethnic minority group enrolled at four-year colleges and universities (Fry & López, 2012), with a significant proportion enrolling at Hispanic-Serving Institutions (HSIs). In fall 2008, approximately 35% of all Latina/o undergraduates at four-year institutions were enrolled at colleges or universities where at least 25% of the students were Latina/o (National Center for Educational Statistics, 2009), a criterion of HSI eligibility. Given the enrollment-based definition of HSIs and the projected growth of the Latina/o population in the United States, more postsecondary institutions will presumably become HSIs. Colleges and universities with Latina/o student populations approaching the 25% threshold are commonly referred to as emerging HSIs (Santiago & Andrade, 2010). Despite an increasing representation of HSIs and emerging HSIs in the higher education landscape, knowledge of the factors that influence Latina/o student enrollment at these institutions and non-HSIs is just evolving. Similarly, our understanding of the influence of these institutional contexts on Latina/o student experiences and outcomes is limited (Nora & Crisp, 2009), but also beginning to develop.

To promote the educational, societal, and political advancement of Latinas/os, it is critically important to understand the extent to which the unique institutional contexts at four-year HSIs, emerging HSIs, and non-HSIs academically develop and empower Latinas/os. The findings in this chapter come from a two-part national study using data from the Cooperative Institutional Research Program (CIRP) at the University of California, Los Angeles (Cuellar, 2012). This chapter first examines the factors that influence Latina/o student enrollment in these three institutional contexts. It then considers how these contexts influence two outcomes—academic self-concept and social agency—which I argue represent student success and empowerment when a positive change is observed during college.

What We Know about Latina/o Students at HSIs, Emerging HSIs, and Non-HSIs

Perhaps not surprisingly, Latinas/os are more likely to enroll at HSIs than their non-Latina/o peers (Núñez, Sparks, & Hernández, 2011; Núñez & Bowers, 2011). In addition, they generally enter HSIs with different predispositions than their counterparts at non-HSIs. For instance, Latinas/os attending baccalaureate-granting HSIs are more likely to have parents with lower educational backgrounds and be older, part-time, and/or transfer students than those attending non-HSIs (Bridges, Kinzie, Nelson Laird, & Kuh, 2008). Also, Latinas/os at four-year HSIs typically want to live closer to home (Núñez & Bowers, 2011). Location and affordability are consequently key factors in Latinas/os' decisions to enroll at HSIs (Santiago, 2007). Moreover, students attending high schools with larger enrollments, higher proportions of underrepresented minorities, and more Latina/o teachers, as well as students with lower standardized math test scores, are more likely to enroll at HSIs (Núñez & Bowers, 2011). Overall, Latina/o students enter HSIs with lower levels of academic capital than their peers who enroll elsewhere, and these institutions thus provide postsecondary opportunities for a more diverse Latina/o student population.

Research on Latina/o student experiences and outcomes in these institutional contexts is less conclusive. Differences in educational experiences may be anticipated since Latinas/os at non-HSIs are more likely than their counterparts at HSIs to live on campus and be involved in co-curricular activities (Bridges et al., 2008). Yet, Latinas/os at HSIs and non-HSIs do not significantly differ on their perceptions of a supportive campus environment, faculty interactions, or overall college satisfaction (Nelson Laird, Bridges, Morelon-Quainoo, Williams, & Holmes, 2007). In fact, Latina/o students at HSIs are actually more involved in collaborative learning and report larger gains in overall development (Nelson Laird et al., 2007). That said, two major limitations of previous work stem from the cross-sectional nature of data that do not control for pre-college dispositions related to outcomes as well as a lack of information on emerging HSIs. Also, scholars question the equity of access and success for Latinas/os at HSIs because of observably lower graduation rates compared to their peers at non-HSIs (Contreras, Malcom, & Bensimon, 2008). Much of this gap is due to differences in institutional selectivity and resources, however, highlighting the importance of funding for additional services to increase Latina/o success (García, 2013).

Student Success Through a Traditional Lens

Most scholars consider degree attainment to be the definitive sign of student success (Kuh, Kinzie, Buckley, Bridges, & Hayek, 2006), with persistence and retention as indicators of progress towards this goal (Braxton, 2000; Nora, 2003). Academic achievement (such as college grades and graduate exam scores) and post-college outcomes (such as employment and graduate school enrollment) are also traditionally recognized as signs of success (Kuh et al., 2006). These concepts are easily measurable and confer tremendous economic and social returns to individuals and society. These forms of success do not, however, gauge the depth of learning or quality of the college experience.

To further tap into the impact of higher education, student success is also often represented as the development students undergo during college. Bowen (1977), for example, outlined the types of outcomes college students should develop. He argued that the educational task of colleges and universities is to promote cognitive learning, as well as emotional and moral development, in conjunction with practical skills. Furthermore, college students should develop an openness to change and become involved in public affairs. Individual gains on these outcomes cascade into greater benefits for society because college graduates may influence non-college educated individuals to adopt socially conscious values and behaviors. Thus, Bowen's view of student success places responsibility on colleges and universities to holistically prepare students for advancement in American society.

Broader notions of student success as development can be classified as cognitive or affective in nature (Astin, 1993a). The cognitive dimension represents outcomes associated with knowledge acquisition and higher order thinking skills, such as reasoning and decision making, whereas the affective dimension involves students' attitudes, values, beliefs, and self-concepts. More recently, scholars have considered how holistic development models may differ for racial/ethnic minority students, such as Latinas/os, given that experiences with race and racism may positively and negatively affect cognitive, intrapersonal, and interpersonal development (Torres & Hernández, 2007). Further, the Association of American Colleges and Universities (2002) has affirmed that all students need an education that prepares them for personal success and that fosters a democratic society by empowering them to change information into knowledge and action, develop multicultural and global competencies, and take responsibility for social justice. While many institutions tend to avoid *assessing* affective outcomes to measure these forms of student learning and development, colleges and universities usually aim to develop them (Astin, 1993a).

Although the aforementioned conceptualizations of success are important, scholars have advocated for more expansive definitions of student success that are representative of a more diverse college population (Kuh et al., 2006; Rendón, 2006), especially for students who attend HSIs (Malcom, Bensimon, & Dávila, 2010; Santiago, Andrade, & Brown, 2004). Concurrently, scholars have called for the development of theories for diverse students that incorporate more critical perspectives and acknowledge the distinct backgrounds and experiences of underrepresented students, such as Critical Race Theory (Carter & Hurtado, 2007; Rendón, 2006; Solórzano, 1998). Given the historically marginalized status of Latinas/os in the United States, it is essential that they leave college not only with baccalaureate degrees and the requisite knowledge to excel professionally, but also with a sense of empowerment that positions them for success in

American society. Outcomes that represent empowerment can thus also serve as indicators of Latina/o student success.

Expanding Success as Empowerment for Latinas/os

Notions of success as empowerment can be conceptualized through a Critical Race Theory (CRT) lens and its extensions. CRT builds on the principle that racism in American society is real as it centers the experiences of people of color and examines the ways that racial oppression has historically created inequalities (Taylor, 1998). Educational scholars use CRT to examine how educational structures and practices create inequities for students of color (Solórzano, 1998). Through its commitment to social justice, CRT in education acknowledges the personal discriminatory experiences that racial/ethnic groups often face in the United States and proposes that education should empower disenfranchised students. It calls for outcomes that are empowering for oppressed groups, regardless of their benefits to society at large, simply because it is ethical. Grounded in these principles, higher education should better serve Latina/o students by developing educational environments that empower them on multiple levels at college entry and throughout the college experience.

With this mind, it is critical for two reasons to acknowledge and understand the various forms of capital that inform Latina/o students' college choices. First, their enrollment decisions have led to the development of HSIs and emerging HSIs—these institutions simply would not exist without the critical mass that stems from Latinas/os' enrollment decisions. Thus, understanding Latinas/os' choice processes will enhance our understanding of how student characteristics shape diverse institutional contexts. Second, we must understand the various forms of capital that Latinas/os possess at the beginning of college in order to better serve them.

Yosso (2005) challenged traditional notions of cultural capital in relationship to students of color because of assumptions that they enter educational environments with cultural deficiencies. She argued that students of color possess cultural assets, described as *community cultural wealth*, which represent an array of knowledge, skills, abilities, and networks that communities of color draw upon in order to resist macro and micro forms of oppression. Colleges and universities can build on these influential entering characteristics and empower Latinas/os during college by promoting a positive campus racial climate and providing a variety of curricular and co-curricular experiences.

Empowerment through higher education can be assessed by accounting for students' pre-college characteristics and the extent to which institutional contexts have enhanced outcomes by the end of the college experience. Positive changes during college on academic self-concept and social agency can represent student empowerment. Academic self-concept is associated with persistence and retention

(Robbins et al., 2004), and it is particularly important for Latinas/os because they generally enter higher education with lower levels of academic self-concept than their peers (Contreras, 2005; Núñez, 2009). This can be traced to their lower status position in American society, underrepresentation on many college campuses, and the disconnect between cultural expectations at colleges and universities and home cultures (Oseguera, Locks, & Vega, 2009). Likewise, social agency, which represents the desire to change society through sociopolitical engagement, is important because commitment to these ideas can advance the social status of a racial/ethnic group. As Latinas/os express more interest in creating social change, presumably they will demonstrate more civic involvement and increased political standing. Consequently, the extent to which institutions enhance these outcomes for Latina/o college students indicates how successful they are at talent development, which demonstrates institutional success on measures broader than degree completion (Astin, 1993a).

Data Sources and Analyses

Two datasets from the Cooperative Institutional Research Program (CIRP) at the Higher Education Research Institute (HERI) at the University of California, Los Angeles (UCLA) were utilized to explore student characteristics and outcomes at HSIs, emerging HSIs, and non-HSIs. CIRP, a national longitudinal study of the U.S. higher education system, has collected data annually on college students since 1966. Student responses from the CIRP's The Freshman Survey (TFS) in 2004 provided pre-college student information, particularly about Latinas/os' college choice of HSIs, emerging HSIs, or non-HSIs. The 2008 College Senior Survey (CSS) captured students' college experiences four years after they entered. The longitudinal 2004–2008 TFS/CSS dataset was used to examine how Latina/o students changed on two measures representing success and empowerment—academic self-concept and social agency—within the three institutional types. Thus, the study had two components: a college choice model and a student success/empowerment model.

HSIs and emerging HSIs were coded according to Latina/o full-time equivalent (FTE) enrollments in 2006–2007, in part because this period aligned with the third year that students were enrolled in college—enough time to establish the influence of the institutional context. Colleges and universities on the U.S. Department of Education's 2006–2007 list of Institutions with High Hispanic Enrollment (U.S. Department of Education, n.d.) were identified and then cross-referenced with Title V grant recipients between 2004 and 2008. Thus, HSIs in the sample had a Title V grant and/or were on the federal list of institutions that enrolled a high number of Latinas/os. Next, *Excelencia* in Education's list of colleges and universities that had between 15% and 24% Latina/o FTE undergraduates in 2006–2007 was used to identify emerging HSIs (Santiago & Andrade,

2010). Lastly, all remaining institutions were classified as non-HSIs if they had 10% or less Latina/o enrollment based on 2006–2007 fall data. This limit allowed for a more discrete differentiation between emerging HSIs and non-HSIs.

Students self-reported their racial/ethnic membership in the 2004 TFS, and the survey allowed them to mark multiple groups. Those who marked only that they were "Mexican American/Chicano," "Puerto Rican," or "Other Latino" were coded into these Latina/o ethnic categories. Those who marked a Latina/o ethnic group and another racial/ethnic group were classified into a multiracial Latina/o category to further explore the diversity among Latinas/os. Student- and institutional-level classifications yielded a significant number of Latinas/os at the three institutional types for the 2004 TFS as well as the 2008 CSS. The college choice model analysis sample represented a total of 5,079 Latinas/os at 21 four-year HSIs; 3,699 Latinas/os at 23 emerging HSIs; and 17,138 Latinas/os at 619 non-HSIs. For the success models, there were 314 Latinas/os at 18 HSIs; 359 Latinas/os at 14 emerging HSIs; and 1,451 Latinas/os at 217 non-HSIs.

Descriptive analyses and ANOVA with post hoc tests were performed for all variables in both the college choice and student success models in the three institutional contexts. Longitudinal t tests were also performed for the success outcomes. These initial analyses were utilized to identify any differences on these measures among Latina/o students in the three institutional contexts. Thereafter, different multivariate analyses were employed for the college choice and success components of the study.

For the college choice model, a multinomial logistic regression was used to determine which variables increased the likelihood of Latina/o enrollment at an HSI, emerging HSI, or non-HSI. The categorical dependent variable was enrollment at an HSI, emerging HSI, or non-HSI, for which non-HSIs served as the referent group. The overall model fit and Wald tests were assessed for the most significant variables associated with the decision to enroll at an HSI, emerging HSI, or non-HSI.

The college choice model also contained four blocks of independent variables that have been associated with Latina/o college enrollment: background characteristics, past capital accumulation, college considerations, and anticipated college conversion (McDonough, Núñez, Ceja, & Solórzano, 2003; Núñez, McDonough, Ceja, & Solórzano, 2008). The background characteristics block contained gender and language background in conjunction with traditional forms of capital, such as cultural capital (parental education) and economic capital (financial support). Measures representing Yosso's (2005) six forms of community cultural wealth (aspirational, familial, social, navigational, resistant, and spiritual) were also included. For example, familial capital referred to cultural knowledge that is nurtured by the family and carries a sense of community history; it was captured through the influence of family on the pursuit of a college education. Also, resistant capital, the knowledge and skills that challenge inequality through behaviors, was represented through participation in organized demonstrations, discussions of politics, and a belief that racial discrimination still exists. The college considerations set of variables accounted for factors important in college selection, such as the influence of teachers and counselors and institutional reputation. The last block, anticipated college conversion, represented outcomes students hoped to gain from their college experiences, including their desire to employ and gain social capital through engagement with faculty, student organizations, and racially/ethnically diverse peers.

The dependent variables for the student success models were academic self-concept and social agency. Academic self-concept comprised four items representing students' self-ratings of academic abilities and confidence in the academic environment. Students rated themselves in comparison to an average person their age on four traits: academic ability, drive to achieve, mathematical ability, and intellectual self-confidence. The social agency variable comprised six items that measured the extent to which students valued political and social involvement as a personal goal. These items included the following: participating in community action programs, influencing social values, keeping up to date with political affairs, becoming a community leader, helping others who are in difficulty, and helping to promote racial understanding. Both of these variables were CIRP constructs measured on the 2004 TFS and 2008 CSS and validated through item response theory (Sharkness, DeAngelo, & Pryor, 2010).

Independent variables for the student success models were chosen based on the Multi-contextual Model for Diverse Learning Environments (MMDLE)[1] (Hurtado, Álvarez, Guillermo-Wann, Cuellar, & Arellano, 2012) and because they are influential predictors of academic self-concept and social agency. Independent variables were organized into three blocks based on background characteristics and capitals, institutional characteristics, and student experiences (campus racial climate, curricular, and co-curricular). Ethnicity, gender, socioeconomic status, pre-college academic self-concept and social agency, and familial and spiritual capital were among the background characteristics and capitals accounted for in the models. Institutional contexts included private/public control and a dummy coded variable for designation as an HSI or emerging HSI. Student experiences with the campus racial climate, such as positive and negative interactions with diverse peers, were included. Curricular variables (e.g., enrollment in ethnic and women's studies courses) were also included. Co-curricular experiences that may foster academic self-concept or social agency, such as hours spent studying or volunteering, were also included in the respective models. (For more information on the variables used in the models, please refer to Cuellar, 2012.)

Hierarchical multiple regressions were conducted to allow for a temporal ordering of blocks of independent variables to assess the influence of inputs and environments on outcomes (Astin & Dey, 1997). The regression models for academic self-concept and social agency were analyzed in two stages. First, a preliminary blocked forced entry multiple regression analysis was conducted with independent variables on the entire sample of Latinas/os at HSIs, emerging HSIs, and non-HSIs. The second stage of analysis entailed running the same blocks of variables for the sample within each institutional type separately, in order to assess the predictive power of variables within each context and also to allow for comparisons of results across groups. Further, given the small sample size for Latinas/os at HSIs and emerging HSIs, the p value was set moderately lower for these samples ($p < .05$), while the significance level for the non-HSI sample was set at a higher threshold ($p < .01$). Finally, an equality test of coefficients (Paternoster, Brame, Mazerolle, & Piquero, 1998) was conducted to assess whether coefficient differences were significant across the institutional context models.

Factors Influencing Latina/o College Choices

Notable differences in the factors influencing the likelihood of Latina/o enrollment at four-year HSIs, emerging HSIs, and non-HSIs are shown in Table 6.1. There were enrollment differences based on gender, language background, and ethnic sub-group membership. Females were more likely to enroll at HSIs compared to their male counterparts, who were more likely to enroll at non-HSIs. Also, controlling for all other factors, Latinas/os whose first language was English were more likely to enroll at HSIs as compared to non-HSIs, but more likely to enroll at non-HSIs as compared to emerging HSIs. In addition, "Other Latinas/os" were more likely to enroll at HSIs, and multiracial Latinas/os at non-HSIs, as compared to Mexican Americans and Chicanas/os. On the whole, these differences suggest that the representation of Latinas/os was distinctive across the three institutional contexts and, as such, may create different educational environments, experiences, and outcomes for students.

Traditional measures of academic and social capital were largely associated with Latina/o enrollment decisions at HSIs, emerging HSIs, and non-HSIs. For example, Latinas/os at non-HSIs possessed more academic capital at the beginning of college; those with higher GPAs were more likely to enroll at these colleges and universities. Further, social capital played an important role for Latinas/os at HSIs and non-HSIs, but in diverse ways. Latinas/os who indicated that their academic networks (teachers and counselors) encouraged them to attend the college where they enrolled were more likely to attend HSIs. At the same time, students who spent more time at a teacher's home during high school were more likely to enroll at non-HSIs. Thus, in comparison to Latinas/os attending HSIs, those choosing non-HSIs appear to have had more extensive relationships with teachers and more access to social capital. In general, Latinas/os at HSIs possessed less academic and social capital than their counterparts at emerging HSIs and non-HSIs, as found in earlier research (Núñez & Bowers, 2011).

Economic and cultural capital were also largely associated with Latina/o students' enrollment decisions. For example, those from lower income backgrounds were more likely to enroll at HSIs and emerging HSIs than were their counterparts from higher income brackets. Latinas/os wanting to live closer to home

TABLE 6.1 *Multinomial Logistic Regression Models for Latina/o Enrollment at HSIs and Emerging HSIs (referent: non-HSIs = 16,828)*

Variable	HSIs (N = 4,962)			Emerging HSIs (N = 3,625)			
	B	SE	Exp(B)	B		SE	Exp(B)
Demographics							
Ethnicity (Mexican American/ Chicano referent)							
Puerto Rican	-0.02	0.09	0.98	0.18	*	0.09	1.20
Other Latina/o	0.13 *	0.06	1.14	0.14	*	0.06	1.15
Multiracial Latina/o	-0.87 ***	0.06	0.42	-0.26	***	0.06	0.77
Gender							
Male (Female referent)	-0.24 ***	0.05	0.79	-0.31	***	0.05	0.74
Language Background							
Native English speaker	0.24 ***	0.05	1.28	-0.31	***	0.05	0.74
Past Capital Accumulation							
Cultural Capital							
Mother's highest level of education (Graduate level referent)							
Less than high school	0.07	0.09	1.08	0.58	***	0.09	1.79
High school graduate	0.13	0.08	1.14	0.38	***	0.08	1.46
Some college	0.02	0.08	1.02	0.29	***	0.08	1.34
College graduate	-0.03	0.08	0.98	-0.09	***	0.09	0.92
Income Quartile (Upper income referent)							
Low-income	1.13 ***	0.08	3.08	0.72	***	0.08	2.05
Lower middle-income	0.78 ***	0.08	2.17	0.59	***	0.07	1.81
Upper middle-income	0.49 ***	0.08	1.64	0.42	***	0.07	1.52
Academic Capital							
Average high school GPA	-0.24 ***	0.02	0.79	-0.16	***	0.02	0.85
Familial Capital							
Parents wanted me to go to college	0.27 ***	0.03	1.31	0.11	***	0.03	1.12
Social Capital							
Was a guest in a teacher's home	-0.27 ***	0.05	0.77	-0.19	***	0.05	0.83
Resistant Capital							
Racial discrimination is still a major problem in America	-0.16 **	0.06	.83	0.03		0.06	1.03
Economic Capital							
Parental financial support	-0.15 ***	0.02	0.86	-0.02		0.02	0.98
Grant aid	-0.26 ***	0.02	0.77	-0.19	***	0.02	0.82

(Continued)

TABLE 6.1 (Continued)

Variable	HSIs (N = 4,962)			Emerging HSIs (N = 3,625)		
	B	SE	Exp(B)	B	SE	Exp(B)
College Considerations						
Reason for choosing this particular college:						
Academic Reputation Factor	-0.30 ***	0.02	0.74	-0.25 ***	0.02	0.78
College visit	-0.28 ***	0.03	0.76	-0.09 **	0.03	0.92
Influence of Academic Network Factor	0.10 ***	0.02	1.10	0.03	0.02	1.03
Not offered aid at first choice	0.36 ***	0.05	1.44	0.11 *	0.05	1.12
Wanted to live near home	0.53 ***	0.03	1.70	0.43 ***	0.03	1.54
Anticipated Capital Conversion						
Personal Goal: Being very well off financially	0.33 ***	0.03	1.39	0.19 ***	0.03	1.21

$***p < .001, **p < .01, *p < .05.$

were also more likely to enroll at HSIs and emerging HSIs. Echoing previous research (Núñez & Bowers, 2011; Santiago, 2007), for Latinas/os who chose to enroll at HSIs, issues of affordability were more pronounced. In contrast, Latinas/os who had more financial support from family were more likely to enroll at non-HSIs. Indeed, other research has shown that the availability of financial aid and affordability are generally critical components of Latinas/os' decisions about which colleges to attend (Kim, 2004). With respect to cultural capital, Latinas/os with mothers who had less formal education were more likely to enroll at emerging HSIs than non-HSIs. Although this cultural capital variable was not a significant predictor for Latinas/os who enrolled at HSIs instead of non-HSIs, it appears that this was largely due to the overpowering nature of the economic measures for these students. Overall, the findings suggest that Latinas/os entered HSIs and emerging HSIs with less access to economic and cultural capital than their non-HSI counterparts.

Familial capital, one of the main elements of community cultural wealth, was a highly significant factor in Latinas/os' college choice. While the operationalization of the variable did not directly tap into cultural knowledge, it did measure the importance of family as a motivating factor in pursuing postsecondary education, which can also encourage Latinas/os to succeed in college (Nora, 2003) and ultimately serve as a form of capital. Latina/o students across institutional contexts acknowledged that parents and family were a fairly important reason for pursuing postsecondary education; for Latinas/os at HSIs and emerging HSIs, however, this factor increased the likelihood of enrollment at these institutions, which confirms previous research on the strong influence of family and the desire to stay close to home in the choice to enroll at an HSI (Núñez & Bowers, 2011; Santiago, 2007) and extends this finding to students at emerging HSIs. Altogether, this finding counters the deficit-minded myth that Latina/o families deter their children from college and shows that parental encouragement is important in getting students to college in the first place (Gándara, 1995). By extension, the inclusion of families in the college experience, particularly at HSIs and emerging HSIs, may further bolster Latina/o student success.

Resistant capital, also within the community cultural wealth framework, refers to the knowledge and skills to challenge inequality through behaviors, which can increase the likelihood of college enrollment for Latinas/os. Latinas/os who believed that racial discrimination was still a pervasive problem in the United States were more likely to enroll at non-HSIs than HSIs. There were no differences on this measure for Latinas/os' choices between emerging HSIs and non-HSIs, indicating that students at these institutional types essentially possessed similar and higher levels of resistant capital than their counterparts at HSIs. Further, these findings suggest that Latinas/os who enrolled at emerging HSIs and non-HSIs were critical of the inequities within American society. Thus, enrolling at a college or university where they would be numerically underrepresented may have been a conscious way to challenge existing racial inequalities and promote social change in the future.

Overall, these findings represent a potential conjoining influence of familial, resistant, social, cultural, economic, and academic capital that creates distinct educational contexts for Latina/o college students. The forms of capital Latinas/os possessed within the three institutional contexts support the notion of a cascading effect (Flores & Morfin, 2008) of race and ethnicity within higher education, specifically in relation to enrollment decisions at HSIs and non-HSIs. Here, the cascading effect refers to racial/ethnic stratification based on institutional selectivity; Latinas/os are increasingly more likely to enroll at less selective institutions that are HSIs in states where they predominate, and this may increase the potential for stratification of educational outcomes (Flores & Morfin, 2008). The findings of the present study further indicate that this stratification overlaps with socioeconomic background. Therefore, it appears that the sorting of Latinas/os based on previously established forms of capital is informed by different dispositions, such as a preference to stay close to home during college (Núñez & Bowers, 2011). Consequently, Latina/o student experiences and outcomes may differ based on enrollment at an HSI, an emerging HSI, or a non-HSI.

In sum, the Latinas/os in this study who entered HSIs, emerging HSIs, and non-HSIs generally possessed different types and levels of capital at the beginning of college. A better understanding of how they made their decisions to enroll in these institutional contexts matters tremendously for the future success of Latinas/os. Traditional notions of excellence may fail to capture the potential of Latinas/os at HSIs (Núñez & Bowers, 2011; Santiago et al., 2004) since Latinas/os enter HSIs with different forms of capital than their emerging HSI and non-HSI counterparts. Institutions should therefore consider the various forms of capital that students possess at college entry to truly capture the value added by the end of the college experience (Astin, 1993b; Núñez & Bowers, 2011). Presumably, there is potential for more growth on student outcomes when institutions incorporate culturally sensitive practices (Laden, 2004; Santiago et al., 2004) that build on the extensive forms of capital that students possess (Yosso, 2005).

Latina/o Student Outcomes at HSIs, Emerging HSIs, and Non-HSIs

Latina/o students had different levels of growth across institutional contexts, depending on the outcome being assessed. While change on academic self-concept was more pronounced for Latinas/os at HSIs, students showed growth on social agency across all institutional types. Further, their characteristics and college experiences influenced their academic self-concept differently. The results for academic self-concept and social agency are discussed separately to highlight changes on these two outcomes.

Academic Self-Concept

Latinas/os entered HSIs, emerging HSIs, and non-HSIs with varying levels of academic self-concept (see also Cuellar, 2014). Those at HSIs and emerging HSIs entered college with lower levels of academic self-concept than their peers at non-HSIs, with Latinas/os at HSIs expressing the lowest average. Despite these significant differences at the beginning of college, the gaps were greatly diminished four years later. Toward the end of college, there were only differences between Latinas/os at emerging HSIs and non-HSIs on academic self-concept, with those at emerging HSIs indicating a lower average academic self-concept than their peers at non-HSIs. By contrast, although the average academic self-concept after four years for Latinas/os at HSIs was still slightly lower than for those at non-HSIs, the differences were insignificant. In other words, Latinas/os at HSIs and non-HSIs had surprisingly comparable levels of academic self-concept by the end of college. Upon further examination, Latinas/os at HSIs, on average, increased their academic self-concept during their years at HSIs, while academic self-concept for Latinas/os at non-HSIs actually decreased during that time span. Collectively, the positive change on academic self-concept for Latinas/os as a whole at HSIs indicates that these institutions were strongly developing Latina/o students' academic potential and self-perception of academic abilities as compared to students who attended emerging HSIs and non-HSIs.

Differences on the explanatory power of background characteristics and various forms of capital further highlight how Latina/o student experiences at HSIs can significantly shape their academic self-concept. At emerging HSIs and non-HSIs, Latinas/os' entering college characteristics explained most of the variance on their academic self-concept, while less of the variance on this outcome was explained by incoming student characteristics for those at HSIs. Latinas/os may have entered HSIs with lower self-perceptions of their academic abilities than their counterparts who attended other institutions, but they left these institutional contexts with a stronger sense of their academic potential as a result of some of their experiences during college. Thus, these federally designated HSIs did quite a bit of talent development and empowered Latina/o students.

Not surprisingly, pre-college academic self-concept was the strongest explanatory variable for growth in academic self-concept across all institutional contexts. For Latinas/os at HSIs, however, academic self-concept at the beginning of college was slightly less predictive of future academic self-concept as compared to Latinas/os at emerging HSIs and non-HSIs. In addition, some factors were associated with growth in two of the three institutional contexts. For example, females attending HSIs and non-HSIs were more likely to have lower levels of academic self-concept than their male peers. In addition, "Other Latinas/os" were more likely to report higher levels of academic self-concept than Mexican Americans and Chicanas/os. Moreover, Latinas/os with higher levels of supportive interactions with faculty and who spent more time tutoring other students reported higher levels of academic self-concept. Altogether, these findings suggest that some factors similarly show growth on academic self-concept, regardless of institutional context.

In contrast, other background characteristics and college experiences uniquely influenced change on academic self-concept within specific institutional types. In HSIs, for example, Latinas/os who felt more family support to succeed in college were more likely to indicate higher academic self-concept. Also, Latina/o students at HSIs had higher academic self-concept toward the end of college if they spent more hours on homework every week and had more discussions on course content with peers. Academic factors external to the classroom thus seemed highly influential on Latinas/os' academic self-concept at HSIs, which differed from their counterparts at non-HSIs. Latinas/os attending non-HSIs who did not report their academic self-concept at the beginning of college tended to have lower scores than their peers who did, suggesting that students who did not report academic self-concept entered this institutional context with lower academic self-concept. Latinas/os at non-HSIs also had lower academic self-concept after four years if they felt intimidated by faculty, which shows how faculty can have a positive and a negative influence on Latina/o students' perceptions of their own academic abilities, particularly at non-HSIs.

For Latinas/os at emerging HSIs, three college experiences distinctly shaped academic self-concept. Among curricular experiences, students who asked professors for advice more frequently reported higher levels of academic self-concept. Interestingly, aspects of the campus racial climate were also important within emerging HSIs. Latinas/os who experienced more positive cross-racial interactions were more likely to grow on academic self-concept. Conversely, Latinas/os who participated in ethnic student organizations reported lower academic self-concept after four years of college. The racial/ethnic composition of these contexts, where Latina/o students constituted anywhere between 15% and 24% of the student body, may have uniquely shaped how campus racial climate, assistance from faculty, and participation in ethnic student organizations affected students' academic self-concept.

While other research has indicated that all students generally show increases in self-perceived academic abilities during college (Astin, 1993b), fewer studies have compared Latinas/os across institutional contexts. Overall, the disaggregation of Latina/o college students based on institutional type provides a more comprehensive view of academic self-concept and confirms a positive association between institutions with larger percentages of Latinas/os and increases on academic self-concept (Cole, 2007; Hurtado, Carter, & Spuler, 1996), which may be a proxy for HSIs. When these institutional contexts were disaggregated based on actual federal HSI designation, positive change was observed within HSIs, as they had the largest representation of Latinas/os. Regarding academic self-concept, there was evidently more talent development and empowerment occurring at HSIs.

Importantly, positive changes on academic self-concept may have been associated with the HSI designation specifically. Many HSIs use Title V funding to develop programs designed to increase academic self-confidence and, over the past six years, Title V funds have been increasingly used to develop academic support programs and provide professional development for faculty (Villareal & Santiago, 2012). Latinas/os at HSIs appear to more frequently experience positive interactions with faculty (Dayton, González-Vázquez, Martínez, & Plum, 2004), and these interactions can help Latinas/os increase academic self-concept (Cole, 2007; Núñez, 2009). Moreover, Title V grant funds are often used to develop academic programs to help Latina/o students transition into postsecondary environments (Santiago et al., 2004). As a result, Title V-funded HSIs may very well provide academic programs and services that promote the academic development of Latinas/os.

Social Agency

There were no significant differences on social agency at the beginning of college between Latinas/os at HSIs, emerging HSIs, and non-HSIs, as Table 6.2 shows. Essentially, Latina/o students entered these college environments with similar levels of commitment to social action and increased their commitment to social agency at comparable levels. Consequently, HSIs, emerging HSIs, and non-HSIs provided learning environments where Latinas/os were equally empowered to value political and social engagement, thus effectively developing our future citizenry.

Several key background characteristics and forms of capital significantly influenced growth on Latina/o social agency across institutional types. As might be

TABLE 6.2 *Dunnett T-3 Post Hoc Test of Mean Difference for Social Agency and Longitudinal Paired Sample* t *Tests by Institutional Context*

Student Samples	2004		2008		M_D	
	M	SD	M	SD		
HSIs	50.96	9.08	54.57	10.66	3.61	***
Emerging HSIs	50.74	9.06	54.56	10.59	3.82	***
Non-HSIs	51.00	9.30	54.06	10.14	3.06	***

*** $p < .001$.

expected, the pre-college measure of social agency was the most significant factor on future social agency. Also, students who entered college aspiring to obtain higher educational degrees, such as PhDs, showed higher levels of social agency four years later. Perhaps Latina/o students who aspired to obtain advanced degrees used this approach as a way to challenge negative racial/ethnic perceptions and change society in the future (Solórzano & Delgado Bernal, 2001). Moreover, students who frequently discussed spirituality or religion with their families during high school were more likely to value future social action, substantiating previous research that Latinas/os draw on spiritual capital to challenge social inequities (Solórzano & Delgado Bernal, 2001).

A multitude of college experiences can enhance Latinas/os' social agency across institutional types. Interestingly, Latina/o students attending private institutions were less likely to show growth on social agency as compared to their peers who attended public institutions, regardless of HSI designation. Curricular activities, such as frequent interaction with faculty and completion of an ethnic studies course, enhanced social agency for Latinas/os. Additionally, activities outside of the classroom also positively influenced social agency—for example, participation in political demonstrations, attendance at cultural awareness workshops, and volunteering. Further, Latinas/os who experienced more negative cross-racial interactions valued social action more, perhaps suggesting that these negative exchanges developed their resistant capital to challenge racial inequities.

The longitudinal findings support the notion that these three institutional contexts differentially influenced the development of college outcomes that represent empowerment for Latinas/os. There were some common factors that influenced growth on outcomes of empowerment across all three contexts, but there were others that were solely predictive of change within one or two. The findings clearly show that these institutional types represent distinct institutional contexts that differentially empowered Latinas/os in terms of academic self-concept and social agency. As such, it is important to distinguish between these three institutional types whenever possible in order to better understand how background characteristics and college experiences impact educational outcomes for Latinas/os.

Implications for Research, Practice, and Policy

Future studies on Latina/o college students should further consider how student experiences and outcomes may differ at HSIs, emerging HSIs, and non-HSIs. Latinas/os clearly enter these college environments with different pre-college characteristics and, after four years, show different levels of growth on outcomes representing success and empowerment. In addition, demographic characteristics within Latina/o ethnic sub-groups influence whether students enroll at HSIs, emerging HSIs, or non-HSIs, as well as subsequent changes on outcomes. For instance, in the current study, "Other Latinas/os" were more likely to enroll at HSIs and emerging HSIs and, on average, showed more gains on academic self-concept than their Mexican American and Chicana/o peers. Also, Latinas were more likely to enroll at HSIs and emerging HSIs, yet they were also more likely to report decreases on self-perceived academic abilities within HSIs and non-HSIs. These distinctions highlight the complexity of race/ethnicity among Latinas/os and the intersectionality of social identities that may influence college choice and outcomes. As such, equity in college access and success within the monolithic Latina/o group are critical issues for further exploration.

Interestingly, the differential gains on academic self-concept after controlling for background characteristics indicate that distinct elements within institutional contexts may impact outcomes for Latinas/os. Overall, the findings suggest that different Latina/o student experiences in college do indeed shape distinct outcomes at HSIs, emerging HSIs, and non-HSIs. Future studies should therefore extend the current research by including other outcomes and by considering how these institutional contexts influence educational experiences and outcomes for students from other racial/ethnic groups.

There are also direct implications for practice. Latinas/os enter each educational environment with different levels and forms of capital, and this impacts their experiences and outcomes in distinct ways. For example, their experiences with the campus racial climate and specific elements of the learning environment may differ. Thus, practitioners and faculty at HSIs, emerging HSIs, and non-HSIs should understand who their Latina/o students are in order to develop curricular and co-curricular programs that positively influence the types of outcomes they aim to develop in students. More targeted approaches should be employed based on research that reflects students and their institutional contexts. Further, faculty and staff need to recognize the diverse forms of capital that Latinas/os possess, including familial and resistant capital, since these are associated with change in educational outcomes.

The findings support continued federal funding for HSIs, especially with regard to Title V. HSIs represent some of the most poorly resourced institutions with large proportions of first-generation and low-income students, who often possess fewer resources than their peers at non-HSIs (see Chapters 3, 4, 9, and 11, this volume). As such, there are inequities at both the institutional and student level. Despite these challenges, HSIs are performing above expectations and tremendously developing the academic self-concept and social agency of Latinas/os—two outcomes that are directly and indirectly connected to national interests. Growth on both of these outcomes for Latinas/os within HSIs offer an example of the positive impact that these institutions can have on advancing educational opportunities. Furthermore, while there is evidence that talent development occurred for Latinas/os across the three institutional contexts, the growth was more pronounced for Latinas/os at HSIs. In short, these lower resourced institutions were outperforming more highly resourced colleges and universities. Thus, the empowerment Latinas/os demonstrated in the HSI context in particular shows the importance of continued support for Title V funding.

As Latinas/os enroll in higher education in greater numbers, an understanding of what factors motivate their pursuit of postsecondary education can help colleges and universities better serve and empower them, creating more equitable outcomes. Through more nuanced approaches, HSIs, emerging HSIs, and non-HSIs can prepare Latinas/os for long-term success with stronger academic self-confidence and more interest in social action. This understanding is essential to ensure that Latinas/os leave colleges and universities not only with degrees but also with a quality education that empowers them on academic and social levels. This will enable institutions of higher education to fulfill their basic function of developing individuals who positively enhance American society.

Notes

This manuscript is based on Marcela Cuellar (2012), *Latina/o student success in higher education: Models of empowerment at Hispanic-Serving Institutions (HSIs), emerging HSIs, and non-HSIs* (Unpublished dissertation). University of California, Los Angeles, CA.

1 The MMDLE illustrates how external and institutional contexts shape student outcomes, particularly for historically underrepresented racial/ethnic groups. Within the institutional context, the campus climate for diversity, also known as the campus racial climate, frames the curricular and co-curricular dimensions of students' experiences. For a detailed description, see Hurtado et al. (2012); for its application specifically to HSIs, see Hurtado and Ruiz Alvarado, Chapter 2, this volume.

References

Association of American Colleges and Universities. (2002). *Greater expectations: A new vision for learning as a nation goes to college.* Washington, DC: Author.

Astin, A.W. (1993a). *Assessment for excellence: The philosophy and practice of assessment and evaluation in higher education.* Westport, CT: The Oryx Press.

Astin, A.W. (1993b). *What matters most in college: Four critical years revisited.* San Francisco, CA: Jossey-Bass.

Astin, A.W., & Dey, E. (1997). *Causal analytic modeling via blocked regression analysis (CAMBRA): An introduction with examples.* Los Angeles, CA: UCLA.

Bowen, H.R. (1977). *Investment in learning: The individual and social value of American higher education*. San Francisco, CA: Jossey-Bass.

Braxton, J.M. (Ed.). (2000). *Reworking the student departure puzzle*. Nashville, TN: Vanderbilt University Press.

Bridges, B.K., Kinzie, J., Nelson Laird, T.F., & Kuh, G.D. (2008). Student engagement and student success at Historically Black and Hispanic-Serving Institutions. In M. Gasman, B. Baez, & C.S.V. Turner (Eds.), *Understanding minority-serving institutions* (pp. 217–236). Albany, NY: SUNY Press.

Carter, D.F., & Hurtado, S. (2007). Bridging key research dilemmas: Quantitative research using a critical eye. In F.K. Stage (Ed.), *Using quantitative data to answer critical questions* (New Directions for Institutional Research No. 133, pp. 25–35). San Francisco, CA: Jossey-Bass.

Cole, D. (2007). Do interracial interactions matter? An examination of student-faculty contact and intellectual self-concept. *Journal of Higher Education, 78*(3), 249–281. doi: 10.1353/jhe.2007.0015

Contreras, F.E. (2005). Access, achievement, and social capital: Standardized exams and the Latino college-bound population. *Journal of Hispanic Higher Education, 4*(3), 197–214. doi: 10.1177/1538192705276546

Contreras, F.E., Malcom, L.E., & Bensimon, E.M. (2008). Hispanic-Serving Institutions: Closeted identity and the production of equitable outcomes for Latina/o students. In M. Gasman, B. Baez, & C.S.V. Turner (Eds.), *Understanding minority-serving institutions* (pp. 71–90). Albany, NY: SUNY Press.

Cuellar, M. (2012). *Latino student success in higher education: Models of empowerment at Hispanic-Serving Institutions (HSIs), emerging-HSIs, and non-HSIs* (Unpublished doctoral dissertation). University of California, Los Angeles, CA.

Cuellar, M. (2014). The impact of Hispanic-Serving Institutions (HSIs), emerging HSIs, and non-HSIs on Latina/o academic self-concept. *Review of Higher Education, 37*(4), 499–530.

Dayton, B., González-Vázquez, N., Martínez, C.R., & Plum, C. (2004). Hispanic-Serving Institutions through the eyes of students and administrators. In A.M. Ortiz (Ed.), *Addressing the unique needs of Latino American students* (New Directions for Student Services No. 105, pp. 29–40). San Francisco, CA: Jossey-Bass.

Flores, S.M., & Morfin, O.J. (2008). Another side of the percent plan story: Latino enrollment in the Hispanic-Serving Institutions sector in California and Texas. In M. Gasman, B. Baez, & C.S.V. Turner (Eds.), *Understanding minority-serving institutions* (pp. 141–155). Albany, NY: SUNY Press.

Fry, R., & López, M.H. (2012). *Now largest minority group on four-year colleges and campuses: Hispanic student enrollments reach new highs in 2011*. Washington, DC: Pew Hispanic Center.

Gándara, P. (1995). *Over the ivy walls: The educational mobility of low-income Chicanos*. Albany, NY: SUNY Press.

García, G.A. (2013). Does percentage of Latinas/os affect graduation rates at 4-year Hispanic serving institutions (HSIs), emerging HSIs, and non-HSIs? *Journal of Hispanic Higher Education, 12*(3), 256–268.

Hurtado, S., Álvarez, C.L., Guillermo-Wann, C., Cuellar, M., & Arellano, L. (2012). A model for diverse learning environments: The scholarship on creating and assessing conditions for student success. In J.C. Smart & M.B. Paulsen (Eds.), *Higher education: Handbook of theory and research* (Vol. 27, pp. 41–122). New York, NY: Springer.

Hurtado, S., Carter, D.F., & Spuler, A. (1996). Latino student transition to college: Assessing difficulties and factors in successful college adjustment. *Research in Higher Education, 37*(2), 135–157.

Kim, D. (2004). The effects of financial aid on students' college choice: Differences by racial groups. *Research in Higher Education, 45*(1), 43–70.

Kuh, G.D., Kinzie, J., Buckley, J.A., Bridges, B.K., & Hayek, J.C. (2006). *What matters to student success: A review of the literature.* Washington, DC: National Postsecondary Education Cooperative.

Laden, B.V. (2004). Hispanic-Serving Institutions: What are they? Where are they? *Community College Journal of Research and Practice, 28*(3), 181–198.

Malcom, L.E., Bensimon, E.M., & Dávila, B. (2010). *(Re)constructing Hispanic-Serving Institutions: Moving beyond numbers toward student success* (Vol. 6). Ames, IA: Iowa State University, Education Policy and Practice Perspectives.

McDonough, P.M., Núñez, A.-M., Ceja, M., & Solórzano, D. (2003). *A model of Latino college choice.* Paper presented at the meeting of the Association for the Study of Higher Education, Portland, OR.

National Center for Education Statistics. (2009). *Fall enrollment of specific racial/ethnic groups in degree-granting institutions, by type and control of institution and percentage of students in the same racial/ethnic group: 2008.* Washington, DC: Author. Retrieved from http://nces.ed.gov/programs/digest/d09/tables/dt09_230.asp?referrer=list

Nelson Laird, T.F., Bridges, B.K., Morelon-Quainoo, C.L., Williams, J.M., & Holmes, M.S. (2007). African American and Hispanic student engagement at minority-serving and predominantly White institutions. *Journal of College Student Development, 48*(1), 39–56.

Nora, A. (2003). Access to higher education for Hispanic students: Real or illusory? In J. Castellanos & L. Jones (Eds.), *The majority in the minority: Expanding the representation of Latina/o faculty, administrators and students in higher education* (pp. 47–68). Sterling, VA: Stylus.

Nora, A., & Crisp, G. (2009). Hispanics and higher education: An overview of research, theory, and practice. *Higher education: Handbook of theory of research, 24*, 317–353. doi: 10.1007/978-1-4020-9628-0_8

Núñez, A.-M. (2009). Modeling the effects of diversity experiences and multiple capitals on Latina/o college students' academic self-confidence. *Journal of Hispanic Higher Education, 8*(2), 179–196. doi: 10.1177/1538192708326391

Núñez, A.-M., & Bowers, A.J. (2011). Exploring what leads high school students to enroll in Hispanic-Serving Institutions: A multilevel analysis. *American Educational Research Journal, 48*(5), 1–29.

Núñez, A.-M., McDonough, P., Ceja, M., & Solórzano, D. (2008). Diversity within: Latino college choice and ethnic comparisons. In C. Gallagher (Ed.), *Racism in post-race America: New theories, new directions* (pp. 267–284). Chapel Hill, NC: Social Forces Publishing.

Núñez, A.-M., Sparks, P.J., & Hernández, E.A. (2011). Latino access to community colleges and Hispanic-Serving Institutions: A national study. *Journal of Hispanic Higher Education, 10*(1), 18–40.

Oseguera, L., Locks, A.M., & Vega, I.I. (2009). Increasing Latina/o students' baccalaureate attainment. *Journal of Hispanic Higher Education, 8*(1), 23–53. doi: 10.1177/1538192708326997

Paternoster, R., Brame, R., Mazerolle, P., & Piquero, A. (1998). Using the correct statistical test for the equality of regression coefficients. *Criminology, 36*(4), 859–866.

Rendón, L.I. (2006). *Reconceptualizing success for underserved students in higher education.* Washington, DC: National Postsecondary Education Cooperative.

Robbins, S.B., Lauver, K., Le, H., Davis, D., Langley, R., & Carlstrom, A. (2004). Do psychosocial and study skill factors predict college outcomes? A meta-analysis. *Psychological Bulletin, 130*(2), 261–288. doi: 10.1037/0033-2909.130.2.261

Santiago, D.A. (2007). *Choosing Hispanic-Serving Institutions (HSIs): A closer look at Latino students' college choices.* Washington, DC: *Excelencia* in Education.

Santiago, D.A., & Andrade, S.J. (2010). *Emerging Hispanic-Serving Institutions: Serving Latino students.* Washington, DC: *Excelencia* in Education.

Santiago, D.A., Andrade, S.J., & Brown, S.E. (2004). *Latino student success at Hispanic-Serving Institutions: Findings from a demonstration project.* Washington, DC: *Excelencia* in Education.

Sharkness, J., DeAngelo, L., & Pryor, J. (2010). *CIRP construct technical report.* Los Angeles, CA: Higher Education Research Institute.

Solórzano, D.G. (1998). Critical Race Theory, race and gender microaggressions, and the experience of Chicana and Chicano scholars. *International Journal of Qualitative Studies in Education, 11*(1), 121–136.

Solórzano, D.G., & Delgado Bernal, D. (2001). Examining transformational resistance through a Critical Race and Latcrit Theory framework: Chicana and Chicano students in an urban context. *Urban Education, 36*(3), 308–342.

Taylor, E. (1998). A primer on Critical Race Theory. *The Journal of Blacks in Higher Education, 19*, 122–124.

Torres, V., & Hernández, E. (2007). The influence of ethnic identity on self-authorship: A longitudinal study of Latino/a college students. *Journal of College Student Development, 48*(5), 558–573.

U.S. Department of Education. (n.d.). *Institutions with high Hispanic enrollment from IPEDS spring 2007 survey (Fall Enrollment 2006).* Washington, DC: Author. Retrieved from http://www2.ed.gov/about/offices/list/ocr/edlite-minorityinst-list-hisp-tab.html

Villareal, R., & Santiago, D. (2012). *From capacity to success: HSIs and Latino student success through Title V.* Washington, DC: *Excelencia* in Education.

Yosso, T.J. (2005). Whose culture has capital? A Critical Race Theory discussion of community cultural wealth. *Race, Ethnicity, and Education, 8*(1), 69–91.

7

THE HORIZON OF POSSIBILITIES

How Faculty in Hispanic-Serving Institutions Can Reshape the Production and Legitimization of Knowledge Within Academia

Leslie D. Gonzales

This chapter was guided by the pragmatic phrase "horizon of possibilities" (Rosiek, 2013), which is intended to orient one toward the future without dismissing the importance of the past. This notion inspired me to consider the possibilities that lie within Hispanic-Serving Institutions (HSIs), particularly in relation to the role of faculty. To develop my argument, I lean on scholarship related to "funds of knowledge," which suggests that all communities, especially underserved communities such as Latinas/os who enroll in HSIs, hone historically, culturally, and socially relevant knowledge, which is often dismissed by mainstream educational institutions. One of the central goals of the funds of knowledge scholarship is to have this knowledge recognized and validated (Moll, Amanti, Neff, & González, 1992; Ríos-Aguilar & Kiyama, 2012; Ríos-Aguilar, Kiyama, Gravitt, & Moll, 2011; Yosso, 2005).

Following this line of thinking, I argue that HSI faculty members have extraordinary potential to (re)shape the production and legitimization of knowledge inside academia. Although there are potential parallels and insights applicable to two-year college settings and relevant to part-time faculty, my argument here focuses on tenure-track faculty within four-year institutions, where there is considerably more emphasis on research activity. While I readily acknowledge that the production of knowledge unfolds across many contexts and is crafted by all individuals, my focus on tenure-track faculty at four-year institutions is rooted in the assumption that these professors are much more likely to be heavily involved in creating and disseminating new knowledge that will eventually inform teaching, learning, and research inside of higher education, as well as policy formation outside of academia.

This chapter is organized as follows: First, I briefly set faculty work roles and rewards in context. Second, I describe the HSI faculty landscape and offer a more thorough description of the funds of knowledge framework. Third, to present my argument, I revisit compelling findings from existing scholarship to show how funds of knowledge can work in practice, and I highlight the powerful impact that faculty can have if and when they work from a funds of knowledge perspective. In this discussion I draw heavily from my own experience as an undergraduate, master's, and doctoral student, and as an adjunct instructor, all within HSI contexts. I offer additional implications in the concluding section of the chapter.

Faculty Roles and Rewards in Academia

Any study that considers the impact and potential contribution of faculty members—whether inside or outside of HSIs—must first set faculty roles in context. Higher education researchers have long acknowledged the importance of earning distinction (Bourdieu, 1988), prestige (Gardner, 2010; Jencks & Riesman, 1968; Lewis, 1996), or legitimacy (Gonzales, 2012, 2013; Rusch & Wilbur, 2007) within academia. On this note, scholars have widely acknowledged that when it comes to earning distinction, prestige, and legitimacy in academia, engagement in research-related activities is privileged (Baez, 2000; Boyer, 1990; Henderson, 2009; O'Meara, 2002; Terosky, 2005, 2010; Wright, 2005). In fact, Fairweather (1993, 2005) and Melguizo and Strober (2007) have shown how faculty rewards (e.g., salary, merit raises) are based on faculty research productivity, even inside liberal arts colleges and universities where the mission is assumed to be holistic student development and instruction. And beyond the general privilege allotted to research over teaching and service work, there is mounting evidence that particular methodological approaches and topics are further privileged.

Stanley (2007), for example, documented how the production of knowledge (via publication processes) centers the grand narratives developed by White men who live(d) comfortably in the canons of academia. Indeed, this was the exact sentiment that spurred Patricia Hill Collins's (1986) writing on Black feminist thought and Dorothy Smith's (1987) critique of sociology. Providing very similar descriptions of how faculty work is rewarded, Baez (2000), Delgado Bernal (2008), and González (2008) all noted how academia rewards research methods embedded in a scientific (detached, objective) epistemology, as well as individualism over collectivism and the scholarship of discovery (Boyer, 1990) over applied research (Gonzales & Rincones, 2011; Neumann, 1999). Such tendencies can influence scholars to orient their work toward pure research, rather than toward research that seeks to address social problems for historically underrepresented groups or in local communities (Gonzales & Núñez, 2014; González, 2008; Jaeger & Thornton, 2006; Welner, 2012).

Relatedly, other scholars have noted how faculty are often rewarded for developing national and international reputations, while those who focus on more local or applied problem-based research are given less credit (Gonzales, 2012, 2013; Gouldner, 1957, 1958; Jaeger & Thornton, 2006; Rhoades, Kiyama,

McCormick, & Quiroz, 2008). On this point, Rhoades and colleagues (2008) argued that such cosmopolitan orientations can mean that opportunities to produce new and nuanced forms of knowledge anchored in and/or relevant to local communities are overlooked. In sum, the major insight from this literature is that faculty socialization and faculty rewards processes are governed by deeply institutionalized norms that seem to privilege very particular tasks and approaches to those tasks. This insight is further addressed later in this chapter as it yields implications for the larger argument. Next, however, I provide a description of HSIs and the HSI professoriate before reviewing the limited literature on faculty roles within these institutions.

The HSI Faculty Landscape

Based on the 2011 Integrated Postsecondary Education Data System (IPEDS; U.S. Department of Education–Institute of Education Sciences National Center for Education Statistics, 2011), there were 8,199 tenure-track faculty members serving at the 18 research universities designated as HSIs and 11,980 tenure-track professors serving at the 70 master's colleges/universities with this classification. Thus, taken together, there were roughly 20,000 tenure-track professors serving in four-year HSIs in 2011. Table 7.1 provides additional demographic details about tenure-track faculty across the four-year sector of HSIs.

In terms of work experiences, HSI faculty, like their counterparts at other institutions, are expected to balance teaching, research, and service responsibilities. However, as is the case across all of higher education, HSI professors report growing expectations for research productivity (Gardner, 2013; O'Meara & Bloomgarden, 2011). For example, in the state of Texas, several public universities, including several four-year HSIs, are competing for state funds to establish themselves as "top tier" or "national tier one" research universities (Gonzales, 2010).

Doing more with less is not unique to HSI faculty, yet the growing expectations can be particularly daunting in universities like HSIs that receive far fewer resources than other institutions—according to Calderón Galdeano, Flores, and Moder (2012), when all federal funding is accounted for, HSIs receive only $0.69 for every $1.00 that other institutions receive. More specifically, because HSIs serve populations that have historically and systematically been underserved, it is not uncommon for these institutions to receive large numbers of students who are less academically prepared for college-level work (Núñez & Bowers, 2011). Serving a large number of students who require cross-cutting support services—including developmental education—demands resources of all kinds (e.g., fiscal, human, space, technology) (see Scherer & Anson, 2014). Without such support, faculty members are likely to report increased dissatisfaction and stress, as well as a higher likelihood of departure (Rosser, 2005).

To this point, and in light of the relatively limited financial resources within HSIs (see Ortega et al., Chapter 9, this volume), Hubbard and Stage (2009) found

TABLE 7.1 *Characteristics of Full-Time Tenure Track Faculty at Four-Year HSIs by Institutional Type*

	HSI Research Universities[a] (N = 18)		HSI Master's Colleges and Universities[b] (N = 70)	
	#	%	#	%
Total full-time tenure-track faculty	8,199	100%	11,980	100%
Men	5,099	62.19%	6,655	55.55%
Women	3,100	37.81%	5,325	44.45%
White	4,280	52.20%	7,441	62.11%
Latina/o	2,091	25.50%	1,787	14.92%
Latino men	1,138		887	
Latina women	953		900	
American Indian or Alaska Native	58	.71%	51	0.43%
Asian American	854	10.42%	1,426	11.90%
Black or African American	189	2.31%	569	4.75%
Native Hawaiian or Other Pacific Islander	4	.05%	27	0.23%
Two or more races	21	0.26%	78	0.65%
Race/ethnicity unknown	449	5.48%	331	2.76%
Nonresident alien total	253	3.09%	270	2.25%

Source: 2011 Integrated Postsecondary Education Data System (IPEDS) database.
[a] Totals are based on the following: (1) total full-time instruction/research/public service, tenured total, and (2) total full-time instruction/research/public service, non-tenured on tenure track total. All but one of 18 universities reported totals for both variables.
[b] Eight out of 70 institutions did not report data. An additional eight institutions reported on only one variable (7 reported a tenured total; 1 reported a non-tenured on tenure track total).

that HSI faculty members were less satisfied with their students and, compared with faculty at Historically Black Colleges and Universities (HBCUs) and predominantly White institutions (PWIs), preferred to spend less time on teaching undergraduates. Yet they also found that HSI faculty were more likely than their HBCU and PWI counterparts to say that, if they had to choose again, they would still choose a career in academia.

Although limited, the qualitative scholarship on HSI faculty helps to illuminate such paradoxical insights. For example, Ek, Quijada Cerecer, Alanís, and Rodríguez (2010); Murphy, Araiza, Cárdenas, and Garza (2013); and Gonzales (2014) have all suggested that HSI faculty find a great sense of purpose in their work, largely because they understand that most of their students are first-generation college-going students who tend to come from underserved geographical regions.

Having a sense of their students' historical and economic backgrounds and the greater regional history surrounding HSIs can inform understandings of student ability and potential (Garza, 2007; Ramírez-Dhoore & Jones, 2007). For example, Gonzales (2012, 2014) and Gonzales and Terosky (2013) highlighted how such contextual knowledge can prevent faculty from assigning blame to students if they struggle with college-level work, and instead to understand students more holistically, as part of larger societal structures and cultures, where there is inequitable access to educational, medical, and other important social services. For example, in one of these studies (Gonzales, 2014), a professor explained that when she designed her course syllabi, she tried to account for the realities of her students' lives. She acknowledged that many of her doctoral students held down full-time jobs off campus and maintained families, which led her to be very intentional about the workload and nature of assignments that she designed for the class.

McCracken and Ortiz (2013) agreed that having such contextual knowledge is very important because it accounts for the responsibilities and challenges that many students in HSIs face. They warned, however, that if institutional personnel are not diligent in testing their own assumptions, such background information can lead them to cast students in a deficit perspective. As an example, McCracken and Ortiz noted that students at the University of Texas-Pan American are often described with value-laden labels or references such as "first-generation," "largely minority," and students who are "'not quite ready' for college writing and reading assignments" (n.p.). They rightly argued that if these labels are not historically situated as a reflection of long-running systemic inequalities, then "not being ready" becomes the fault of the student. They further argued that it is possible to recognize students' contextual and historical backgrounds while resisting widely accepted deficit-oriented and marginalizing labels (see also Cortez, Chapter 8, this volume). Specifically, McCracken and Ortiz described a highly challenging writing program in which they asked their students to draw from personal experience in their assignments. In this way, they accounted for and valued students' personal and community histories. Based on examples like this, in the remainder of this chapter I advance an argument about the opportunities and possibilities that HSI faculty have available for reshaping the production and legitimization of knowledge within academia.

The Horizon of Possibilities: HSI Faculty Roles

HSIs are spaces where a critical mass of underrepresented students (e.g., Latina/o, first-generation, working class) can be encouraged to see themselves as knowers, thinkers, and theorists in their own right (Anzaldúa, 1987). Key to this process are faculty who are positioned to (re)shape the production and legitimization of knowledge inside academia in big and small ways. These perspectives, which underline my argument, are anchored in funds of knowledge scholarship (Moll et al., 1992; Ríos-Aguilar et al., 2011; Ríos-Aguilar & Kiyama, 2012), insights from research on faculty careers (inside and outside of HSIs), and my own experiences as a student (undergraduate, master's, and doctoral) and adjunct instructor within HSIs.

Funds of Knowledge

Funds of knowledge theory grew from studies centered on the historical experiences and home lives of working-class Latinas/os in the southwestern United States (Moll et al., 1992). The notion of "funds" refers to "the competence and knowledge embedded in the life experiences of underrepresented [communities]" (Ríos-Aguilar et al., 2011, p. 164). A typical study by funds of knowledge researchers might consider how labor and/or immigration histories, as well as communal, cultural, and spiritual traditions, provide individuals with skills or dispositions that allow them to navigate life. Funds of knowledge researchers would also consider how these skills or dispositions are likely to be dismissed by mainstream institutional measures of ability, intelligence, or projected success (Ríos-Aguilar et al., 2011). In this way, funds of knowledge research has very often been used to facilitate paradigmatic shifts among K–12 educators to help them see that students bring diverse and not always traditionally recognized forms of knowledge to the classroom.

Funds of knowledge researchers stress that this type of knowledge can be folded into curriculum offerings to make learning more relevant to students (e.g., Ríos-Aguilar et al., 2011). Ríos-Aguilar and colleagues (2011) have argued, however, that most scholars have not considered how to transform funds of knowledge into specific strategies that can be leveraged to achieve important educational outcomes (e.g., graduation rates, self-efficacy in schools). To address this gap, they proposed to shift the funds of knowledge scholarship closer to a "capital" perspective and generate "a more nuanced understanding of the processes of converting funds of knowledge into different forms of capital . . . [to deal with] issues of power within educational settings . . . to explore how power dynamics within educational settings influence the conversion or transformation process" (p. 164). More specifically, they suggested four steps to tap into the potential of various funds of knowledge to effect positive educational outcomes: (1) recognition, (2) transmission, (3) conversion, and (4) mobilization. I discuss each of these in turn, offering examples of how HSI faculty can incorporate these steps into their work.

Recognition

Recognition involves the processes where funds of knowledge are actually identified and acknowledged. The research suggests that, within the context of an HSI, a prerequisite to recognition is an understanding of the HSI's institutional, local, and community contexts (Hurtado & Ruiz, 2012; Hurtado & Ruiz Alvarado, Chapter 2, this volume). For example, in one study of a partnership that brought math, science, and education professors at an HSI together, Gonzales and Rincones (2011) found that the most involved faculty members demonstrated an intimate knowledge of the schools within the community and the resource constraints of those schools. Many of these professors, including those from outside of the discipline of education, could talk about the complexities that arose around schooling when there were misunderstandings between schools and families. The findings showed that these professors spent time in the schools and the broader community, which allowed them to formulate a more holistic picture of their students. Consequently, they were committed to efforts to improve public education by working with in-service and pre-service teachers.

Another study revealed how HSI faculty at one institution were highly aware that most of their students were first-generation college-going students, and that most graduated from poorly funded local high schools (Gonzales, 2014). One professor noted that a majority entered the university with literacy skills below the high school level. As he described the difficulties that this posed for college-level writing assignments, he simultaneously referred to the history of the regional population, the labor market in the area, and underfunded schools. He also talked about the work ethic of the students and families in the area, as if to soften his earlier comments. These studies provide good examples of how contextual knowledge can provide fundamental insights to faculty about their students, and how faculty can frame students' limited skill sets not in terms of some innate lack of ability, but rather in terms of historically inequitable social, economic, and educational contexts.

Ríos-Aguilar and colleagues (2011) noted that students and communities must have opportunities and space to recognize the knowledge and skills embedded in their histories and experiences. This means that faculty could open up space for students to articulate their histories and lived experiences within their classrooms. For example, HSI faculty could consider having students incorporate and share their personal and familial experiences in relation to course topics. Furthermore, having students journal about their experiences can help professors understand students' histories in a more intricate way. This is especially important because Latinas/os are not a monolithic demographic group (Núñez, 2014), although dominant stereotypes and taken-for-granted assumptions suggest that they are quite homogenous (Espino, 2012).

Other HSI faculty have employed ethnographic and action-based research to address how they have opened up spaces to learn from their students (Murakami, Núñez, & Cuero 2010). For example, some faculty at an HSI described how they invited students to discuss their personal biographies and social identities within the context of broader community histories, opening the potential for faculty and students to teach and learn from one another about historically marginalized identities or about social issues such as privilege and activism.

Inspired by the visit of well-known Nuyorican poet Tato Laviera to their South Texas campus near the U.S.–Mexico border, faculty at another HSI developed an advanced composition course that focused on the work and life experiences of migrant students who attended the institution. Students wrote and performed their stories through the method of *testimonio* (Moll et al., 1992), and professors and students (together with Laviera, during his later visits) co-created historical and current knowledge about the experiences of the students and their families in migrating and laboring in agriculture (Álvarez & Martínez, 2014). Participating in this course allowed students to document their own and their families' stories of immigration and migration, as well as their contributions to the economy, cultural richness, and social opportunities of the United States.[1] Beyond this, student class members expressed feeling more confident, connected to, and recognized within their university setting (Álvarez & Martínez, 2014). Providing space for students to understand their life experiences as a form of valid knowledge is the first significant step toward reshaping the production and legitimization of knowledge within academia. Since recognition is a step that is probably most easily facilitated in classrooms, this is relevant for two-year and four-year faculty, regardless of tenure status.

Transmission

Ríos-Aguilar et al. (2011) explained that after funds of knowledge are recognized, "underrepresented students [should be provided] the cultural and ideological tools to transform" them into capital for useful purposes (p. 177). In this way, faculty can encourage students to explore literature and to develop research projects and questions that address their histories, their heritage, and related cultural traditions. They may also theorize from their "place identity" (Romero, 2004), which assumes that "land-based cultures [and] place knowledge shape people's ethnic identity formation" (p. xi), and also serves as a unique store of knowledge.

In terms of application, HSI faculty can make efforts to provide students with readings that allow them to grapple with their own experiences and set their experiences in relation to history or broader phenomena. This does not mean that all readings have to be by Latina/o scholars or even about Latinas/os. Faculty might include material that addresses other common characteristics of HSI student bodies, including being first-generation, working class, bilingual, or from immigrant or migrant families. From such readings, students can be encouraged to develop research and writing projects (McCracken & Ortiz, 2013) or art-based projects.

For example, an HSI faculty member described developing in- and out-of-classroom activities that connected students to their families' farming and ranching pasts (Gonzales & Terosky, 2013). As an anthropologist, this professor took students out to a nearby farming community to demonstrate the history of land rights in the area. The students then explored current land and resource use policies, and read history and policy that reflected their own and their families' histories, including the political savvy of their families in negotiating land and resource rights. In these ways, students from rural areas realized that they had knowledge about land and water use as it related to critical public policy issues. In the classroom, they used this new knowledge to supplement reading materials and classroom discussions, and to form new questions. In another example, professors and students in the advanced composition class described earlier engaged middle school students in documenting their testimonies as migrant workers. Accordingly, the college students served as role models to show the middle school students that they, too, could attend college someday (Álvarez & Martínez, 2014). While students in such courses learned about their families' contributions to U.S. society, the professors also expressed how insights gleaned in such courses could inform and transform their research, teaching, and service activities.

Professors across many disciplines can conduct similar activities. Biologists, anthropologists, public health professors, and educational researchers could all encourage students to develop small projects in which they explore achievements, opportunities, or challenges that are relevant to them, their friends, their families, or the greater regional community. They could also ask students to interview individuals from their communities who might have been involved in local government, politics, farming and ranching, or business development. Additionally, students could seek out elders within the community to ask them to share their life stories in oral history projects. Such work could focus on the personal, public, and political, and on other experiences that might otherwise go undocumented.

Conversion and Mobilization

The third and fourth mechanisms (conversion and mobilization), as advanced by Ríos-Aguilar et al. (2011), represent the most powerful opportunities for HSI faculty to affect the production and legitimization of knowledge. *Conversion* "is the process in which students and families convert their funds of knowledge into forms of capital" (p. 177). In *mobilization*, individuals apply knowledge or capital to achieve a specific goal. In academia, the conversion and mobilization of funds into capital can entail helping students move research projects toward presentation, publication, and wider dissemination so that they may claim spaces of knowledge production within academia, allowing them to enter, challenge, or even slightly shift discourse. Anzaldúa (1987) described how powerful and meaningful entering the discourse can be:

> When Chicanas started reading [my book] . . . it somehow legitimated them. . . . [It] gave them permission [to write] about all the issues they have to deal with in daily life. To them, it was like somebody was saying: You are just as important as a woman as anybody from another race. And the experiences that you have are being told and written about.
>
> *(p. 232)*

Keeping Anzaldúa's writing in mind, faculty members can use their knowledge of the field of academia in conversion and mobilization as they help students navigate the research and publication processes. This might begin, as noted previously, with faculty support of students in the research process.

A key step is helping students identify friendly outlets or platforms that will allow them to develop their academic confidence and identity. Writers who challenge majoritarian knowledge by illuminating cultural and locally situated knowledge might find that mainstream outlets are less receptive to their work (e.g., Delgado Bernal & Villalpando, 2002). Thus, it is key that faculty members help them position their work in smart ways. Identifying journals with a social justice bent or outlets that are focused on regional issues are both potentially beneficial strategies. Moreover, faculty members could help students connect to professional and community organizations, such as the American Association of Hispanics in Higher Education (AAHHE) or the National Association of Chicana and Chicano Studies (NACCS), where their approach to knowledge production is more likely to be supported and nurtured. Of course, this does not mean that all HSI students maintain critical or even non-mainstream political, cultural, or social outlooks, but in the cases where they do, such strategies could be empowering.

Another example of faculty members assisting students in the conversion and mobilization of knowledge comes from a few professors with whom I interacted during my graduate school experience at an HSI. These professors collaborated on research projects with students in Mexico, and they frequently published their work in both Spanish and English. This strategy was in line with funds of knowledge work and changed the production and dissemination of knowledge in three ways. First, it honored students whose first language was Spanish. Second, it demonstrated that, although it is often not recognized as such in the United States, bilingualism can serve as a valuable form of capital in academic settings, especially from a more global and international perspective (e.g., Gándara & Hopkins, 2010). Finally, the work (knowledge) reached a broader and more diverse set of audiences.

Ultimately, faculty members in HSIs have the opportunity to leverage spaces like their classrooms, conferences, and academic journals to support students in the articulation and dissemination of knowledge. Not only can they strategize to help students see themselves as legitimate knowers on an individual level, but with the massive number of Latinos and Latinas who attend HSIs, faculty have the opportunity to reshape the production and legitimization of knowledge within academia. Specifically, questions, methods, and theories, if shaped by funds of knowledge thinking, could support underrepresented groups—like Latina/o, working class, and/or first-generation students—by establishing welcoming spaces of knowledge production within academia. In this way, faculty in Hispanic-Serving Institutions have the opportunity to develop future scholars who feel confident drawing from their funds of knowledge, thereby shining light on problems or opportunities that are of direct relevance to them and their communities.

Before closing, it is important and fair to acknowledge that the funds of knowledge framework will likely resonate with some faculty more than others. Some might not see it as relevant, and others may apply it to varying degrees. Some might never move beyond the development of contextual knowledge and awareness. Faculty members who are less engaged in research might focus only on awareness and recognition work. Some might only go as far as to provide space for students to relate their experiences to course topics or to have students interview local community members or family members in order to shed light on existing course topics. At the same time, other faculty members might move beyond the development of contextual knowledge to explore with students, in a more nuanced way, funds of knowledge within the community. Regardless of how the approach is applied, it is critical that higher education faculty who wish to support their students in this way are also supported by institutional leadership (see Cortez, Chapter 8, this volume).

Supporting HSI Faculty: Implications for Practice and Leadership

The potential for faculty in Hispanic-Serving Institutions to apply a funds of knowledge framework in teaching and learning requires conceptual shifts, not only by faculty and students, but also by institutional leaders. Junior faculty are often discouraged from engaging in "non-conventional" forms of faculty work, including action research (O'Meara, 2002), civic engagement work (Jaeger & Thornton, 2006), scholarship that challenges majoritarian knowledges and episte- mology (Delgado Bernal & Villalpando, 2002), and work that is anchored in locally defined, participatory action research, as noted by González (2008). As such, HSI leaders must create supports and reward systems that recognize socially-, cultur- ally-, and, indeed, politically-grounded faculty work. As outlined in the literature review, these reward systems must act as buffers against the normative and profes- sional pressures that faculty members face from the larger higher education field.

HSIs that want to move toward a funds of knowledge perspective for faculty roles must acknowledge the entrenched and narrow notions of legitimacy within the academic profession before asking or expecting their faculty to follow such paths. To this end, faculty and administrators who sit on tenure committees must have an understanding that the profiles of faculty who follow a funds of knowl- edge approach may have a different bent, but their work should be viewed as ten- ureable as well as promotable. Specifically, those engaged in funds of knowledge work might publish more often with students, and they might publish in regional outlets as often as they do in national journals. They might present their work in local venues more often than at national or international conferences. Thus, fac- ulty and administrators must think differently about incentives in the traditional rewards systems and reform them accordingly, including recognizing the impor- tance of community-oriented research, teaching, and service.

Funds of knowledge literature and scholarship on faculty rewards should be shared and read among faculty and leaders so that individuals can determine if and to what extent they are interested in such work. Faculty with greater interest could develop work plans that align with the kinds of activities demanded by funds of knowledge work. As Murphy et al. (2013) showed, not all HSI faculty will believe that it is necessary or even ethical to develop work practices based around one particular group (in this case, Hispanics). Those interested and invested in funds of knowledge work, however, may ask themselves such questions as the following: How do we ensure that faculty work that is focused on the development of our students and the greater community is rewarded? If faculty are not publishing in mainstream journals, but they are publishing with their students in local outlets, how can we provide fair evaluations? And how do potential faculty members understand and apply the HSI designation in their research, teaching, and service?

These sorts of shifts take time. They require deep transformations in how faculty carry out their roles. Not everyone will support the notion that faculty need to be more responsive to their communities, including Latina/o students and their families. In light of the colorblind meritocracy that serves as a prominent ideology in today's society (Alemán, Sálazar, Rorrer, & Parker, 2011; Murphy et al., 2013), some will question the need to make specific efforts to address the needs of Latina/o students and communities. However, the research described in this chapter suggests that HSIs can be sites where new knowledge that advances alternative perspectives can be created, rather than where existing knowledge is reproduced as if it is a static and objective good that never changes and must simply be dispensed to students.

This proposed approach to faculty work is unique. Its legitimization in faculty evaluation will signal that an institution is committed to serving an important purpose in the field of higher education. Faculty in Hispanic-Serving Institutions have the opportunity to have their own processes of knowledge creation transformed via interaction and collaboration with their students (Álvarez & Martínez, 2014; Núñez, Murakami Ramalho, & Cuero, 2010). They have the opportunity to open up new possibilities for advancing Latina/o students as knowers, thinkers, and theorists in their own right, thereby reshaping academia in significant ways.

Note

1 See www.utpa.edu/cosechavoices for digital examples.

References

Alemán, E., Jr., Sálazar, T., Rorrer, A., & Parker, L. (2011). Introduction to postracialism in U.S. public school and higher education settings: The politics of education in the age of Obama. *Peabody Journal of Education, 86*(5), 479–487. doi:10.1080/01619 56X.2011.616129

Álvarez, S., & Martínez, J.L. (2014). La palabra, conciencia, y voz: Tato Laviera and the Cosecha Voices Project at The University of Texas-Pan American. In S. Álvarez & W. Luis (Eds.), *The AmerRícan poet: Essays on the work of Tato Laviera* (pp. 204–239). New York, NY: Hunter College Center for Puerto Rican Studies Press.

Anzaldúa, G. (1987). *Borderlands/La frontera*. San Francisco, CA: Aunt Lute.

Baez, B. (2000). Race-related service and faculty of color: Conceptualizing critical agency in academe. *Higher Education, 39*(3), 363–391.

Bourdieu, P. (1988). *Homo academicus*. Stanford, CA: Stanford University Press.

Boyer, E. (1990). *Scholarship reconsidered: Priorities of the professoriate*. Lawrenceville, NJ: Princeton University Press.

Calderón Galdeano, E., Flores, A.R., & Moder, J. (2012). The Hispanic Association of Colleges and Universities and Hispanic-Serving Institutions: Partners in the advancement of Hispanic higher education. *Journal of Latinos and Education*, 11(3), 157–162.

Collins, P.H. (1986). Learning from the outsider within: The sociological significance of Black feminist thought. *Social Problems*, 33(6), S14–S32.

Delgado Bernal, D. (2008). La trenza de identidades: Weaving together my personal, professional, and communal identities. In K.P. González & R.V. Padilla (Eds.), *Doing the public good: Latina/o scholars engage civic participation* (pp. 134–148). Sterling, VA: Stylus.

Delgado Bernal, D., & Villalpando, O. (2002). An apartheid of knowledge in academia: The struggle over the "legitimate" knowledge of faculty of color. *Equity and Excellence in Education, 35*(2), 169–180.

Ek, L.D., Quijada Cerecer, P.D., Alanís, I., & Rodríguez, M.A. (2010). "I don't belong here": Chicanas/Latinas at a Hispanic-Serving Institution creating community through Muxerista mentoring. *Equity and Excellence in Education, 43*(4), 539–553.

Espino, M. (2012). Seeking the "truth" in the stories we tell: The role of critical race epistemology in higher education research. *The Review of Higher Education, 36*(1), 31–67.

Fairweather, J.S. (1993). Faculty reward structures: Toward institutional and professional homogenization. *Research in Higher Education, 34*(5), 603–623.

Fairweather, J.S. (2005). Beyond the rhetoric: Trends in the relative value of teaching and research in faculty salaries. *The Journal of Higher Education*, 76(4), 401–422.

Gándara, P., & Hopkins, M. (2010). *Forbidden language: English learners and restrictive language policies*. New York, NY: Teachers College Press.

Gardner, S.K. (2010). Keeping up with the Joneses: Socialization and culture in doctoral education at one striving institution. *Journal of Higher Education, 81*(6), 728–749.

Gardner, S.K. (2013). Women faculty departures from a striving institution: Between a rock and a hard place. *The Review of Higher Education, 36*(3), 349–370.

Garza, E. (2007). Becoming a border pedagogy educator: Rooting practice in paradox. *Multicultural education, 15*(1), 2–7.

Gonzales, L.D. (2010). *Faculty inside a changing university: Constructing roles, making spaces* (Unpublished doctoral dissertation). University of Texas, El Paso, TX.

Gonzales, L.D. (2012). Stories of success: Latinas redefining cultural capital. *Journal of Latinos and Education, 11*(2), 124–138.

Gonzales, L.D. (2013). Faculty sensemaking and mission creep: Interrogating institutionalized ways of knowing and doing legitimacy. *The Review of Higher Education, 36*(2), 179–209.

Gonzales, L.D. (2014). Framing faculty agency inside striving universities: An application of Bourdieu's theory of practice. *Journal of Higher Education, 85*(2), 193–218.

Gonzales, L.D., & Núñez, A.-M. (2014). The ranking regime and the production of knowledge: (Re)shaping faculty work? *Education Policy Analysis Archives, 22*(31). Retrieved from http://dx.doi.org/10.14507/epaa.v22n31.2014

Gonzales, L.D., & Rincones, R. (2011). Interdisciplinary scholars: Negotiating legitimacy at the core and from the margins. *Journal of Further and Higher Education, 36*(4), 495–518.

Gonzales, L.D., & Terosky, A. (2013). *From the faculty perspective: A multi-site study of legitimacy*. Paper presented at the meeting of the American Educational Research Association, Philadelphia, PA.

González, K. (2008). In search of praxis: Legacy making in the aggregate. In K.P. González & R.V. Padilla (Eds.), *Doing the public good: Latina/o scholars engage civic participation* (pp. 125–135). Sterling, VA: Stylus.

Gouldner, A.W. (1957). Cosmopolitans and locals: Toward an analysis of latent social roles—I. *Administrative Science Quarterly, 2*(3), 281–306.

Gouldner, A.W. (1958). Cosmopolitans and locals: Toward an analysis of latent social roles—II. *Administrative Science Quarterly, 2*(3), 444–480.

Henderson, B.B. (2009). Mission creep and teaching at the master's university. *College Teaching, 57*(4), 185–187.

Hubbard, S.M., & Stage, F.K. (2009). Attitudes, perceptions, and preferences of faculty at Hispanic-Serving and Predominately Black Institutions. *Journal of Higher Education, 80*(3), 270–289.

Hurtado, S., & Ruiz, A. (2012). Realizing the potential of Hispanic-Serving Institutions: Multiple dimensions of institutional diversity for advancing Hispanic higher education. Sacramento, CA: Hispanic Association of Colleges and Universities. Retrieved from http://www.hacu.net/images/hacu/OPAI/H3ERC/2012_papers/Hurtado%20 ruiz%20-%20realizing%20the%20potential%20of%20hsis%20-%20updated%202012.pdf

Jaeger, A.J., & Thornton, C.H. (2006). Neither honor nor compensation: Faculty and public service. *Educational Policy, 20*(2), 345–366.

Jencks, C., & Riesman, D. (2002/1968). *The academic revolution.* New Brunswick, NJ: Transaction.

Lewis, L.S. (1996). *Marginal worth: Teaching and the academic labor market.* New Brunswick, NJ: Transaction Books.

McCracken, I.M., & Ortiz, V. (2013). Latino/a student (efficacy) expectations: Reacting and adjusting to a writing-about-writing curriculum change at an Hispanic-Serving Institution. *Composition Forum, 27.* Retrieved from http://compositionforum.com/ issue/27/

Melguizo, T., & Strober, M.H. (2007). Faculty salaries and the maximization of prestige. *Research in Higher Education, 48*(6), 633–668.

Moll, L., Amanti, C., Neff, D., & González, N. (1992). Funds of knowledge for teaching: A qualitative approach to developing strategic connections between homes and classrooms. *Theory into Practice, 31*(2), 132–141.

Murakami Ramalho, E., Núñez, A., & Cuero, K.K. (2010). Latin@ advocacy in the hyphen: Faculty identity and commitment in a Hispanic Serving Institution. *International Journal of Qualitative Studies in Education, 23*(6), 699–717.

Murphy, S.W., Araiza, I., Cárdenas, H., Jr., & Garza, S. (2013). When I grade a paper, I do not look at the name. I grade the paper for content: Teacher perceptions of students at a Hispanic-Serving Institution. *Journal of Border Educational Research, 7*(1), 133–144.

Neumann, A. (1999). Inventing a labor of love: Scholarship as a woman's work. In M. Romero & A.J. Stewart (Eds.), *Women's untold stories: Breaking silence, talking back, voicing complexity* (pp. 243–255). New York, NY: Routledge.

Núñez, A.-M. (2014). Employing multilevel intersectionality in educational research: Latino identities, contexts, and college access. *Educational Researcher, 43*(2), 85–92.

Núñez, A.-M., & Bowers, A.J. (2011). Exploring what leads high school students to enroll in Hispanic-Serving Institutions: A multilevel analysis. *American Educational Research Journal, 48*(6), 1286–1313.

Núñez, A.-M., Murakami-Ramalho, E.M., & Cuero, K.K. (2010). Pedagogy for equity: Teaching in a Hispanic-Serving Institution. *Innovative Higher Education, 35*(3), 177–190.

O'Meara, K. (2002). Uncovering the values in faculty evaluation of service as scholarship. *The Review of Higher Education, 26*(1), 57–80.

O'Meara, K., & Bloomgarden, A. (2011). The pursuit of prestige: The experience of institutional striving from a faculty perspective. *Journal of the Professoriate, 4*(1), 39–73.

Ramírez-Dhoore, D., & Jones, R. (2007). Discovering a "proper pedagogy": The geography of writing at the University of Texas-Pan American. In C. Kirklighter, D. Cárdenas, & S. Wolff Murphy (Eds.), *Charting new terrains of Chicana/o/Latina/o education* (pp. 1–34). Creskill, NJ: Hampton Press.

Rhoades, G., Kiyama, J.M., McCormick, R., & Quiroz, M. (2008). Local cosmopolitans and cosmopolitan locals: New models of professionals in the academy. *The Review of Higher Education, 31*(2), 209–235.

Ríos-Aguilar, C., & Kiyama, J.M. (2012). Funds of knowledge: An approach to studying Latina(o) students' transition to college. *Journal of Latinos and Education, 11*(1), 2–16.

Ríos-Aguilar, C., Kiyama, J.M., Gravitt, M., & Moll, L.C. (2011). Funds of knowledge for the poor and forms of capital for the rich? A capital approach to examining funds of knowledge. *Theory and Research in Education, 9*(2), 163–184.

Romero, E. (2004). Learning Manito discourse: Children's stories and identity in northern New Mexico. In R. DeAnda (Ed.), *Chicanos and Chicanas in contemporary society* (2nd ed., pp. 39–55). New York, NY: Rowman and Littlefield.

Rosiek, J. (2013). *Contemporary pragmatism, epistemology and methodology.* Paper presented at the meeting of the American Educational Research Association, San Francisco, CA.

Rosser, V. (2005). Measuring the change in faculty perceptions over time: An examination of their work-life and satisfaction. *Research in Higher Education, 46*(1), 81–107.

Rusch, E.A., & Wilbur, C. (2007). Shaping institutional environments: The process of becoming legitimate. *The Review of Higher Education, 30*(3), 301–318.

Scherer, J.L., & Anson, M.L. (2014). *Community colleges and the access effect: Why open admissions suppresses achievement.* New York, NY: Palgrave Macmillan.

Smith, D. (1987). *The everyday world as problematic: A feminist sociology.* Toronto, Canada: University of Toronto Press.

Stanley, C.A. (2007). When counter narratives meet master narratives in the journal editorial-review process. *Educational Researcher, 36*(1), 14–24.

Terosky, A.L. (2005). *Taking teaching seriously: A study of university professors and their undergraduate teaching* (Unpublished doctoral dissertation). Teachers College, Columbia University, New York, NY.

Terosky, A.L. (2010). How do they do it? Career strategies of university professors noted for taking teaching seriously. *Journal on Excellence in College Teaching, 21*(1), 121–145.

U.S. Department of Education–Institute of Education Sciences National Center for Education Statistics. (2011). *Fast facts: Characteristics of postsecondary education faculty* [Data file]. Retrieved from http://nces.ed.gov/programs/digest/d11/tables/dt11_268.asp

Welner, K.G. (2012). Scholars as policy actors: Research, public discourse, and the zone of judicial constraints. *American Educational Research Journal, 49*(1), 7–29.

Wright, M. (2005). Always at odds?: Congruence in faculty beliefs about teaching at a research university. *The Journal of Higher Education, 76*(3), 331–353.

Yosso, T.J. (2005). Whose culture has capital? A Critical Race Theory discussion of community cultural wealth. *Race Ethnicity and Education, 8*(1), 69–91.

8

ENACTING LEADERSHIP AT HISPANIC-SERVING INSTITUTIONS

Laura J. Cortez

Scholars cannot ignore the significant role of institutional leaders in shaping environments that will increase college success for students (Bensimon, 2007; Stanton-Sálazar, 2001). In order to prepare for the future of higher education, leaders must embrace new concepts and acquire new abilities (Kezar, 2009). Leaders at HSIs, in particular, must respond to the needs of a growing yet historically underserved population in higher education and in the United States. They face the challenge of effecting institutional transformation to serve these students in the face of changing demographics and declining funding in public higher education (see Ortega et al., Chapter 9, this volume).

To date, the organizational identity and make-up of Hispanic-Serving Institutions has rarely been studied or documented. In fact, Hurtado and Ruiz Alvarado (Chapter 2, this volume) contend there is little evidence regarding the kinds of transcultural changes institutions have undergone or will need to undergo in order to become "Hispanic-serving." Furthermore, they assert that additional evidence is needed to explain how these transformative changes occur within an institution. Studies of HSIs have tended to focus solely on students' experiences and outcomes (e.g., Bridges, Kinzie, Nelson Laird, & Kuh, 2008; Cuellar, 2014), faculty (Hubbard & Stage, 2009), or presidents (de los Santos & Vega, 2008; Santiago, 2009; Santiago, Andrade, & Brown, 2004). And research that has focused on HSI leadership has tended to address challenges faced (e.g., de los Santos & Cuamea, 2010; de los Santos & de los Santos, 2003) rather than the strategies that leaders develop and employ to respond to these challenges (for an exception, see Santiago, 2009).

To address the relative scarcity of literature on these strategies, the current chapter describes how five institutional leaders at one HSI described organizational change on their own campus, and how they implemented changes to improve outcomes for both students and the organization. I examined the leadership approaches, skills, and practices of a range of administrators who varied in age, ethnicity, and gender. What they shared was the common goal of improving the educational experiences of students, and they all intentionally utilized their roles to implement change.

Their stories of advocating and championing for students, particularly Latinas/os, represent a form of "grassroots leadership" (Kezar & Lester, 2011). This type of leadership moves away from crediting traditional hierarchical positions with the role and responsibility of change, but rather promotes the notion that other individuals within the organization can contribute to change (Astin & Leland, 1991; Pearce & Conger, 2003). Given the growing number of institutions that are becoming HSIs, there is an urgency to demonstrate what type of leadership is necessary in institutions that seek to become truly "Hispanic-serving."

In this chapter, I also explore how these institutional leaders made sense of the term "Hispanic-Serving Institution." Laden (2004) asserted that the term "HSI" is evolving, but often never truly focuses on the needs of Latina/o students. García (2013) recently found evidence to contest this "manufactured identity" hypothesis, however, arguing that "sensemaking and sensegiving are important in the co-construction of the organizational identity of HSIs" (p. iii). Ultimately, this chapter sheds light on how institutional leaders make sense of their HSI status, how they utilize their positions to enact change, and what organizational programs and services they believe are necessary to help Latina/o students succeed.

Regional, State, and National Context

The current study took place at a four-year HSI in Texas's Rio Grande Valley. Informally known as the "Valley," the region is located along the southern tip of Texas and consists of a stretch of land that embodies four counties: Cameron, Hidalgo, Starr, and Willacy. More importantly, it lies along the northern bank of the Rio Grande River, across the border from Mexico. Currently, 11% of the total Latina/o population in Texas is located in the Valley, and 95% of the region's K–12 population is Latina/o (Santiago, 2012).

Texas is home to 68 HSIs, the second highest number of any state in the country (Calderón Galdeano & Santiago, 2014). Four of these HSIs are located in the Rio Grande Valley, including two 4-year institutions (University of Texas at Brownsville and University of Texas—Pan American) and two 2-year community colleges (Texas State Technical College and South Texas College). Degree attainment among Latinas/os in the Rio Grande Valley lags behind national indicators: Only 16% of adult Latinas/os age 25 and older hold at least an associate's degree, compared to 20% of Latinas/os nationwide (Santiago, 2012; National Center for Education Statistics [NCES], 2013).

Despite these obstacles, one institution in particular has seen success: the University of Texas—Pan American (UTPA). With 15,806 undergraduates and 1,885 graduate students, UTPA is the second highest among all U.S. universities in the number of Hispanic undergraduate students enrolled (UTPA OIRE, 2013a). It is third in the nation for the number of bachelor's and graduate degrees awarded to this racial/ethnic group, and 57% of all UTPA students who apply to medical school have been accepted, compared to the state average of 34% (UTPA OIRE, 2013a). The full-time undergraduate enrollment of Latinas/os at UTPA (91% of the entire student body) surpasses both the national and the state average for full-time undergraduate Latina/o HSI enrollment (47% each) (Calderón Galdeano & Santiago, 2014).

The UTPA campus can best be described as a commuter college with a high concentration of low-income, first-generation, and non-traditional students. More than one-half (55%) of the students commute at least 10 miles or more daily, and 75% report living at home with three to six members in their household (UTPA OIRE, 2013b). Many students report caring for extended family members (i.e., grandparents, aunts, and parents), as well as their own children. A full 75% are first-generation college students, 71% come from low-income backgrounds, and 20% are parents (UTPA OIRE, 2013a). Additionally, approximately 39% of full-time and part-time faculty and 79% of the administration are Hispanic. Therefore, UTPA is undoubtedly impacting a region of the country and a segment of the Latina/o population that are most in need.

According to *Hispanic Outlook in Higher Education* magazine, UTPA ranks among the top 100 best U.S. colleges for Hispanics in terms of enrollment of Latinas/os, relatively low cost of tuition, and degree completion rates (Cooper, 2013; UTPA OIRE, 2013a). The university has also shown progress in its first-year, first-time student retention rate—from 68% in 2005 to 76% in 2013 (UTPA OIRE, 2013a). This signifies a commendable increase, given that UTPA's student population consists largely of non-traditional students, who often leave college within their first year (Gilardi & Guglielmetti, 2011; UTPA OIRE, 2013a). UTPA's six-year graduation rate of 44% exceeds the average six-year graduation rate for large comprehensive regional universities in Texas (39%) (Texas Higher Education Coordinating Board [THECB], 2014). Lastly, it is important to note that between 2000 and 2010, UTPA showed an increase in its four-year graduation rate—from 6% to 18%—denoting that students at UTPA are now finishing college within a shorter period of time than their counterparts a decade before (UTPA OIRE, 2012). All these achievements indicate that UTPA is enacting changes that are impacting retention and degree attainment for the better.

Setting the Stage

In this study, university officials demonstrated a keen awareness of the population they serve, and they indicated they are openly committed to creating an educated populous in the Rio Grande Valley that fosters the cultural, economic, and social well-being of the region. In fact, their work has been quite intentional, through a

mission to "direct academic, budgetary, research, and all other decisions" in a manner that will "graduate as many students as we can, as quickly as we can, with the
very best education we can provide" (UTPA OIRE, 2012, p. 3).

Given the relative success of UTPA in serving its students, I sought to discover the factors that the institution's leaders believe are critical in increasing
college completion rates. More importantly, this study explored how leaders have
intentionally created institutional change at an HSI, and how these changes may
impact students and the overall outcomes for the university. Data were collected
through individual interviews with administrators who held high-level positions
at the university. Their experiences allowed them to speak directly from an institutional and leadership perspective on how the university has been meeting its
goals and overcoming challenges. All of the participants were members of the
President's Cabinet (i.e., student services, provost's office, development, enrollment services, and student affairs). These institutional leaders had worked at the
university between 2 and 10 years. Two were natives of the Rio Grande Valley, and
all happened to be the first in their families to graduate from college. They represented various areas of campus and ethnic backgrounds, as well as both genders.

Table 8.1 provides a snapshot of the administrators' profiles. It is important to
note that University of Texas—Pan American officials approved and encouraged
the use of the university's name in this chapter. To protect individual participants'
privacy, however, I indicate the types of positions they held, but refer to them with
pseudonyms.

Each participant provided a unique and enriching perspective on UTPA and
its students. For instance, the administrator from enrollment services provided
information on how UTPA recruits and retains Latina/o students, as well as on
changes in the institution's admissions policies and how they have affected students and the region. The day-to-day involvement of Latina/o students on campus
was captured in an interview with an administrator in student affairs. In addition,
an academic affairs administrator provided a broad but historical description of
Latina/o students and UTPA's involvement with the surrounding community.
Finally, the administrator in the provost's office provided information about academic support programs and the key factors that help students persist, shedding

TABLE 8.1 *Administrator Profiles*

Pseudonym	Gender	Ethnicity	Department	Years of Service
Dr. Isa Chapa	Female	Latina	Enrollment Services	5 years
Ms. Jane Howard	Female	White	Development	10 years
Dr. Paloma Jiménez	Female	Latina	Provost's Office	9 years
Dr. Kevin Johnston	Male	Black	Student Services	2 years
Dr. Edward Lewis	Male	White	Student Affairs	10 years

light on how UTPA utilizes its HSI status to obtain Title V funds that impact services to students. Overall, each institutional leader provided a rich history that greatly contributed to learning more about the integral role of leadership at this Hispanic-Serving Institution.

This study utilized a *funds of knowledge* framework, which is based on the premise that "people are competent, they have knowledge, and their life experiences have given them that knowledge" (González, Moll, & Amanti, 2005, pp. ix–x). In particular, this assets-based approach assumes that Latina/o children and their families have "historically developed and accumulated strategies (skills, abilities, ideas, practices) or bodies of knowledge that are essential to a household's functioning and well-being" (González et al., 2005, p. 92). By incorporating such a framework, the data reflect the intellectual and social knowledge that campus administrators possess concerning Latina/o students and the region.

A funds of knowledge lens was also helpful in capturing the culture of the Rio Grande Valley, particularly since it has a significant influence on the way the institution, staff, faculty, and students engage with one another. For example, the institutional leaders shared how the culture, values, and norms of the region have affected the students and the university. For instance, participants described the perception in the Valley that attending a local college like UTPA is not prestigious and alluded to students' perceptions that they might not receive an education comparable to what they would at other universities outside of the Valley. These institutional leaders shared how they have tried to combat and change such stereotypes.

Findings

Administrators who participated in this study described three institutional structures and practices they found critical in their efforts to create a supportive campus environment for Latina/o students: (1) culturally sensitive leadership, (2) student-centered services, and (3) intensive academic and career advising.

Culturally Sensitive Leadership

For Latina/o students, mentoring can have an overall positive impact on degree and career aspirations, academic achievement, and success during college (Bordes & Arredondo, 2005; Crisp & Cruz, 2010; Santos & Reigadas, 2002). However, leaders must not only mentor students, but must also remain sensitive to context and culture, ethics, emotion, and values (Kezar, 2009). Administrators in this study shared that culturally relevant leadership was an especially important inspiration for new programs and changes. As Dr. Isa Chapa, a senior administrator in enrollment services, explained, "I am them."

Growing up in the Valley, Dr. Chapa's parents did not go to college. Her mother had a sixth-grade education, and her father was educated in Mexico; together they taught her the value of an education at an early age. Her family earned a modest wage but believed that education was the social equalizer:

> I grew up in a very small town. I grew up with hard work. I wouldn't say that we were poor, but if you strictly looked monetarily, yeah, I think my dad made $12,000 a year. But we weren't poor in the sense that the idea of education was something that our parents instilled in us very young. Even though my parents weren't educated, they understood the value of education.

Due to her own personal life experiences, Dr. Chapa was able to relate to the struggles and hardships of UTPA's Latina/o students. As an enrollment administrator, she understood that her role was to ensure students were prepared and would be successful at the institution. She did not take lightly the impact that admissions decisions (positive or negative) had on students and their families: "Every day that I see a student, have an appeal on my desk, or that I'm looking at numbers—I don't look at them as solely a number. I look at them as if they were me, just a few years ago."

Dr. Paloma Jiménez, a senior administrator in the provost's office, shared a similar story. As the oldest of six children, she had dedicated her life to helping her younger brothers and sisters by putting them all through college. Without children of her own, she wanted to see her siblings "achieve their goals and dreams." As she explained it, "once all six of them became professionals, then I did the same for my seven nieces and nephews." Dr. Jiménez's dedication and compassion transcended to her work with students at UTPA. Describing what motivates her to do her work, she tearfully said, "I'm inspired when I see the light in students' hearts and eyes. When they've felt proud of themselves, they've felt successful, and they've felt accomplished, I can't even put it into words."

Dr. Jiménez also had a mantra—"we can never rest"—and a legacy she wanted to be remembered for: "I want my legacy to be that I have given 24/7, my life, to help others achieve their goals and their dreams." She believed it is the responsibility of campus leaders to "never take the finger off the switch" and to always be re-looking, re-thinking, and re-organizing, so that momentum toward supporting student success is not lost. In other words, it is the administrators' responsibility to bridge the gap between Latina/o students' desires to come to college and their preparation for that goal:

> We did a very good job of getting the students here, and many of them were not ready to be here. They were not ready because they did not have clear goals for why they wanted to be here. They just knew they wanted to go to school. And so they came. We gave financial assistance, and so they came. But they did not have a clear idea as to what it would take to be successful.

And to be successful meant getting a degree. So that's where we come in, and it's like we try to help bridge that gap.

As Dr. Jiménez explained, however, getting students to UTPA is only part of the equation. The other pieces of the puzzle include providing direction, giving them the resources they need, and teaching them the skills they need to finish the endeavor. With more than 10 years of experience, Dr. Jiménez has been involved with implementing support structures and programs to assist Latina/o students, both locally and nationally, from working with state organizations such as the Texas Higher Education Coordinating Board (THECB) to improve retention and graduation rates, to assessing student learning outcomes and institutional changes for accreditation with the Southern Association of Colleges and Schools (SACS).

Drawing from similar cultural and personal experiences, Drs. Chapa and Jiménez were both able to relate to students and serve as role models and advocates. This supports the literature that asserts that Latina/o administrators are important agents in the retention and success of Latina/o students (Castellanos & Jones, 2003) and in the facilitation of the educational socialization process for students (Anaya & Cole, 2003). The role that institutional leaders play in becoming cultural translators, mediators, and facilitators can advance the bicultural development and understanding of the students they serve. It is evident that these administrators' backgrounds and experiences serve as lifelines that allow them to connect with and better understand their Latina/o students at UTPA.

Student-Centered Services

Students are the focus at UTPA. It is clear that administrators at all levels are engaged with students and have a commitment to garnering their input and feedback. As Ms. Jane Howard shared, "Our president is so empathic for our students." The president grew up in the mountains of Montana, and he often shared with students that his destiny was to become a blacksmith, but he was good at taking exams and that took him out of his own "Valley." As Ms. Howard explained, the president believes students are central to all the work at UTPA:

> It's all about the kids. Now, that kid might be 50 years old, working on a master's degree, but [the president believes] it's all about the students. While he can't necessarily make everybody believe the way he does, that's how he operates.

UTPA offers a wealth of activities and student support services that are culturally relevant, and administrators involve students in many of their decision-making processes, including faculty and administrative searches. They have found simple yet effective ways to solicit student feedback and create change. For instance, student surveys have led to the development of an on-campus child care center and a self-imposed student fee to create a new recreational center. Dr. Edward Lewis, a senior administrator in student affairs, shared the following:

> One of the first things we do is we look at our population. We had a survey that looked at our students and it said that 20% are parents. And we didn't have a child day care center, so we built a child care center. It holds 140 kids, and it's pretty close to being full all the time with a waiting list. The need was there and it's allowed hundreds of students to take their baby or their child so they can study, work, and stay on campus, rather than staying home to care for the child.

In addition to these student services, Dr. Lewis realized students needed a space where they could spend time when they were not studying. He believed, if you "get a student engaged in anything, you're better off and he or she is better off." After noticing that the current student union was not serving students' needs, he proposed the idea of a recreational center for students that would allow them the space and opportunity to remain on campus and stay engaged:

> We started a survey with students, and they voted to impose a fee on themselves, and that's how we got the [recreation] center. We have had a huge increase in the number of students, not only going over to the facility, but engaged in intramural and club sports and those kinds of things. It's been a huge increase.

Dr. Kevin Johnston, a senior administrator in student services, further explained the reasoning for the center:

> We're trying to build some traditions, because it's one of the things students say—we haven't done a good job in identifying those traditions. And for us it's a little hard, because some of those traditions are tied directly to sports. We don't have big sports here, but we got a new recreational center and we're trying to get more students involved with it.

Now, with foot traffic in the recreation center reaching 1,500 to 2,000 students each day, UTPA has created a healthy opportunity for student engagement.

UTPA has also begun providing students with more traditional activities, including an orientation for first-year students. In years past, students would typically arrive on campus with no formal introduction to the university or its traditions. Dr. Johnston noted that the students they serve are changing, and, as more traditional-aged students are admitted, they want to be more involved: "We are moving more and more towards similar norms that most institutions have, where they have robust orientations." He described the possibility of creating a three- to four-day orientation where students could stay on campus and become engaged early in various university programs:

> We are starting to see more types of programs that are going in that direction, and we're grappling [with] whether they can work here. I think it can, and we're trying to sell a different message, even down [to] our marketing materials, which is to "Come and experience UTPA, it's a great experience."

Intensive Academic and Career Advisement

Dr. Jiménez noticed that, after intensive support during their first year, sophomores were dropping out of UTPA. She explained,

> One of the things that we needed to do to retain kids is take them by the hand, if you will, and teach them the ropes and how to navigate the system. And that requires teaching them how to transition from high school to college, and how to be engaged in an intrusive advisement process.

Thus, in 2005, through the support of a Title V grant, a new advising system was devised to allow first-year and first-time students to be assigned to an undergraduate counselor who could provide them with a degree plan and assist them with registering for courses. Sophomores are assigned to professional guidance counselors in their major departments. In their junior and senior years, students engage with faculty mentors. "So today," Dr. Jiménez explained, "we have a very systematic, comprehensive plan and . . . [we] give them a four-year road map."

With such an "intrusive" advising process, Dr. Lewis noted, "You can't let down. You can't say, 'Well, we're not going to do that this year.' It's an everyday, day in and day out process." These systematic processes are in place to ensure students don't fall through the cracks, particularly when first-generation Latina/o students feel academic guidance is critical to their success and to completing their degrees (Solórzano, Villalpando, & Oseguera, 2005). This approach has allowed UTPA to combat the commuter environment and keep students engaged.

Another helpful benefit of the advisement process is that it gives students the academic and professional support they need to really understand the importance of their degrees. Nevertheless, Dr. Jiménez confirmed that career guidance is something that can be improved:

> We need to help students make better choices and decisions of what they want to do with their lives, and that's career development. We've been guiding them for majors they think they want, but eventually, halfway down the

road, they decide "this is not for me," so they change again and we lose out [in retaining students] again.

Dr. Jiménez said she believes career development should begin early, in middle school or even earlier. In fact, the philosophy of providing students in the Valley with early guidance is reflected in the creation of UTPA's Visitor Center. In order to establish a culture around college and careers, UTPA welcomes school children to the campus Visitor Center year-round. UTPA creates lesson plans around school requirements, such as the Texas Essential Knowledge and Skills (TEKS), and invites school districts from across the Valley to visit. As Dr. Lewis explained, the message behind the Visitor Center is to "get students at a young age to see themselves on a college campus and to believe that he/she belongs on a college campus." Dr. Chapa, the administrator in enrollment services, agreed: "Once we get them here, we begin to discuss this is a college campus and college is attainable." The Visitor Center is booked all year, and in fall 2010 about 25,000 students visited over a period of four months. Students who come to the Visitor Center are, ultimately, potential UTPA students who have now had early exposure to the idea that college can be their next step. Through the Visitor Center, Dr. Lewis believes, "we have probably done more than any university in the state to grow our own students."

In 2009, the University Retention and Advisement office at UTPA created the Sophomore Advising and Mentoring Program, which pays sophomores to mentor first-time students. A year later, in 2010, the university hired 75 mentors to provide on-going activities and support for entering students. According to Dr. Jiménez, since the inception of the program, about 1,100 students have been affected. The program has benefits for students who are mentored as well as those who are hired to be mentors: By paying students a wage, UTPA is able to "keep students in college because they are here and they don't have to work outside of the university." Indeed, the literature shows that, because Latina/o students are more likely than others to work during college (Dowd & Malcom, 2012), and because working off-campus is negatively related to outcomes like academic performance and persistence (Bozick, 2007; Darolia, 2014; Pascarella, Edison, Nora, Hagedorn, & Terenzini, 1998), offering such opportunities to Latina/o students is critical for their success (Núñez, Hoover, Pickett, Stuart-Carruthers, & Vázquez, 2013).

Institutional leaders at UTPA believe that intensive academic and career advisement is important. By taking students by the hand, administrators are ensuring that students are given a roadmap to be successful and not slip through the cracks. Dr. Jiménez asserted, "Students at UTPA value education and want to get an education." The important job is that "we meet them halfway and provide the necessary support and resources to ensure they get there." Throughout the study, it was evident that UTPA's institutional leaders have compassion for and a true understanding of their students. As first-generation students themselves, they could relate to the challenges their students faced in college and at home. On several occasions, they described how their own personal experiences and backgrounds influenced how they approached and performed their jobs. By conducting their work in a manner that was supportive of students and by utilizing their own funds of knowledge, they were able to create a student-focused environment.

Enacting Institutional Identity at an HSI: Challenges and Opportunities

This study afforded the opportunity to learn how key administrators at UTPA understood the institutional identity of their campus. They described a clear understanding of the history and purpose of being a Hispanic-Serving Institution (Perrakis & Hagedorn, 2010). It appears to be part of their institutional identity, as some referred to UTPA as an HSI without being prompted. They also discussed the challenges of being an HSI and truly understanding its role, however, particularly noting the variation among faculty and administrators' perceptions of such a designation. Dr. Jiménez explained,

> Of course, faculty know that we are a Hispanic-Serving Institution, but I don't know if they understand the benefits of being a Hispanic-Serving Institution. I think they hear about grants, but I'm not sure they get it.

Administrators raised concerns about the perceptions that stakeholders—including alumni and members of the Valley community—had about UTPA being an HSI. For instance, Dr. Johnston shared that he received a call from a community member who was upset that UTPA had been designated as "Hispanic-Serving." Even though the gentleman was a graduate of another HSI, he felt UTPA was discriminating against other students by calling itself an HSI:

> He called me and he said he got his degree from [a different university]. I said, "Okay," and he goes on that he was upset about, "What's this about Hispanic-Serving Institution?" So he's drilling me down, and I said, "It's just a designation it doesn't mean—" "Well, it sounds a lot to me that you are all about this Hispanic thing." I'm on the phone saying, "Sir, no, it's a designation that the federal government gives, and the majority of people here happen to be of that race or ethnicity. But nowhere does it say that we only accept those individuals or we're not a campus that is open." [He said] "Well, I feel that." And I said, "Sir, did you know that [your alma mater] is a Hispanic-Serving Institution?"

HSIs are not required to publicly announce their designation as such, and, in fact, some may shy away from publicizing their institutional type for fear of losing prestige or, as illustrated in the previous anecdote, communicating an external message that they serve Hispanic students to the exclusion of other students (Contreras, Malcom, & Bensimon, 2008; Dwyer, 2014). Therefore, despite the legitimacy of HSIs as a federally recognized institution type, there is evidence that institutions internally construct the meaning of this designation differently, leading administrators to determine how an institution should embrace or acknowledge such an institutional identity (García, 2013).

Although UTPA is located in an area that has historically had fewer resources to afford local residents postsecondary opportunities, administrators at UTPA felt their students should be afforded educational opportunities of the highest caliber. Dr. Lewis contended that just because students are attending their local college does not mean they do not deserve the best:

> These students deserve what they would get if they were going up to UT Austin or Texas A&M, or Texas Tech. They deserve the best. Just because they are here [in the Valley] doesn't mean we shouldn't be giving them the best.

Importantly, these administrators were keenly aware that not all HSIs are the same. In the late 1980s when the Hispanic Association of Colleges and Universities (HACU) lobbied Congress to create an official designation for two-year and four-year not-for-profit postsecondary institutions with high concentrations of Latina/o students, some campuses were already serving Latina/o student populations far beyond the 25% threshold. For institutions like UTPA, whose Hispanic population is over 90%, this has created an interesting predicament. As Dr. Jiménez explained, "We have always been an HSI, and there needs to be a different designation for us, who are doing it with greater numbers." For example, there are tensions around the value and recognition that other HSIs are afforded despite their more limited Latina/o student populations:

> I've been on national task forces where we've gone to look at universities that are doing really good work with Hispanic populations, and they have been identified as HSIs with 25% of students. Here I am with [a] 90% [Latina/o] student body and I have not been identified as someone doing great things. This population that they have, they are only doing it with 25%. That just doesn't add up.

She went on to describe the tensions they have when competing for financial resources. She called it a "very good thing" that "Congress has designated Hispanic-Serving Institutions and has put money into it." But HSIs of all types (private, public, four-year, and two-year) compete for Title V funding. Therefore, the money allocated by the Department of Education is split between institutions with widely varied Hispanic populations. Dr. Jiménez admitted, "If the University of Texas at Austin and UT Pan Am were competing for the same monies, we would never win, because UT Austin has more power and resources." While the University of Texas at Austin is an emerging HSI and does not currently compete for these funds, flagship institutions often do have the financial and institutional resources, and the grant-writing expertise, to secure them.

Despite these challenges, UTPA has been successful in securing grants. Title V monies have helped them fund programs like an all-freshman course called "Learning Frameworks," which was recognized by *Excelencia* in Education as being effective in serving Latina/o students (Santiago, 2012). In 2005, UTPA developed the course as a retention mechanism to help students acquire the skills they needed to navigate through their first year of college. Title V money allowed them to hire additional faculty solely dedicated to teaching the course, rather than assigning faculty from other departments to split their teaching course loads. Since the grant supported this initiative for five years, UTPA was able to slowly integrate the expense into their main budget. Today, the new faculty and the course have been fully integrated, and both are part of the institution's budget.

Conclusion

The goal of this chapter was to provide an example of the type of leadership that can be found at Hispanic-Serving Institutions. It sought to show the role of leadership in organizational change on a single campus, and how institutional leaders have implemented policies and programs to improve outcomes for both students and the organization. Leaders at UTPA exhibited a form of "grassroots leadership" by going above and beyond the call of duty, engaging their own personal experiences to guide decision-making, and staying ahead of the curve to support and engage students. This chapter suggests that these institutional leaders have created a space in keeping with Paulo Freire's (1985) idea of education as a mechanism for social change. More specifically, Freire saw education as a terrain where "values engage and respond to the deeper beliefs about the very nature of what it means to be human, to dream, and to name and struggle for a particular future and way of life" (Giroux, 1985, p. xiii). It was evident that each of these leaders had a profound respect for the university and cared deeply about students' progress.

It is important to note that while the University of Texas—Pan American is unique, the issues leaders on this campus have faced with regard to retention, persistence, and completion of Latinas/os are not. These leaders have confronted the same challenges as other universities, particularly with respect to developing a campus climate that is conducive to and supportive of diverse populations (Hurtado, 1994; Hurtado & Ruiz Alvarado, Chapter 2, this volume). Leaders at UTPA found that progress can be made for non-traditional students when a cultural sensitivity toward their needs is maintained, and when leaders create academic and social programs that keep students one step ahead of the curve.

Administrators at UTPA employed culturally relevant approaches by drawing upon their own funds of knowledge (Moll, Amanti, Neff, & González, 1992). While the individuals who participated in this study were not all Latina/o, they addressed the types of leadership skills and institutional practices that have proven instrumental in the persistence and completion of Latina/o students (Núñez et al., 2013). They described how, in order to improve Latina/o retention and completion, they needed to integrate strategies that would work best for their specific populations of students. Furthermore, as with many HSIs that play an important role in enrolling local students (Vega & Martínez, 2012), institutional leaders understood that context matters and that programs and services must remain sensitive to the needs of not only Latinas/os, but also the area more broadly. This resonates with the notion of placing Latina/o student identity at the center of practice at an institution (see Hurtado & Ruiz Alvarado, Chapter 2, this volume). They acknowledged that Latina/o students' needs are distinct and if institutions, specifically HSIs, are not willing to be creative or flexible, it will be difficult to enact change.

With these findings in mind, this study has important implications for research. Given the evolution of HSIs, scholars need to continue learning how institutions respond to this new identity. Leaders in this study struggled with the "authenticity" of being an HSI, especially since they were serving Latinas/os long before the HSI designation was created. UTPA is not the only HSI with this type of history—in fact, there are a handful of universities in Puerto Rico and the mainland United States that were specifically created to serve Latinas/os. However, these differences are important, and as scholars expand research in this area, they need to develop a common language to discuss, categorize, and describe HSIs. As Dr. Jiménez expressed, if there were distinctions among HSIs, then competition for Title V funds might be distributed more equitably among similar types of institutions.

Furthermore, with the total number of HSIs on the brink of 400, scholars need to carefully analyze the various regional contexts in which these institutions exist (Calderón Galdeano & Santiago, 2014). For instance, in past studies, UTPA has been categorized as a "border HSI." Santiago (2010) found that, including UTPA, there are eight such institutions along the Texas–Mexico border, and they enroll 5% of all Hispanic undergraduates in the United States. Context matters, and scholars need to be aware that, many times, HSIs are a reflection of their local communities. Although geographically concentrated in certain states, HSIs vary markedly in their enrollment size, urbanicity, and local economic conditions (Núñez, Crisp, & Elizondo, in press, and Chapter 3, this volume; Núñez & Elizondo, Chapter 4, this volume). These diverse economic and social conditions that different HSIs inhabit must be considered in research, scholarship, and practice. At UTPA, administrators took into account the cultural influences the Valley has on students and were able to adjust and adapt their leadership approaches accordingly. Indeed, this study—in concert with Chapter 2 in this volume—underscores that sociohistorical context matters in how institutional personnel construct the institutional identity of an HSI. Scholars should be cautious in defining HSIs as isolated entities, and instead be mindful that they are often extensions of their local communities.

In the end, this qualitative study sheds light on the integral role of five administrators who reflected, in their own ways, a leadership style that can be adapted to other institutional settings. While there is still an urgent need to expand the research on leadership at HSIs, this is a starting point for current HSIs, emerging HSIs, and predominantly White institutions (PWIs) that are struggling to find systematic ways to support Latina/o students during their transitions into and through the postsecondary experience.

References

Anaya, G., & Cole, D. (2003). Active involvement in Latina/o student achievement. In L. Jones & J. Castellanos (Eds.), *The majority in the minority: Retaining Latina/o faculty, administrators, staff, and students in the 21st century* (pp. 95–108). Sterling, VA: Stylus.

Astin, H., & Leland, C. (1991). *Women of influence, women of vision.* San Francisco, CA: Jossey-Bass.

Bensimon, E.M. (2007). The underestimated significance of practitioner knowledge in the scholarship on student success. *The Review of Higher Education,* 30(4), 441–469.

Bordes, V., & Arredondo, P. (2005). Mentoring and 1st-year Latina/o college students. *Journal of Hispanic Higher Education,* 4, 114–133.

Bozick, R. (2007). Making it through the first year of college: The role of students' economic resources, employment, and living arrangements. *Sociology of Education,* 80(3), 261–285.

Bridges, B.K., Kinzie, J., Nelson Laird, T.F., & Kuh, G.D. (2008). Student engagement and student success at historically Black and Hispanic Serving Institutions. In M. Gasman, B. Baez, & C.S.V. Turner (Eds.), *Understanding minority-serving institutions* (pp. 217–236). Albany, NY: SUNY Press.

Calderón Galdeano, E., & Santiago, D.A. (2014). *Hispanic-Serving Institutions (HSIs) fact sheet: 2012–2013.* Washington, DC: *Excelencia* in Education.

Castellanos, J., & Jones, L. (Eds.). (2003). *The majority in the minority: Expanding the representation of Latina/o faculty, administrators, and students in higher education.* Sterling, VA: Stylus.

Contreras, F.E., Malcom, L.E., & Bensimon, E.M. (2008). Hispanic-Serving Institutions: Closeted identity and the production of equitable outcomes for Latina/o/a students. In M. Gasman, B. Baez, & C.S.V. Turner (Eds.), *Interdisciplinary approaches to understanding minority serving institutions* (pp. 71–90). Albany, NY: SUNY Press.

Cooper, M.A. (2013, May). A portrait of Hispanics in Higher Education by numbers. *Hispanic Outlook in Higher Education,* 23, 9–17.

Crisp, G., & Cruz, I. (2010). Confirmatory factor analysis of a measure of "mentoring" among undergraduate students attending a Hispanic-Serving Institution. *Journal of Hispanic Higher Education,* 9(3), 232–244.

Cuellar, M. (2014). The impact of Hispanic-Serving Institutions (HSIs), emerging HSIs, and non-HSIs on Latina/o academic self-concept. *Review of Higher Education,* 37(4), 499–530.

Darolia, R. (2014). Working (and studying) day and night: Heterogeneous effects of working on the academic performance of full-time and part-time students. *Economics of Education Review*, 38, 38–50.

de los Santos, A.G., & Cuamea, K.M. (2010). Challenges facing Hispanic-Serving Institutions in the first decade of the 21st Century. *Journal of Latinos and Education, 9*(2), 19–107.

de los Santos, A.G., & de los Santos, G.E. (2003). Hispanic-serving institutions in the 21st century: Overview, challenges, and opportunities. *Journal of Hispanic Higher Education, 2*(4), 377–391.

de los Santos, A. G., & Vega, I.I. (2008). Hispanic presidents and chancellors of institutions of higher education in the United States in 2001 and 2006. *Journal of Hispanic Higher Education, 7*(2), 156–182.

Dowd, A.C., & Malcom, L.E. (2012). *Reducing undergraduate debt to increase Latina and Latino participation in STEM professions.* Los Angeles, CA: University of Southern California.

Dwyer, B. (2014). *Emerging as Hispanic-serving: Students' perceptions of the Hispanic-Serving designation.* Paper presented at the meeting of the American Educational Research Association, Philadelphia, PA.

Freire, P. (1985). *The politics of education: Culture, power, and liberation.* Westport, CT: Bergin & Garvey.

García, G.A. (2013). *Challenging the "manufactured identity" of Hispanic-Serving Institutions (HSIs): Co-constructing an organizational identity* (Unpublished doctoral dissertation). University of California, Los Angeles, CA.

Gilardi, S., & Guglielmetti, C. (2011). University life of non-traditional students: Engagement styles and impact on attrition. *The Journal of Higher Education*, 82(1), 33–523.

Giroux, H. (1985). Introduction. In P. Freire, *The politics of education: Culture, power, and liberation* (pp. xi–xxvi). Westport, CT: Bergin & Garvey.

González, N., Moll, L.C., & Amanti, C. (2005). Preface. In N. González, L. Moll, & C. Amanti (Eds.), *Funds of knowledge: Theorizing practices in households, communities, and classrooms* (pp. ix–xii). Mahwah, NJ: Lawrence Erlbaum Associates.

Hubbard, S.M., & Stage, F.K. (2009). Attitudes, perceptions, and preferences of faculty at Hispanic-Serving and predominantly black Institutions. *The Journal of Higher Education*, 80(3), 270–289.

Hurtado, S. (1994). The institutional climate for talented Latino students. *Research in Higher Education*, 35(1), 21–41.

Kezar, A.J. (2009). *Rethinking leadership practices in a complex, multicultural, and global environment: New concepts and models for higher education.* Sterling, VA: Stylus.

Kezar, A.J., & Lester, J. (2011). *Enhancing campus capacity for leadership. An examination of grassroots leaders in higher education.* Redwood City, CA: Stanford University Press.

Laden, B.V. (2004). Hispanic-Serving Institutions: What are they? Where are they? *Community College Journal of Research and Practice*, 28, 181–198.

Moll, L.C., Amanti, C., Neff, D., & González, N. (1992). Funds of knowledge for teaching: Using a qualitative approach to connect homes and classrooms. *Theory into Practice, 31*(2), 132–141.

National Center for Education Statistics. (2013). *Digest of Education Statistics, 2013.* (NCES 2014-015). Washington, DC: Author.

Núñez, A.-M., Crisp, G., & Elizondo, D. (in press). Mapping Hispanic-Serving Institutions: A typology of institutional diversity. *Journal of Higher Education.*

Núñez, A.-M., Hoover, R., Pickett, K., Stuart-Carruthers, C., & Vázquez, M. (2013). Latina/os in higher education and Hispanic-Serving Institutions: Creating conditions for success. *ASHE Higher Education Report*, 39(1). San Francisco, CA: Jossey-Bass.

Pascarella, E.T., Edison, M.I., Nora, A., Hagedorn, L.S., & Terenzini, P.T. (1998). Does work inhibit cognitive development during college? *Educational Evaluation and Policy Analysis*, 20(2), 75–93.

Pearce, C.L., & Conger, J.A. (2003). The historical underpinnings of shared leadership. In J.A. Conger (Ed.), *Shared leadership: Reframing the hows and whys of leadership* (pp. 1–13). Thousand Oaks, CA: SAGE.

Perrakis, A., & Hagedorn, L.S. (2010). Latina/o/a student success in community colleges and Hispanic-Serving Institutions. *Community College Journal of Research and Practice*, 34(10), 587–598.

Santiago, D. (2010). *Reality check: Hispanic-serving institutions on the Texas border strategizing financial aid*. Washington, DC: Excelencia in Education.

Santiago, D.A. (2009). Leading in a changing America: Presidential perspectives from Hispanic-Serving Institutions. Washington, DC: *Excelencia* in Education. Retrieved from http://www.edexcelencia.org/research/leading-changing-america-presidential-perspectives-hispanic-serving-institutions

Santiago, D.A. (2012). *Latina/o college completion: Rio Grande Valley*. Washington, DC: *Excelencia* in Education.

Santiago, D.A., Andrade, S.J., & Brown, S.E. (2004). *Latino student success at Hispanic-Serving Institutions*. Washington, DC: *Excelencia* in Education.

Santos, S.J., & Reigadas, E.T. (2002). Latina/os in higher education: An evaluation of a university faculty mentoring program. *Journal of Hispanic Higher Education*, 1(1), 40–50.

Solórzano, D.G., Villalpando, O., & Oseguera, L. (2005). Educational inequities and Latina/o undergraduate students in the United States: A critical race analysis of their educational progress. *Journal of Hispanic Higher Education*, 4(3), 272–294. doi: 10.1177/1538192705270552776550

Stanton-Sálazar, R.D. (2001). *Manufacturing hope and despair: The school and kin support networks of U.S.-Mexican youth*. New York, NY: Teachers College Press.

Texas Higher Education Coordinating Board. (2014). *University of Texas-Pan American success and key measures*. Retrieved from http://www.thecb.state.tx.us

University of Texas-Pan American Office of Institutional Research. (2012). *Enrollment management plan, 2012–2022*. Retrieved from www.utpa.edu/oire

University of Texas-Pan American Office of Institutional Research. (2013a). *Factbook: Stats at a glance*. Retrieved July 4, 2014, from www.utpa.edu/oire

University of Texas-Pan American Office of Institutional Research. (2013b). *Report on entering students*. Retrieved July 4, 2014, from www.utpa.edu/oire

Vega, A., & Martínez, R. (2012). A Latina/o scorecard for higher education: A focus on Texas universities. *Journal of Hispanic Higher Education*, 11(1), 41–54. doi: 10.1177/1538192711435554

PART III

Building Capacity and Accountability in Hispanic-Serving Institutions

9

EXAMINING THE FINANCIAL RESILIENCE OF HISPANIC-SERVING INSTITUTIONS

Noe Ortega, Joanna Frye, Christopher J. Nellum, Aurora Kamimura, and Angela Vidal-Rodríguez

This chapter examines the effects of the recent decline in public investment in U.S. public colleges and universities on Hispanic-Serving Institutions (HSIs). Our longitudinal analysis of revenue and expenditure trends suggests that among the first institutions to be affected by this continual decline are those that serve the fastest-growing segment of our changing society—Latinas/os. Persistent financial pressures present a specific set of challenges and opportunities for HSIs, and throughout the chapter we highlight some of the efforts made by these colleges and universities to protect the core functions and mission of higher education in order to ensure access and a quality education for Latina/o students. We conclude our discussion with recommendations that will allow HSIs to build on previous efforts to carry this momentum forward. The impetus for this work was the belief that our ability to secure postsecondary opportunities for all capable students is crucial to the future of our nation and will ultimately shape our democracy in generations to come.

Fulfilling a Promise

A college education has long been considered central to the "American dream" of individual achievement, upward social mobility, and progress. Over the past several decades, institutions of higher learning have played an increasingly important role in preparing individuals for civic and economic participation. The very success of colleges and universities in fulfilling this mission has only increased the sizeable expectations of them—expectations that grow amid patterns of changing demographics and economic conditions. It is now an article of faith as well as a demonstrated fact that the American vision for progress can only be fully realized through the continual provision of educational opportunities for all capable students, and this has inspired more than two centuries of public and private investment in higher education (Goldin & Katz, 2009; Thelin, 2005).

Today's assumption that we should embrace postsecondary opportunities for all has evolved after many decades of struggles to make higher learning more inclusive of underrepresented groups that were once restricted from access to its full benefits. There has always been a bias that has favored privileged groups of Americans (and the institutions they attend) over new groups, whether "new" meant literally "new to arrive" or, more symbolically, "new to be recognized." To some degree, this bias still persists. But one of the major developments of higher education during the latter half of the twentieth century was the cultivation of a general consensus that all Americans should have access to the full range of educational opportunities available in our society (Cohen, 2008).

Financial resources for higher education have been significantly reduced in the past decade, and institutions are being forced to do more with less. Public colleges face a growing demand for what they promise within rapidly changing socioeconomic and political contexts, both of which have created greater competition for government and private investment (Zumeta, 2005). Even with the recent gradual economic recovery, persistent declines in state funding observed in the last several years threaten our nation's historic commitment to access to higher educational opportunities, and in all likelihood will disproportionately affect opportunities for groups that have historically been underrepresented in our colleges and universities. As postsecondary educational attainment increases in its value and the resources to provide it are increasingly constrained, competition for access to resources becomes increasingly political and potentially divisive.

Theoretical Rationale

Concerns over resources have a long history in the literature on strategic management in the field of organizational studies. Scholars tend to use open system theories of organizations, such as transaction-cost economics (Williamson, 1975), new institutional theory (Meyer & Rowan, 1977), population ecology (Hannan & Freeman, 1977), and resource-dependence theory (Pfeffer & Salancik, 1978) to understand the restructuring of higher education. These perspectives emphasize the importance of organizations' pursuit of "environmental fit" and adaptation to constraints and uncertainties in their changing social and political contexts (Gumport & Pusser, 1999; Pfeffer & Salancik, 1978; Scott, 1998; Slaughter & Leslie, 1997). However, many of these theories remain relatively silent about how resource differences among organizations affect their relative propensity for change and about alternative strategies that are chosen over time (Kraatz & Zajac, 2001; Pfeffer & Salancik, 2003).

Much of the work on strategic management in organizational studies has drawn attention to how resources contribute to sustained performance, figure prominently in strategic decision making, and ultimately help to secure the success of an organization (Barney, 1991; Mahoney & Pandian, 1992; Wernerfelt, 1984). While the theoretical framing adopted for this study builds on some of the propositions and assumptions found in open system theories of organizations, it draws specifically from the insights provided by the literature on *resource heterogeneity*, which focuses on differences between organizations that can be measured monetarily, such as endowments, and in less tangible ways, such as institutional reputation or prestige (Kraatz & Zajac, 2001; Zajac, Kraatz, & Bresser, 2000). This theoretical rationale allows researchers, institutional leaders, and policymakers to better understand why institutions that face similar circumstances sometimes adopt different strategies for dealing with fiscal challenges. It also sheds light on why those with more institutional resources may be better insulated from environmental threats or are better able to engage in inefficient practices for quite some time before experiencing significant threat to their survival (Cyert & March, 1963; Singh, 1986). Given the significant differences between institutional revenue among postsecondary institutions, the impact of resources on the adaptive behaviors of colleges and universities warrants further consideration, particularly during times of persistent disinvestment in higher education.

The unequal distribution of monetary resources among colleges and universities can be best characterized by the "Matthew effect," a phenomenon that describes how the rich get richer while the poor get poorer (Merton, 1968; Trow, 1988). Researchers examining how resource constraints affect the restructuring of higher education have suggested that institutions positioned advantageously relative to others enjoy certain competitive benefits. Cheslock and Gianneschi (2008) determined that, during periods of economic uncertainty, highly selective institutions enjoy a greater advantage in generating alternative sources of revenue. Similarly, Bastedo and Bowman (2010) found that institutional prestige, as measured by college rankings, influences an institution's ability to generate and acquire additional resources. Kraatz and Zajac (2001) examined the effects of institutional resources, such as endowments, on the propensity for change at liberal arts colleges and universities in the United States between 1971 and 1986, and they found that institutions with greater resources were less likely to change in response to periods of fiscal instability. They also determined that monetary advantages provide institutions with greater discretion over certain adaptive behaviors that may result from economic challenges (Kraatz & Zajac, 2001). A key takeaway from these findings is that institutions of all types respond to changes in their circumstances over time (or fail to survive), but wealthier institutions have the opportunity to do so on their own terms—often from positions of strength—in ways that may even extend competitive advantage.

The findings reported by each of these studies raise new questions and concerns over how colleges and universities mediate fiscal challenges, as well as about how resource heterogeneity may influence or constrain strategic decisions as they relate to the ability to generate or secure alternative sources of revenue. Among the numerous studies we reviewed, few examined this problem from the perspective of Minority-Serving Institutions (MSIs), and even fewer examined it as it relates to Hispanic-Serving Institutions (HSIs). This is of particular concern, given how the unequal distribution of resources renders HSIs especially vulnerable to economic pressures. Even during times of economic upswing, the comparatively limited financial resilience of these institutions raises further concerns over student retention, as it drains faculty reserves, starves program investment, distorts institutional priorities, and ultimately stymies state and national commitments to provide postsecondary opportunities to all capable students.

Considered in full, the existing literature from organizational research and higher education makes clear that resources provide advantages to institutions, improve the likelihood of sustained performance, and figure prominently into decision making during periods of general fiscal constraint (e.g., Zumeta, 2005). In the case of HSIs—which historically have been underresourced (Núñez, Hurtado, & Calderón Galdeano, chapter 1, this volume)—it should come as no surprise that many of these institutions are redistributing resources away from programs and practices that have proven to effectively recruit, retain, and graduate students who balance on the margin of success. Indeed, it is a case of a double bind—the most vulnerable students are often the most expensive to serve adequately (Webber & Ehrenberg, 2009), and the most vulnerable institutions have the least resilience to withstand threats in their financial environments (Zumeta, 2005). Institutions with even moderate resources are afforded the opportunity to redirect funds and to continue to invest in essential programs, while those with more modest resources may be more likely to direct those funds toward the protection of basic operations in an effort to attempt to ride out the storm and simply survive. The result is that students from low- to moderate-income families pay the price for their institutions' struggles to meet basic operating expenses.

Federal Investment in Hispanic-Serving Institutions

Latinas/os represent the largest group of students of color on postsecondary campuses, but even after increasing by an unprecedented 50% between 2006 and 2010, the share of Latina/o college graduates remains below that of their non-Latina/o peers (Fry & López, 2012). In the 2012–2013 academic year, more than half (59%) of Latinas/os were enrolled at HSIs (Calderón Galdeano & Santiago, 2014). Given the relationship between institutional resources and student success, this situation leaves the prospect of postsecondary educational attainment for the rapidly growing Latina/o population uncertain and contingent upon the changing financial conditions of the United States (Braxton, Hirschy, & McClendon, 2011). Increased investment in higher education will be needed to ensure that postsecondary institutions successfully recruit, retain, and graduate more Latina/o students.

Despite a commitment by Congress in the latter part of the twentieth century to invest in HSIs, federal appropriations have failed to keep pace with the growing number of federally recognized institutions (Figure 9.1). The number of HSIs

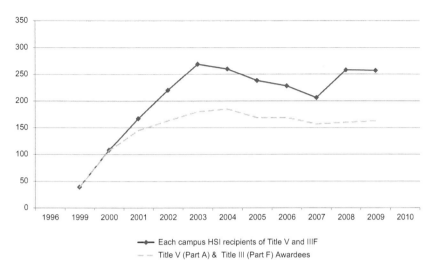

FIGURE 9.1   Total Number of HSIs and Total Number of Title V (Part A) & Title III (Part F) Awardees, 1996–2010

Sources: National Forum on Higher Education for the Public Good analysis of U.S. Department of Education's historical lists of Developing Hispanic-Serving Institutions Program (Title V, Part A), 1999–2010; National Center for Education Statistics (NCES) HSI Statistical Trends, 1990–1999; and NCES Integrated Postsecondary Education Data System (IPEDS), 2000–2010.

that received Title V (Part A) appropriations peaked in 2004, at 185 (about 70% of all HSIs that year), and that number declined to 163 (56%) in 2009. Moreover, the average award to institutions has only increased slightly, despite growing enrollments—from $407,487 in 1999 to $600,000 in 2007. The total amount of appropriations made available to HSIs has consistently remained around $92–$94 million, despite the marked increase in the number of HSIs during the past few years (Ortega, Frye, Nellum, Kamimura, & Vidal-Rodríguez, 2013).

In 2008, the U.S. Department of Education (ED) released new awards available to HSIs in the areas of science, technology, engineering, and mathematics (STEM) under its Title III (Part F) program. As a result, HSIs experienced a significant increase in grant amounts, which averaged nearly $1.2 million per institution annually in 2008 and 2009 (Figure 9.2); the continued investment in this program by Congress remains uncertain, however. It is also important to note that, in 2009, nearly half of all HSIs (44%) still did not receive any Title V federal grant awards. Thus, while Title V appropriations have provided HSIs with some financial relief during periods of fiscal constraint, attempts by the federal government to remedy the historic neglect of HSIs by state governments have been unevenly realized, raising concerns over the long-term sustainability of initiatives designed to facilitate the postsecondary success of Latina/o students.

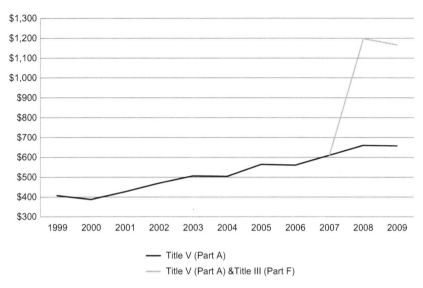

FIGURE 9.2 Average Yearly Amount Awarded to Title V (Part A) & Title III (Part F) Recipients, 1999–2009 (in Thousands)

Source: National Forum on Higher Education for the Public Good analysis of U.S. Department of Education historical lists of Developing Hispanic-Serving Institutions Program (Title V, Part A & Title III, Part F), 1999–2009.

Changes in national and regional economies will affect both the demand and availability of funding for HSIs, as Title V appropriations continue to come under severe scrutiny and face persistent threats of reduction or even elimination. The continual increase in the number of HSIs further exacerbates the uncertain status of Title V funding for these institutions. As of 2010, an additional 242 institutions that enroll between 15% and 24% Latinas/os have been designated as "emerging HSIs" (Santiago & Andrade, 2010), and many of these will certainly cross the 25% threshold and become HSIs in the near future. Given recent demographic shifts, the growing importance of a postsecondary education, and the fiscal challenges faced by a number of colleges and universities, the number of HSIs that compete for discretionary supplemental funding will grow, leading to very uncertain outcomes for these institutions. Therefore, the question remains: Will HSIs have the financial resilience in the coming years to meet their missions, priorities, and goals?

Examining the Financial Resilience of Hispanic-Serving Institutions

Historically, public colleges and universities have come to rely on various sources of revenue to maintain affordability and provide quality educational opportunities for students. Figure 9.3 provides a snapshot of the traditional revenue sources that

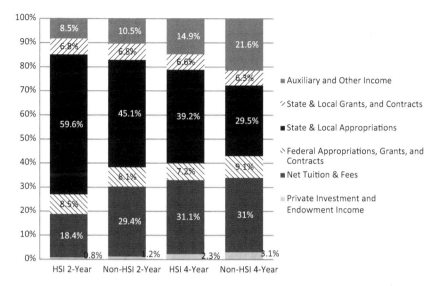

FIGURE 9.3   Revenue Shares at All Public HSIs & Non-HSIs, 2010

Source: National Forum on Higher Education for the Public Good analysis of Delta Cost Project Database, 2010.

were available at all public two- and four-year institutions in 2010. On average, the majority of revenue at public postsecondary institutions was obtained from government sources (i.e., combined revenue from federal and state grants, contracts, and appropriations). Specifically, these revenue sources represented more than half of all revenue shares at public four-year HSIs (53%), two-year HSIs (76%), and two-year non-HSIs (60%). The shares of revenue from these sources were slightly lower at public four-year non-HSIs, yet still accounted for nearly half (45%) of all operating funds.

The largest single share of revenue obtained from government sources at public institutions came from state and local appropriations. In 2010, these appropriations represented 60% of the revenue shares at public two-year HSIs and 45% at public two-year non-HSIs. Public four-year HSIs received, on average, 39% of their revenue from state and local appropriations, while public four-year non-HSIs received 30% of their funds from this source.

On average in 2010, HSIs were 12% more dependent on government sources of revenue than non-HSIs, and this level of dependency makes them especially vulnerable to continual declines in state and federal investment in higher education. It also raises concerns about whether HSIs have the fiscal resilience to overcome sustained periods of constrained resources while continuing to serve the growing number of Latina/o students demanding access to postsecondary education. The problem of resource constraints is not unique to HSIs, yet we posit that declining public investment in higher education affects different institutions differently. Indeed, when one considers the historical context of HSIs (Núñez, Hurtado, & Calderón Galdeano, chapter 1, this volume), it should come as no surprise that they continue to find themselves further constrained with regard to the strategies they pursue to generate "new" sources of revenue.

This claim is perhaps best illustrated by the recession experienced at the turn of the twenty-first century. During this period there was unyielding pressure on public postsecondary institutions to offset declines in state and federal support with revenue from alternative sources (e.g., private investment endowment income, tuition and fees, etc.). For example, in response to a sharp decline in per student appropriations between 2000 and 2010, a number of public colleges and universities increased their reliance on revenue from net tuition and fees (Baum & Ma, 2012). At two-year HSIs and non-HSIs, tuition revenue accounted for 18% and 29% of operating revenue, respectively; revenue from tuition and fees at public four-year HSIs and non-HSIs accounted for 31% of each of their total operating budgets (Figure 9.3). As a result, a greater percentage of the cost share at public postsecondary institutions was passed on to students and their families. And, for the first time since World War II, the average share of revenue received from tuition and fees at public four-year non-HSIs exceeded the share of revenue acquired from state and local appropriations (30%). Many public four-year HSIs are on pace to pass this threshold as well. Given that many students enrolled at HSIs are from low socioeconomic status families, and HSIs tend to enroll students who are most likely to apply for and receive federal financial aid (de los Santos & Cuamea, 2010; Flores, Horn, & Crisp, 2006; Nora & Crisp, 2009), these findings highlight the practical limitations of alternative revenue generating strategies at institutions where affordability is of primary concern.

This close examination of revenue shares at all public college and universities for a single year (2010) sheds light on the inequitable distribution of resources among public HSIs and their non-HSI counterparts. With few exceptions, public two- and four-year HSIs have been forced to do more with less, as they continue to provide educational opportunities for underrepresented, low-income, and first-generation students (a case that can be similarly made for community colleges). This snapshot also illustrates differences in the abilities of public HSIs and non-HSIs to diversify their revenue sources in order to account for decreasing public investment in higher education. Public non-HSIs have generally been more successful than public HSIs at increasing their share of revenue received from tuition and other sources, which provides them with some level of protection from states' financial stress.

There are of course limitations to the claims that can be made with regard to funding inequities between public HSIs and non-HSIs through the use of a single year of data. In an effort to further explicate the disparities across various revenue sources, the sections that follow provide a longitudinal analysis of institutions by sector and type and compare revenue across these institutions according to a full-time equivalent (FTE) student. Examining data by FTE (also referred to as per student expenses) allows for better comparisons among institutions with respect to available resources.

Trends in Revenues

State and Local Funding

Although state and local funds continue to be an important source of revenue across all public institution types, per student state and local appropriations to public two- and four-year HSIs and non-HSIs declined steadily between 1999 and 2010 (Figure 9.4). A closer examination of this trend reveals persistent gaps in per student state and local appropriations between public HSIs and non-HSIs at the four-year level: Public four-year HSIs averaged $1,274 less per student than public four-year non-HSIs over the 11-year period ($8,639 versus $9,913, respectively). While public four-year HSIs received fewer per student state and local appropriations than four-year non-HSIs in all years of our analysis, this gap widened threefold between 1999 and 2010, from $580 to $1,827.

Among public two-year institutions over the same period, the trends are reversed. Public two-year HSIs averaged about $573 more in state and local revenue per student than two-year non-HSIs ($7,120 versus $6,547, respectively). Although it is encouraging to find that public two-year HSIs have not experienced the troubling disparities in state and local appropriations witnessed at the

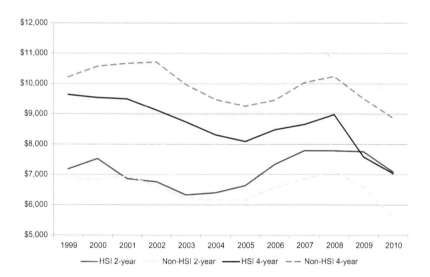

FIGURE 9.4 State and Local Appropriations at All HSI and Non-HSI Public Colleges and Universities, 1999–2010 (by FTE and 2010 Dollars)

Source: National Forum on Higher Education for the Public Good analysis of Delta Cost Project Database, 1999–2010.

four-year level, these institutions also receive significantly fewer tuition dollars per student than their non-HSI peers, a point that will be further elaborated on in the following section. Interestingly, while the gap between private two- and four-year non-HSIs in per student state and local appropriations has remained constant over time, it appears to have closed between public two- and four-year HSIs. Public four-year HSIs now receive about the same amount of state and local funding per student as public two-year HSIs, while public four-year non-HSIs receive nearly 60% more state and local appropriations per student than public two-year non-HSIs.

Consistent reductions in state and local funding for postsecondary education signal a move toward "state assisted" rather than "state supported" public higher education (Hearn, 2006). This new era in financing is characterized by increased competition for state funds and changing attitudes about higher education (St. John & Parsons, 2005; Zumeta, 2005). Some policymakers and other stakeholders have also asserted that public institutions can and should pursue alternate sources of revenue, primarily through increases in tuition and private support (Doyle & Delaney, 2009; Hearn, 2006). This trend is particularly precarious for HSIs because they typically are unable to generate enough supplemental revenue to offset losses in government support, due to the characteristics of the students they serve (Núñez & Elizondo, 2012; Santos & Sáenz, 2013).

Tuition and Fees

As previously discussed, a common strategy adopted by public institutions to mitigate declines in state support is to increase revenue from tuition and fees. As one might expect, for the past several years, the increase in average tuition at public four-year institutions has been higher than the average increase at private non-profit four-year institutions (Baum & Ma, 2012). Between 1999 and 2010, four-year public institutions increased their average share of revenue from net tuition and fees per student by at least 58%. In other words, they generated 58% more revenue from tuition and fees per student than they did a decade earlier. Figure 9.5 illustrates changes in per student tuition and fees revenue at public two- and four-year HSIs and non-HSIs between 1999 and 2010. While the per student growth rate in tuition and fees was similar for public four-year HSIs and non-HSIs over the 11-year time period, HSIs consistently averaged fewer tuition dollars per student than non-HSIs ($4,134 versus $5,699, respectively).

At the public two-year level, increases in per student tuition and fees revenue occurred at a much slower rate, despite the sharp declines in state and local revenue described earlier. In general, public two-year institutions are less able than four-year institutions to raise tuition and fees to compensate for losses in state investment (Núñez, Sparks, & Hernández, 2011). Trends in the public two-year sector reflect even greater inequality in the ability of HSIs to raise tuition and fee revenue per student relative to non-HSIs. Specifically, the per student tuition and

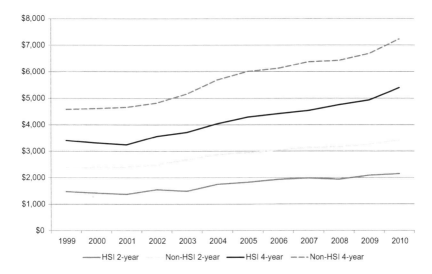

FIGURE 9.5   Net Tuition & Fees at All HSI and Non-HSI Public Colleges and Universities, 1999–2010 (by FTE and 2010 Dollars)

Source: National Forum on Higher Education for the Public Good analysis of Delta Cost Project Database, 1999–2010.

fee revenue disparity between public HSIs and non-HSIs at the four-year level was, on average over the 11 years, 37%; at the two-year level, the gap was 62%. As we will explore later in this chapter, these disparities may have troubling consequences for institutional expenditures.

In sum, the share of institutional revenue generated from net tuition and fees has increased across public two- and four-year institutions, but to a lesser degree at public HSIs. Such changes represent a fundamental reallocation of financial responsibility for higher education from public sources to students and their families. As Rodríguez and Calderón Galdeano assert (Chapter 11, this volume), for institutions like HSIs that serve a large percentage of low-income first-generation students, this revenue-generating strategy has its own practical limitations, particularly with regard to increasing graduation rates at four-year HSIs.

Voluntary Support and Private Giving

Public colleges and universities have also turned to voluntary support and private giving as another strategy for generating revenue to offset declines in state and local appropriations (Drezner, 2011; Leslie & Ramey, 1988). Voluntary support and private giving are defined as resources gifted to a college or university by an individual, foundation, or corporation to support a variety of functions related to the institutional mission (Cheslock & Gianneschi, 2008). These funds can be used not only to balance institutional budgets and to ensure organizational survival, but also to invest in and improve programs and services that would otherwise be on the chopping block if institutions relied solely on state appropriations and tuition (Leslie & Ramey, 1988). Moreover, private funds can be used to recruit and retain disadvantaged student populations, enhance research activities, and improve the quality and delivery of curriculum and instruction (Rothschild, 1999). The ability to generate private giving and grow an endowment differs considerably by institutional type, however.

Over the period from 1999 to 2010, revenue from voluntary support, private giving, and endowment income generally exhibited a significant downward trend, with a select few institutions rebounding at the end of the decade (see Figure 9.6). This decline reflects not only one or more years of reduced giving, but also depressed returns from endowment income (Cheslock & Gianneschi, 2008; Mulnix et al., 2002). At four-year institutions, average revenue from voluntary support and private giving was about 2.5 times greater per student at non-HSIs than at HSIs ($1,472 versus $543, respectively). At two-year colleges, per student revenue from voluntary support and private giving in the aggregate was quite low; two-year institutions, regardless of HSI status, received fewer dollars from private sources. The revenue disparity favored non-HSIs over HSIs, but the difference per student was negligible ($223 versus $169, respectively). These data point to a possible opportunity to enhance fundraising and endowment management to offset current and future reductions in local and state appropriations.

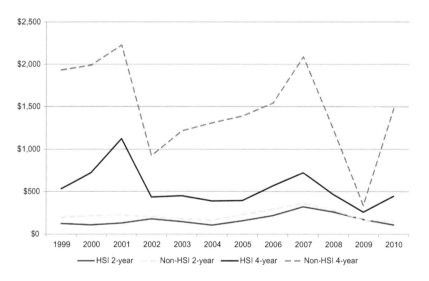

FIGURE 9.6   Average Endowment Assets at All HSI and Non-HSI Public Colleges and Universities, 1999–2010 (by FTE and 2010 Dollars)

Source: National Forum on Higher Education for the Public Good analysis of Delta Cost Project Database, 1999–2010.

The problem of constrained resources is not unique to HSIs, but when one considers the historic patterns of underfunding and recent reductions in government appropriations to these institutions, declines in public and private investment further jeopardize their ability to serve the rapidly growing Latina/o population. In addition, the common strategies available to many institutions to compensate for government disinvestment in higher education do not appear to be commonplace for the majority of HSIs (Cheslock & Gianneschi, 2008; Speck, 2010). Thus, the assumption that all public colleges and universities can generate alternate sources of revenue appears to be inaccurate, particularly when you consider the brief history of institutions such as HSIs, which have been disadvantaged in their ability to acquire additional resources (de los Santos & Cuamea, 2010). It is more feasible to suggest that institutions with more resources are more likely to generate alternative sources of revenue and redirect funds to maintain investment in essential programs and services, while less advantaged institutions are likely to direct their already limited funds toward ensuring immediate survival.

Preserving the Core Purposes and Missions of Public Colleges and Universities

Recent changes in revenue patterns for public colleges and universities are restructuring core priorities at a number of institutions and even threatening the historical function and core mission of higher education more generally. During periods of economic uncertainty, postsecondary institutions that lack financial resilience tend to struggle with issues of student retention, program investment, and affordability (Gumport, 2001; Kraatz & Zajac, 2001). When efforts to secure alternative sources of revenue fail, institutional leaders must consider new structural arrangements that may reshape institutional priorities and ultimately redistribute resources away from programs and practices that effectively recruit, retain, and graduate students.

Trends in Education and Related Expenditures

Restructuring practices at public colleges and universities has an impact on critical areas directly tied to the traditional roles of higher education. In fact, a number of public institutions are beginning to curtail investments in education and related (E&R) expenditures, a spending category that includes instruction, student services, and the share of general associated support and maintenance costs (Desrochers & Wellman, 2011). For the most part, contemporary studies examining expenditure trends at postsecondary institutions tend to focus on the overall bottom line; these analyses remain relatively silent about the history of persistent financial barriers that inhibit the ability of poorly funded institutions to mediate resource constraints. Accounting for these disparities can help us better understand why institutions that face similar circumstances often adopt different strategies when mediating fiscal constraints.

Between 1999 and 2010, despite the fiscal challenges described previously, public four-year non-HSIs increased E&R spending per student by approximately 5%, while public four-year HSIs experienced about a 2% decline in per student E&R investment (Figure 9.7). By the end of the decade, the gap in E&R spending had widened, as public four-year HSIs spent an average of approximately $4,500 less per student on E&R expenditures than public four-year non-HSIs ($11,737 versus $16,318, respectively). At the public two-year level, both HSIs and non-HSIs spent fewer dollars on average per student on E&R in 2010 than they did in 1999. Nonetheless, public two-year HSI expenditures on E&R were, on average, about 11% less per student over the decade than at public two-year non-HSIs ($9,944 versus $11,049, respectively). Similar to the trends observed at the public four-year level, gaps between public two-year HSIs and non-HSIs in per student E&R spending have remained consistent.

These trends in spending on E&R functions suggest that declines in state appropriations to public colleges and universities may affect the quality of education provided. As institutions struggle to diversify sources of revenue to maintain essential programs, many are left with no choice but to reduce expenditures in core areas. Spending per student on E&R expenditures at public HSIs was lower than at public non-HSIs at the two- and four-year levels, and it decreased over the 11-year period from 1999 to 2010. Yet the institutions with the most resources—public four-year non-HSIs—were actually able to increase E&R spending during this time period, likely due to their ability to offset declines in state funding with alternative sources of revenue. Declines in the resources available to public colleges and universities may disproportionately affect students from low- to moderate-income families, who are more likely to attend lower-resourced institutions with fewer revenue alternatives.

It is encouraging, however, that even during a period of significant disruption, institutional leaders made a concerted effort to protect expenditures that were closely related to student success. It is even more impressive that this was true for public two- and four-year HSIs, where limited budgetary safeguards and options for revenue enhancement clearly made financial management even more challenging. To a certain extent, federal support played an important role in helping these institutions achieve some stability in per student E&R expenditures during a period of great economic pressure. And, when available, funds awarded to HSIs through Title V (Part A) and Title III (Part F) of the Higher Education Act provided these institutions with the resources, incentives, and fiscal resilience to continue spending on educational priorities. Unfortunately, this is only one tool (albeit an important one) for maintaining a focus on educational goals, and it is not a tool available to all HSIs. Yet, this speaks to the prudence of federal policy and equally to the vital leadership role played by the boards and presidents of these schools and their emphasis on advancing student educational goals.

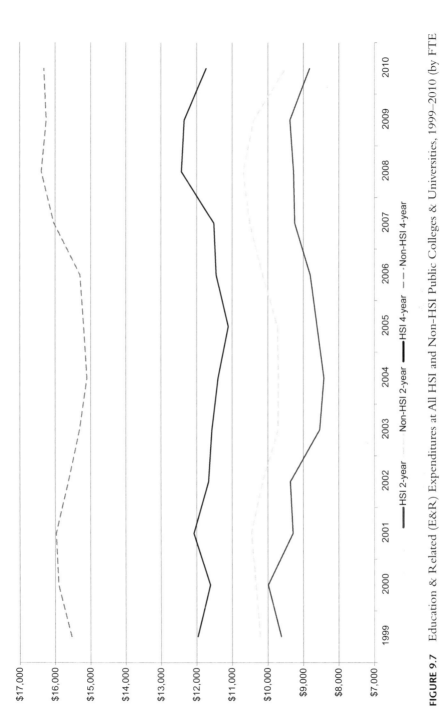

FIGURE 9.7 Education & Related (E&R) Expenditures at All HSI and Non-HSI Public Colleges & Universities, 1999–2010 (by FTE and 2010 Dollars)

Source: National Forum on Higher Education for the Public Good analysis of Delta Cost Project Database, 1999–2010.

Recommendations

There are limits to interpreting or making predictions based on results from an analysis such as this, particularly when economic events weigh so heavily on institutional decisions and interact with so many other factors, including political decisions, a lack of occupational alternatives for those seeking a college education, patterns of international migration, and public fears and attitudes. We do not know if recent reductions in public support signal a permanent change in state and federal appropriations, and it is even harder to conclusively predict their impact on the growing numbers of Latina/o students. But what we can do is begin to take some preliminary steps to help build capacity and resilience at HSIs.

It is important to note that there is no substitute for appropriate and stable state and federal appropriations, especially Title V (Part A) and Title III (Part F) funding, which together offer critical protection for educational priorities at historically underfunded institutions, particularly during periods of fiscal uncertainty. At the same time, increased investment from the private sector and individual institutions will also be needed to ensure the continual provision of a quality education for an expanding segment of our population. With these issues in mind, the following recommendations offer some preliminary steps toward a comprehensive, multifaceted funding approach to adequately serve this new generation of Latina/o college students.

Public Investment

Driven by an increase in the Latina/o population and a growing demand for postsecondary education, the number of HSIs has more than doubled in just 14 years. In 2009, only 163 of 293 colleges and universities designated as HSIs received any federal appropriations (Valle, Nellum, Burkhardt, Ortega, & Frye, 2014). In fact, as noted in Figure 9.1, the proportion of all HSIs receiving federal funding peaked in 2004 and has continually decreased since then. As more Latinas/os pursue postsecondary degrees, HSIs will continue to multiply. As of the 2012–2013 academic year, there are 277 emerging HSIs (with 15%–24% Latina/o enrollment) that are poised to become HSIs, and these institutions will soon complete for already limited funding (Calderón Galdeano & Santiago, 2014).

Recommendation: The Federal Government Should Increase Funding for Title V and Other HSI-specific Grants at a Rate Proportional to the Increase in the Number of HSIs and Their Enrollment

To manage the anticipated demand, the federal government should create a systematic way to increase appropriations for Title V and HSI-specific grants at the Department of Agriculture and the National Endowment for the Humanities. Funding for HSI-specific grants previously authorized (but not currently funded) by the Department of Defense and the Department of Housing and Urban Development should also be reinstated. Moreover, as the Hispanic Association of Colleges and Universities (2011) advocates, the Department of Labor should also establish a competitive grant for HSIs through the Workforce Investment Act (WIA), a program established to train new workers for jobs that require some postsecondary education but not necessarily a four-year degree. Given that more than half of HSIs are community colleges, the availability of this resource can play a fundamental role in workforce development and can further help to ensure that national training needs are met.

Private Investment

In considering the public benefits that HSIs foster, they make an attractive investment for philanthropic foundations. But we preface our recommendations with the assertion that private support should not substitute for public investment in HSIs. In fact, under the present circumstances, this is a strategy that will work for only a small number of institutions. Opportunities for private giving are abundant and could have enormous impact on the budgets of the HSIs we examined. When one also considers the commitment to resilience and efficiency already present at a number of these colleges and universities, even a relatively small private gift could provide great leverage.

Recommendation: Foundations Should Provide Funding to Support Professional Development for Future HSI Leaders

There is no denying the enormity of the challenges faced by the presidents and boards of struggling institutions during periods of fiscal instability. For this reason, investments in leadership development for HSIs will continue to be absolutely vital in preparing future presidents, trustees, and institutional advancement professionals. A number of such programs have been initiated over the last 25 years, only to be discontinued after initial funding dried up. Among the most notable and successful was an innovative program led by the Institute for Higher Education Policy and funded by the W.K. Kellogg Foundation in which future leaders for HBCUs, Tribal Colleges and Universities, and HSIs were trained together (Institute for Higher Education Policy, 2004). Investments like these pay their greatest dividends when leaders are challenged with difficult choices and must act to protect the core values of their institutions. Lessons learned by college leaders who have risen to the challenge under less than favorable circumstances can provide emerging leaders with tools and knowledge to help them better manage their institutions and successfully mediate fiscal constraints. As more Latina/o students transform the student bodies of colleges and universities, it is imperative that we invest in the preparation of the next generation of leaders who will manage HSIs.

Institutional Investment

Projections released by the U.S. Census Bureau (2012) suggest that the Latina/o population will more than double in the coming decades, from 53.3 million in 2012 to 128.8 million in 2060. Nearly one in three U.S. residents will be Latina/o, up from about one in six today (U.S. Census Bureau, 2012). Demographics will remake established colleges and universities in many states; the focus should be on student outcomes, stressing success as well as access.

Recommendation: All Institutions Should Invest in Preparing to Better Serve Latina/o Students and Hold Themselves Accountable for Educational Outcomes

In an effort to understand how public dollars and institutional programs are impacting Latina/o students, HSIs should evaluate and report on the success of their Latina/o students. The HSI community should establish basic indicators of Latina/o student outcomes that enable them to assess effectiveness. This is no less important for non-HSIs, especially those that drift into serving new constituencies through market dynamics rather than in response to their core mission. Moreover, emerging HSIs should thoroughly prepare to serve the growing Latina/o populations that are about to arrive at their institutions. Very few analyses have been conducted on the changes institutions need to undergo to become truly "Hispanic-serving." In an effort to ensure postsecondary success for the growing number of Latinas/os enrolling at U.S. colleges and universities, all HSIs and emerging HSIs should begin to assess their history, culture, assets, and limitations, and create a distinctive mission to guide their changing priorities (Hurtado & Ruiz, Chapter 2, this volume). They should further begin to develop plans for building organizational capacity, realign allocations to reflect their changing mission, reform curriculum, create infrastructures for new strategies and initiatives, and effectively measure organizational performance.

Concluding Thoughts

This analysis was undertaken during a pivotal period of time in modern U.S. higher education history. We conducted our examination of revenue and E&R expenditures at the end of a decade (1999–2010) during which colleges and universities experienced enormous financial challenges and at a point when the national economy was starting to recover. This vantage point allowed us to examine how various institutions mediated fiscal constraints and attempted to maintain focus on investments in educational priorities.

Given the changes in student populations anticipated in the future, we were especially interested in understanding how HSIs, which serve high proportions of Latina/o and low-income students, managed under difficult circumstances over the last decade, and to see how well they might be situated for the important challenges that lie ahead. This approach was premised on the strongly held belief that the United States must make whatever changes are necessary to ensure that all students have equitable access to postsecondary opportunities and that this access is coupled with genuine opportunities for all students to receive an education of the highest possible standard.

Policy decisions result from complicated processes that balance many considerations, and these decisions often do not lend themselves to simple declarations of fact. On the basis of our analysis we can, however, make a few unconditional statements with no fear of reasonable refutation: Latina/o students will increase their participation in U.S. higher education, and such participation is necessary to promote the country's social, political, and economic vitality. Should current trends continue, Latina/o students will be concentrated in the more than 300 Hispanic-Serving Institutions that must strive to serve them well. As such, the strength of these institutions, their viability, their continued improvement, and their educational focus will be increasingly important to educators and to our national future.

As we challenge the remaining barriers that stand in the way of full educational opportunity for all capable students, we must recognize that the institutional settings in which they are educated are diverse and often vulnerable. This chapter provides a glimpse of what may be at stake if, at this pivotal moment in our history, we falter in our commitment to education for all. We should use knowledge gleaned from this chapter—and the limited time we have left to act—to take steps to secure equitable postsecondary educational opportunities for Latina/o students, by ensuring the stability and quality of the institutions that serve them.

Note

The findings and information provided in this chapter were part of larger study funded by the TG Public Benefits Grant program and produced by researchers at the National Center for Institutional Diversity (NCID) and the National Forum on Higher Education for the Public Good at the University of Michigan.

References

Barney, J. (1991). Firm resources and sustained competitive advantage. *Journal of Management, 17*(1), 99–120.

Bastedo, M.N., & Bowman, N.A. (2010). College rankings as an interorganizational dependency: Establishing the foundation for strategic and institutional accounts. *Research in Higher Education, 52*(1), 3–23.

Baum, S., & Ma, J. (2012). *Trends in college pricing, 2012* (Trends in Higher Education Series). New York, NY: College Board Advocacy & Policy Center.

Braxton, J.M., Hirschy, A.S., & McClendon, S.A. (2011). *Understanding and reducing college student departure* (ASHE-ERIC Higher Education Report No. 30). San Francisco, CA: Jossey-Bass.

Calderón Galdeano, E., & Santiago, D.A. (2014). *Hispanic-Serving Institutions (HSIs) fact sheet: 2012–13.* Washington, DC: Excelencia in Education.

Cheslock, J.J., & Gianneschi, M. (2008). Replacing state appropriations with alternative revenue sources: The case of voluntary support. *The Journal of Higher Education*, 79(2), 208–229.

Cohen, A.M. (2008). *The shaping of American higher education: Emergence and growth of the contemporary system.* San Francisco, CA: Jossey-Bass.

Cyert, R.M., & March, J.G. (1963). *A behavioral theory of the firm.* Englewood Cliffs, NJ: Prentice-Hall..

de los Santos, Jr., A.G., & Cuamea, K.M. (2010). Challenges facing Hispanic-Serving Institutions in the first decade of the 21st century. *Journal of Latinos and Education*, 9(2), 90–107.

Desrochers, D.M., & Wellman, J.V. (2011). *Trends in college spending 1999–2009: Where does the money come from? Where does it go? What does it buy?* Washington, DC: Delta Project on Postsecondary Education Costs, Productivity and Accountability.

Doyle, W.R., & Delaney, J.A. (2009). Higher education funding: The new normal. *Change: The Magazine of Higher Learning*, 41(4), 60–62.

Drezner, N.D. (2011). *Philanthropy and fundraising in American higher education: ASHE Higher Education Report.* San Francisco, CA: Jossey-Bass.

Flores, S.M., Horn, C.L., & Crisp, G. (2006). Community colleges, public policy, and Latino student opportunity. In C.L. Horn, S.M. Flores, & G. Orfield (Eds.), *Latino educational opportunity* (New Directions for Community Colleges No. 133, pp. 71–80). San Francisco, CA: Jossey-Bass.

Fry, R., & López, M.H. (2012). *Now largest minority group on four-year college campuses: Hispanic student enrollment reach new highs in 2011.* Washington, DC: Pew Hispanic Center. Retrieved from http://www.pewhispanic.org/files/2012/08/Hispanic-Student-Enrollments-Reach-New-Highs-in-2011_FINAL.pdf

Goldin, C., & Katz, L.F. (2009). *The race between education and technology.* Cambridge, MA: Belknap Press.

Gumport, P.J. (2001). Restructuring: Imperatives and opportunities for academic leaders. *Innovative Higher Education*, 25(4), 239–251.

Gumport, P.J., & Pusser, B. (1999). University restructuring: The role of economic and political contexts. In J.C. Smart & W.G. Tierney (Eds.), *Higher education: Handbook of theory and research* (Vol. 14, pp. 146–200). New York, NY: Springer.

Hannan, M.T., & Freeman, J. (1977). The population ecology of organizations. *American Journal of Sociology*, 929–964.

Hearn, J.C. (2006). Alternative revenue sources. In D.M. Priest & E.P. St. John (Eds.), *Privatization and public universities*, (pp. 87–108). Bloomington, IN: Indiana University Press.

Hispanic Association of Colleges & Universities. (2011). *HACU legislative agenda.* Retrieved from http://www.hacu.net/images/hacu/govrel/2011_legislative_agenda.pdf

Institute for Higher Education Policy. (2004). *Leading the way to America's future: A monograph about the launch and implementation of the Kellogg MSI Leadership Fellow program, 2002–2004.* Washington, DC: Author.

Kraatz, M.S., & Zajac, E.J. (2001). How organizational resources affect strategic change and performance in turbulent environments: theory and evidence. *Organization Science*, 12(5), 632–657.

Leslie, L.L., & Ramey, G. (1988). Donor behavior and voluntary support for higher education institutions. *The Journal of Higher Education*, 59(2), 115–132.

Mahoney, J.T., & Pandian, R. (1992). The resource-based view within the conversation of strategic management. *Strategic Management Journal*, 13(5), 363–380.

Merton, R.K. (1968). The Matthew effect in science. *Science*, 159(3810), 56.

Meyer, J.W., & Rowan, B. (1977). Institutionalized organizations: Formal structure as myth and ceremony. *American Journal of Sociology*, 83(2), 340–363.

Mulnix, M.W., Bowden, R.G., & López, E.E. (2002). A brief examination of institutional advancement activities at Hispanic-Serving Institutions. *Journal of Hispanic Higher Education*, 1(2), 174–190.

Nora, A., & Crisp, G. (2009). Hispanics in higher education: An overview of research, theory, and practice. In J.C. Smart (Ed.), *Higher education: Handbook of theory and research* (Vol. 24, pp. 317–353). New York, NY: Springer.

Núñez, A.-M., & Elizondo, D. (2012). *Hispanic-Serving Institutions in the U.S. mainland and Puerto Rico: Organizational characteristics, institutional financial context, and graduation outcomes*. San Antonio, TX: Hispanic Association of Colleges and Universities. Retrieved from http://eric.ed.gov/?id-ED537723

Núñez, A.-M., Sparks, J., & Hernández, E.A. (2011). Latino access to community colleges and Hispanic-Serving Institutions: A national study. *Journal of Hispanic Higher Education*, 10(1), 18–40.

Ortega, N., Frye, J., Nellum, C.J., Kamimura, A. & Vidal-Rodríguez, A. (2013). *Examining the financial resilience of Hispanic-Serving Institutions (HSIs) as they prepare to serve the next generation of Latino students*. Ann Arbor, MI: National Forum on Higher Education for the Public Good. Retrieved from http://thenationalforum.org/examining-the-financial-resilience-of-hispanic-serving-institutions-hsis/

Pfeffer, J., & Salancik, G.R. (1978). *The external control of organizations: A resource dependence perspective*. New York, NY: Harper and Row.

Pfeffer, J., & Salancik, G.R. (2003). *The external control of organizations: A resource dependence perspective*. Stanford, CA: Stanford University Press.

Rothschild, M. (1999). Philanthropy and American higher education. In C. Clotfelter & T. Ehrlich (Eds.), *Philanthropy and the nonprofit sector in a changing America* (pp. 413–427). Bloomington, IN: Indiana University Press.

Santiago, D.A., & Andrade, S.J. (2010). *Emerging Hispanic-Serving Institutions (HSIs): Serving Latino students*. Washington, DC: Excelencia in Education. Retrieved from http://www.edexcelencia.org/research/hsi/hsi-briefs

Santos, J.L., & Sáenz, V.B. (2013). In the eye of the perfect storm: The convergence of policy and Latina/o trends in access and financial concerns, 1975–2008. *Educational Policy*, 28, 393–424.

Scott, W.R. (1998). *Organizations*. Englewood Cliffs, NJ: Prentice Hall.

Singh, J.V. (1986). Performance, slack, and risk taking in organizational decision making. *Academy of Management Journal*, 29(3), 562–585.

Slaughter, S., & Leslie, L.L. (1997). *Academic capitalism*. Baltimore, MD: Johns Hopkins University Press.

Speck, W.B. (2010). The growing role of private giving in financing the modern university. In J.B. Hodson & B.W. Speck (Eds.), *Perspectives on fund raising* (New Directions for Higher Education No. 149, pp. 7–16). San Francisco, CA: Jossey-Bass.

St. John, E.P., & Parsons, M.D. (2005). *Public funding of higher education: Changing contexts and new rationales*. Baltimore, MD: Johns Hopkins University Press.

Thelin, J. (2005). Higher education and the public trough: A historical perspective. In E.P. St. John & M.D. Parsons (Eds.), *Public funding of higher education: Changing contexts and new rationales* (pp. 21–38). Baltimore, MD: Johns Hopkins University Press.

Trow, M.A. (1988). The analysis of status. In B.R. Clark (Ed.), *Perspectives on higher education: Eight disciplinary and comparative views* (pp. 132–164). Berkeley, CA: University of California Press.

Valle, K., Nellum, C.J., Burkhardt, J., Ortega, N., & Frye, J.R. (2014). *Advancing Hispanic-Serving Institutions: Recommendations for strengthening federal investments.* Ann Arbor, MI: National Forum on Higher Education for the Public Good.

Webber, D.A., & Ehrenberg, R.G. (2009). *Do expenditures other than instructional expenditures affect graduation and graduation rates in American higher education?* Ithaca, NY: Cornell Higher Education Research Institute.

Wernerfelt, B. (1984). A resource based view of the firm. *Strategic Management Journal*, 5(2), 171–180.

Williamson, O.E. (1975). *Markets and hierarchies: Analysis and antitrust implications. A study in the economics of internal organization* (Vol. 46). New York, NY: Free Press.

U.S. Census Bureau. (2012). *U.S. Census Bureau projections show a slower growing, older, more diverse nation a half century from now.* Retrieved from http://www.census.gov/newsroom/releases/archives/population/cb12–243.html

Zajac, E.J., Kraatz, M.S., & Bresser, R.K. (2000). Modeling the dynamics of strategic fit: A normative approach to strategic change. *Strategic Management Journal*, 21(4), 429–453.

Zumeta, W. (2005). State higher education financing: Demand imperatives meet structural, cyclical, and political constraints. In E.P. St. John & M.D. Parsons (Eds.), *Public funding of higher education: Changing contexts and new rationales* (pp. 79–107). Baltimore, MD: Johns Hopkins University Press.

10

ORGANIZATIONAL LEARNING FOR STUDENT SUCCESS

Cross-Institutional Mentoring, Transformative Practice, and Collaboration Among Hispanic-Serving Institutions

Sylvia Hurtado, René A. González,
and Emily Calderón Galdeano

Increasing the success of students from diverse and marginalized communities improves equity and social mobility, democracy, as well as the economy of local communities and the nation at large (Hurtado, Álvarez, Guillermo-Wann, Cuellar, & Arellano, 2012). Students who are low-income, first generation, and racial/ethnic minorities are more likely to begin their studies at Hispanic-Serving Institutions (HSIs) (Hispanic Association of Colleges and Universities [HACU], 2012; Núñez & Bowers, 2011); however, these are also the characteristics of students who tend to have the lowest retention rates at institutions across the country (Titus, 2006). Few institutions, other than Minority-Serving Institutions (MSIs), understand the challenges posed by maintaining a commitment to access and meeting national goals for improving graduation rates. It stands to reason, then, that HSIs face many challenges particular to these student populations that others resolve by limiting access through more selective admissions processes. Institutional agents within HSIs take on the role of assisting students toward degree completion, advocating for students and resources that sometimes must be diverted from other institutional priorities and aspirations. HSIs have to be strategic, and until recently there is very little information about how these institutions learn or innovate in areas related to student success (Bauman, 2005; Bensimon, 2005).

The purpose of this chapter is to provide an asset-based approach to understanding HSIs and to offer evidence of their efforts to improve student success. Most importantly, we illustrate exemplars in practice through a special case of institutional collaboration among HSIs that participated in the MSI Student Success Collaborative (MSISSC). This project was coordinated by the Alliance for Equity in Higher Education, consisting of the American Indian Higher Education Consortium (AIHEC), the Hispanic Association of Colleges and Universities (HACU), and the National Association for Equal Opportunity in Higher

Education (NAFEO), and funded by the Walmart Foundation. The MSISSC project involved 18 colleges and universities (six Tribal Colleges and Universities, six Hispanic-Serving Institutions, and six Historically Black Colleges and Universities).

In this chapter, we report on only the six collaborating HSIs in the partnership coordinated by HACU for nearly three and half years. We document how institutions learned to adapt new strategies at the same time that grassroots leaders (faculty and staff) and administrators gained authentic professional development training in student success. The collaborative project illustrates how and what HSIs learned from each other, despite differences in geographic context, campus culture, institutional type, and resources. The emergent lessons from the collaborative project increase our understanding of the challenges and practices specific to HSIs. While it is too early to determine if all institutions achieved higher completion rates as a result of this collaborative project, agents within these institutions have learned about an array of approaches for improving student success and are empowered to engage in transformative practice.

Organizational Learning

Higher education institutions have typically adapted the innovations of institutions that they aspire to emulate or regard as appropriate role models. This is called *mimetic isomorphism* in organizational theory, which is a tendency for institutions to imitate others and become more alike rather than dissimilar over time (DiMaggio & Powell, 1983). This can lead to widespread adoption of practices that many institutions use to address the same problem, with very little consultation or understanding about whether practices can work for the specific needs of a local student population. While isomorphism occurs informally as institutions look to comparable institutions (or competitors) for solutions to problems, institutional change can also occur as a result of systematic forms of organizational learning that are facilitated by grant-funded research and action projects.

For example, in a project at the Center for Urban Education at the University of Southern California, Bauman (2005) studied 14 institutions (including HSIs) engaged in deliberations regarding Diversity Scorecard student data, observing how campus teams reflected and engaged each other in examining data on inequality in student outcomes across race/ethnicity. Organizational learning occurred among campus teams under three conditions: "the presence of new ideas, the cultivation of doubt in existing knowledge and practices, and the development and transfer of knowledge among actors" (Bauman, 2005, p. 25). In this action research project, Bensimon (2005) identified the key mindsets that underlie practice in institutions, including deficit thinking focused on "fixing the student," diversity mindsets focused on maximizing the educational benefits of a diverse student body, and an equity mindset focused on institutional change and accountability for equity in student outcomes (p. 103). Exposure to new ways of looking at their own student data resulted in conversations and changing mindsets, mobilizing some individuals into action.

Most of the references to learning organizations in higher education refer to the use of data for better information about students as part of creating a culture of evidence (Ewell, 1997). Raising awareness is a critical stage in organizational learning, yet using data is only one way to raise awareness and acquire new knowledge to improve the success of underrepresented groups. Another way to do so is through acquiring in-depth knowledge about how others have dealt with similar challenges to improving student success. Building on Garvin's (1993) conception of organizational learning to summarize the literature on academic accountability and university adaptation, Dill (1999) identified key processes that are actively managed by institutions adept at translating new knowledge into innovative ways of behaving. These activities are (1) exploring new knowledge through problem-solving, learning from one's own experience, and learning from others' experience; (2) experimenting with new processes; and (3) transferring knowledge among actors in units and sub-units within the organization. Most of the literature, however, focuses on individual academic institutions. Little is known about organizational learning that occurs in a collective and across academic institutions using collaborative partnerships, especially among HSIs that serve low-income students and often have fewer resources than other campuses.

Several other concepts are useful to understand how learning occurs in organizations. First, relationships are critical to cultivating, disseminating, and maintaining learning as a way of organizational life (Bokeno & Gantt, 2000). An active community of practice and mentoring are both modes of learning that contribute to the development of actors within the organization. However, in the former, learning occurs in a collaborative group of individuals who may each have different expertise, whereas most learning in a mentoring relationship typically occurs one-on-one with one presumed to have expertise and the other presumed to be a novice. Second, if the goal of a learning organization is continual self-examination and exploration, individuals should seek to learn from difference rather than the sameness that is typically emphasized in mentoring relationships. Bokeno and Gantt (2000) called these *dialogic mentoring relationships*, where differences are appreciated and contradictions are opportunities for exploration and changing viewpoints. Third, the ongoing relationship is characterized by the pursuit of openness and equity of voice in which power asymmetries are removed. In dialogic mentoring relationships, "the role of mentor would be that of constructing organizational reality with the protégé rather than reflecting to or interpreting for the protégé" (Bokeno & Gantt, 2000, p. 252). Before the MSISSC project began, such relationships developed across institutions could not be imagined, but they developed over time as a collaborative mentoring model emerged characterized by a developing community of practice as well as a more intensive dialogic mentoring relationship between HSIs.

Features of the Collaborative

The MSISSC was focused on learning from others' experiences in a cross-institutional mentoring partnership that occurred among institutional pairs within a larger community of practice focused on improving student progress. This overall MSI community of practice included TCUs, HBCUs, and HSIs; but under coordination of each of these organizations, it was thought to be more effective at changing practices if mentor-mentee partner institutions had similar student populations, and/or share common goals and challenges. The project had four major goals: (1) to identify successful intervention strategies for supporting student success among member institutions, (2) to disseminate and support implementation of successful intervention strategies, (3) to build a community of practice among participating MSIs establishing student success, and (4) to increase the number of students who complete programs of study at MSIs.

In the short timeframe of the funded project (three years), the Alliance project team concluded that the fourth goal would be impossible to measure effectively, given that most graduation rates for institutions are measured at the four- and six-year time periods. The Alliance project team decided to focus on the first three goals, and developed a cross-institutional "mentor–mentee" model. The basic assumption for developing the model was that institutions with higher graduation and retention rates would have experienced program staff and faculty who could mentor and/or guide staff and faculty at institutions with lower graduation and retention rates. Another assumption was that the "pairing" of institutions would be of "like or similar" institutions. This meant HACU would select HSI pairs by institutional type—two of each among four-year public institutions, two-year public colleges, and four-year private institutions, for a total of six institutions. As partner institutions learned more about each other, it became clear that there were many more contextual differences that they grew to appreciate as they learned how to problem-solve and confer regarding adaptation of practices.

Selection and Characteristics of the Campuses

Selection of mentor and mentee campuses occurred via a request for proposals (RFPs) that went out to HACU member institutions. The RFPs requested the following information: (1) six-year graduation rates; (2) first year-to-second year retention rates; (3) three-year graduation rates and transfer rates to four-year or other two-year institutions (for two-year candidate institutions); (4) examples of campus-wide planning and implementation to address the issues as well as document resource allocations (e.g., student services expenditures); (5) a statement of the applicant's commitment to participate and support the project, provide mentoring support to the assigned mentee institution, and collaborate with other project institutions; (6) a description of particular challenges faced in increasing Hispanic graduation and retention rates (for mentee candidates); (7) a statement of the applicant's commitment to participate in and support the project, work with their mentor institution, collaborate with other project institutions, and implement promising approaches to improving student success; (8) a budget showing how the $100,000 would be allocated; and (9) other supporting documentation.

An external team rated each proposal using a form, with HACU making the final selection of HSIs based on the review of proposals. Each of the selected six campuses was awarded $50,000 per year, for two years, to improve their student success initiatives. They were required to regularly report on progress and attend meetings (both with the larger MSI community and amongst the HSI group of institutions) held at various locations throughout the country. The mentor institutions were selected first and met in April 2011 to discuss expectations and roles for the project. Following this meeting, the mentee institutions were selected in May of 2011. The six mentee and mentor HSIs selected were New Mexico Highlands University (Las Vegas, NM), paired with California State University-Fullerton; Universidad del Sagrado Corazón (San Juan, Puerto Rico), paired with St. Mary's University (San Antonio, TX); and San Bernardino Valley College (San Bernardino, CA), paired with the Community College of Denver.

Ultimately, even though the mentor–mentee pairings were made by institutional sector (2-year public, 4-year public, and 4-year private), there were many more differences among the collaborating campuses. Table 10.1 illustrates the various institutional characteristics of the HSI mentor and mentee institutions at the start of the collaborative, and several observations are worth mentioning. First, each of the institutional participants had a student body that included nearly one-third or more low-income students, as characterized by their receipt of Pell Grants. Second, each of the mentor institutions had a lower undergraduate Hispanic full-time equivalent (FTE) student percentage than its partner institution. Third, among four-year institutions, there was a double-digit difference in graduation rates between the mentor and mentee institutions. Fourth, among the two-year institutions, it appears that the mentee (San Bernardino Valley College) had a higher graduation rate, but in fact, the Community College of Denver (CCD) had a higher transfer rate as a result of their initiative to move students more quickly through developmental education. Their location on the Auraria Campus of institutions within walking distance of each other facilitates student transfer and is also enhanced by focused programming. In the case of two-year institutions, IPEDS completion data provide a limited view of success.

Setting the Stage for Organizational Learning

At the first meeting of mentor campus representatives and Alliance staff in the three MSI communities, the experience, confidence, leadership, communication, and teamwork skills of the HSI campus project coordinators became clearly evident. They assumed leadership roles in guiding the discussion on mentoring, and they focused the discussion on the mentoring process as a collaborative effort. The participants accepted the definition of the process of mentoring as a collaborative, where each party of the mentor–mentee relationship could learn from

TABLE 10.1 *Institutional Characteristics by Sector and Mentor–Mentee Pairing*

Mentor–Mentee	2-year Public		4-year Public		4-year Private	
	Community College of Denver	San Bernardino Valley College	California State University-Fullerton	New Mexico Highlands University	St. Mary's University	Universidad del Sagrado Corazón
Location	Colorado	California	California	New Mexico	Texas	Puerto Rico
Open Admission	Y	Y	N	Y	N	N
Selectivity[1]	Non-competitive	Non-competitive	Moderately Difficult	Minimally Difficult	Moderately Difficult	Moderately Difficult
Undergraduate Headcount	13,053	12,380	30,782	2,338	2,508	5,521
Undergraduate Hispanic Full-Time Equivalent (FTE) Student Percentage	25	57	34	55	71	100
Percentage of Students Receiving Pell Grants	47	30	40	32	51	63
Percentage of Students Receiving Student Loans	40	0	57	41	72	38
Full-Time Retention Rate Percentage	55	65	84	48	78	73
Part-Time Retention Rate Percentage	42	40	60	39	—	61
Graduation Rate at 100% of Normal Time	7%	3%	16%	5%	31%	2%
Graduation Rate at 150% of Normal Time	9%	13%	52%	19%	57%	40%
Graduation Rate at 200% of Normal Time	13%	19%	59%	23%	58%	46%

Source: Authors' analyses of the 2010–2011 Integrated Postsecondary Education Data System (IPEDS) survey files.

[1] Selectivity determined by Peterson's Admission Difficulty Index (non-competitive, minimally difficult, moderately difficult, very difficult, and most difficult).

the other. This was a fundamental group decision that guided them through the project implementation and provided a framework for effective communication. This framework was grounded in learning created by respect for different campus cultures and respect for each other as professionals facing similar challenges in serving the Hispanic community of students, staff, and faculty. It also provided an opportunity to work through some of the challenges inherent in collaboration between different institutional cultures, a principle for developing an understanding of each other's proposal activities, and a guide for developing specific goals and objectives on their project work.

It is important to note that, although the mentor campuses had experienced some success in developing student interventions, each continued to actively strive to improve their own graduation rates and refine their initiatives due to internal and external pressures to excel. The acceptance of the concept of collaborative mentoring also provided the six HSI project coordinators the flexibility to adapt to challenges and opportunities in working together as the project was implemented. These factors helped to create equity of voice in the relationship between institutions, which fostered mutual organizational learning and helped to focus on building institutional capacity.

Activities were structured by the MSI Alliance and, project-wide, included group meetings at different MSI campuses to allow mentor campuses from HSIs, HBCUs, and TCUs to showcase their practices, and presentations from external experts who provided a national overview of work on student success. This gave campus teams additional cultural and contextual insights into other MSIs' student success initiatives, and was another way to promote organizational learning across institutions serving large numbers of underrepresented students. At these general community meetings, each set of institutions was given opportunities to discuss progress as part of the HACU-coordinated set of HSIs. These partnered HSI institutional teams also took part in carefully planned study tours of their respective campuses, which allowed groups of administrators to meet with their counterparts at the matched institution. It became clear through group presentations and meetings that both the mentor and mentee campuses had assets to contribute to group learning on student success. Relationships were nurtured through these face-to-face team meetings, as well as through regular phone and email contact. In short, each campus extended its resources of information on practice through the social network created by the project. Connecting the institutions to allow for collaboration, both within the group (HSIs only) and across groups (HSIs, HBCUs, and TCUs), provided additional insight; however, the HSI representatives developed closer working relationships with each other.

Method

To gather information for this chapter, all three authors had occasion to observe and speak with representatives from the HSI campuses during all community meetings of the alliance; two participated in regular phone calls with the campus project coordinators; and one had extensive notes from campus visits during the project. All received regular reports from each of the campuses at various phases of the project. This information was aided by the report of another external evaluator assigned to observe, take notes, and make reports on progress. A final interview was conducted with each of the campus project coordinators. Much of the information presented here is based on how participants viewed the collaboration, though some observations by the authors also helped to place each campus in a larger context of HSIs they have worked with or conducted research on in the past. The information gathered was also reviewed in light of guiding theory, which allowed us to confirm concepts and emerging insights. It is important to note that the project was also a learning experience for each of the authors, who worked with the campuses for the duration of the project, and who had a strong interest in building institutional capacity for student success at HSIs. That is, we developed relationships with the educators involved at each of the HSIs—as advisors and coordinators—and the campus teams were aware we served as resources, but two of us were also charged with reporting on their progress.

In the next sections we describe important elements of the collaborative work among the HSIs. First, we describe the successful efforts of mentor campuses, detailing programs and services that have worked in serving their diverse student bodies. Then, we turn our attention to the initiatives put in place by mentee campuses as a result of the collaboration. We specifically describe some of the challenges that these institutions faced as they sought to effectively serve their students. Finally, we describe the key themes of how organizational learning and behavioral change occurred in an HSI community of practice, sharing implications for other institutions.

HSI Mentor Campuses as Assets in the Collaborative

Some of the initiatives were identified early on as assets and examples of transformative practice, which we observed subsequently in group meetings and campus visits. As noted earlier, it is important to regard these examples as developing initiatives that were not without challenges. That said, these efforts were aided by visibility, funding, and responses from researchers and other campuses in the collaborative. It was clear that mentor campuses were also in the midst of improving their practices and introducing new initiatives to their campuses. Thus, while each campus had many initiatives, we feature only a few that have shared a student-centered approach and that were topics of conversation in meetings where participants presented their programs and practices.

Coordinating Student Retention Efforts

St. Mary's University (StMU), in San Antonio, Texas, showcased their retention initiatives at the early stages of the partnership. They began an Office of Student

Retention (OSR), employing an Assistant Vice President for Retention Management who built momentum and a network for advancing student success. The OSR initially hired a coordinator of retention services as a result of the Walmart Foundation grant, and subsequently continued the work on institutional funds. This additional staff allowed the OSR to increase capacity as a unit and to carry out tasks related to student support. The enthusiastic and dynamic individuals in the OSR wore several hats, as case workers for individual student issues, program innovators and coordinators, and institutional change agents whose role was to question existing policies and practices and develop new ones that promote student success. A proactive agent role was key in investigating and coordinating policies and units to improve overall campus retention goals and degree attainment rates.

Recognizing that one small unit cannot be solely responsible for student retention, the OSR collaborated with other offices (e.g., financial aid, registrar) as well as with faculty and advisors to assist students toward completion. When the OSR approach was first presented to the collaborating campuses, it was described as a "high touch" and individualized approach, since handling students' issues was a primary concern. Given the relatively small size of the student body (3,800 undergraduates), some of the other HSIs wondered if it would be possible to adapt such a student-centered approach on large campuses. Programmatic emphases at StMU, such as coordinated orientation, first-year seminars, and mentoring programs, were transferable practices; however, a transformative practice was the principle of creating institutional change by increasing everyone's responsibility for retaining students in a Refer to Retention (R2R) program. This was a campaign-like strategy used to raise awareness and mobilize the campus toward early identification of students who had difficulties in college, encouraging all faculty and staff to refer students to work with the increasingly visible OSR.

Accelerating Student Learning

Many of the campuses brought larger teams to the collaborative meeting held in Denver to learn how to become more effective in improving developmental education. The Community College of Denver (CCD) developed a faculty-driven, student-centered initiative called FastStart, which allowed students to take compressed developmental education coursework in mathematics, writing, reading, and English as a second language. Recognizing that not all students need a term of developmental education, faculty restructured the developmental education courses at CCD. Compressed course pairings (e.g., two levels of math) were co-taught by trained instructors for the program, and a key feature was multiple levels of support for both the students who participated and the faculty who taught in the program. In addition to typical counseling and academic support programs on campus, the program employed case managers to help identify students who could benefit from the accelerated classes, engage them in educational planning, orient them to the program, and coordinate ongoing support for them. Instructors were supported by authentic professional development activities that were central to their daily work, including peer-review observations and participation in faculty learning communities. Part-time faculty were compensated for their time in learning, and both full- and part-time instructors were encouraged to innovate their pedagogy and learn from each other in teaching the restructured courses.

Campus teams across the MSI collaborative were able to speak with CCD faculty, visit several different accelerated classes with engaging pedagogy (offered during the same time of day), and visit the student learning center (where students could prepare before placement) and a center focused on facilitating transfer. CCD is a national leader in this holistic student approach to developmental education, with several studies confirming program effectiveness, cost savings due to improved student retention, and implementation features (e.g., Bragg, Baker, & Puryear, 2010; Edgecombe, Jaggars, Baker, & Bailey, 2013). The FastStart program began in 2005 with external funding and periodic evaluation, and it was subsequently incorporated into the campus budget by 2010. Digital storytelling (DST) was introduced in FastStart learning communities during the project, which uses video editing software to assess students' knowledge of learned concepts, articulated through their writing (script and voice over), combined with images and music. DST was incorporated across disciplinary areas and student services, and, most significantly, the accelerated learning model for developmental education was scaled-up to be implemented across all community colleges in the state of Colorado by the end of the MSISSC project.

Intensive Academic Preparation, Tracking, and Support

Like many large universities, California State University (CSU) Fullerton has many longstanding and relatively new programs to address student success. In addition to comprehensive programs for new students and movement toward integrated and coordinated student academic services, the campus developed new initiatives to promote intensive academic preparation, monitoring, and student support. The focus of externally funded initiatives has been to develop innovative and sustainable programs, systems, and model projects that implement proven strategies for retention, persistence, and graduation in a timely manner. Some of the programs include Project MISS (Mathematics Intensive Summer Session), supplemental instruction (SI), an early warning system, an early alert system, and an integrated academic advising system.

CSU Fullerton showcased two practices at MSI collaborative meetings: its supplemental instruction (SI) program, and a new student success dashboard for monitoring and identifying individual student progress. SI is a model for academic assistance to help students master "bottleneck" and gateway classes that have proven to be difficult for students (e.g., calculus). The approach uses peer learning assistants who help students integrate learning and develop course-specific, content study strategies—connecting *what to learn* with *how to learn*. CSU Fullerton offers 224 sections of SI annually, and each year nearly 3,500 students have access to study group sessions supported by an SI coordinator, faculty liaisons with three units of course release time, and nearly 80 (paid) peer instructors across all disciplines. It is an evidence-based practice (Arendale, 1997) in which the campus has developed a common assessment plan across divisions and regularly disseminates evaluation results showing program effectiveness (Bonsangue et al., 2013; California State University Fullerton, 2011).

To complement early warning and alert systems and academic advising, in the last two years of the MSISSC, the campus also implemented state-of-the-art technology to monitor individual student progress and support students toward completion. The "student success dashboard" provides data from several sources (e.g., degree audit, co-curricular activity) in one system that provides dynamic, timely, and accessible information for staff and administrators who can target students for intervention and/or referral to other support offices. Both SI initiatives and the student success dashboard illustrate collaborations across several student and academic affairs units at CSUF and show how a large campus can implement a strategic individualized approach to student support.

Challenges and Initiatives of Mentee Campuses

The three mentee institutions all had initiatives in place, but New Mexico Highlands University (NMHU), Universidad del Sagrado Corazón (UdSC), and San Bernardino Valley College (SBVC) each faced unique challenges. The project helped them to expand existing programs and create new ones based on mentor campus models. Within the three years of the project, a remarkable amount of organizational change occurred as a result of the organizational learning that took place in the collaborative.

A high proportion of the students at NMHU are first-generation college-going (78%), nearly 61% are from rural counties, and 93% receive grants, loans, or work subsidies. The campus had the lowest tuition rate of any campus in the MSI collaborative and was also open access. NMHU was extremely motivated and had a comprehensive vision based on student development theory, as well as a realistic assessment of the structure and culture of the campus. As a result of working with CSU Fullerton, the campus was able to expand and further develop its new student programs, especially design a first-year experience course, and expand supplemental instruction from STEM classes to other disciplines with student learning assistants. It also developed a campus-wide retention committee, comprising academic and student affairs professionals, who made progress on a tangible retention plan.

UdSC identified two significant challenges: an outdated first-year experience program, and an absence of engaging and interactive online activities to complement its distance learning courses. Project leaders focused on introducing information literacy competencies in several classes and faculty training in web technology, and, as a result of working with StMU, they began to coordinate new student programs and focus on consolidating tutoring and training. They developed an online tutoring initiative and also accelerated the development of the Learning Commons by repurposing physical space in the library. At its dedication, the president used a culturally symbolic metaphor to place student learning at the center of the campus community, stating, "With this facility we have incorporated our cultural preference for a common gathering space, the plaza [town square], onto our campus. . . . We now have created a common learning space indoors" (observation translated from Spanish to English).

SBVC faced severe challenges, including budget cuts from the state, a basic skills mandate, pressure to graduate more students, and turnover in leadership (top administrative positions were filled with interim appointments for most of the project period). There was also further pressure to restrict enrollment at the community college and become selective in admissions. Turnover in project leaders also created some instability in the mentor–mentee relationship, though faculty did their best to remain connected across the campuses. Despite these challenges, they began a student learning community initiative (several linked courses) and experimented with accelerated learning in specific math and reading basic skill courses—changes that were subsequently institutionalized. While budget issues during the time of the project prevented them from adopting the full FastStart model (e.g., trained case managers), they were also able to begin to create faculty learning communities similar to that established at their partner institution.

Themes in a Developing HSI Community of Practice

This section provides information about experiences among participants in the cross institutional mentoring model that influenced change across the campuses. There are several distinctive features that emerged from the participants' experiences, including building relationships, changing mindsets, and mutual encouragement toward action that also began a "ripple effect" on campuses.

Cross Institutional Mentoring: Building Relationships

Campus teams were paired at meetings and discussed their proposed plans for the student success. Each meeting was an opportunity to learn about institutional context differences and gain insight into how another campus was working toward achieving overall retention goals. As it turned out, "like pairings" were very different in terms of enrollment size, resources, and type of geographic region served (rural/suburban vs. urban), requiring mentors and mentees to problem solve together to adapt similar practices across distinct contexts. The collaborative mentoring model was described by some as developing "much like a successful interpersonal relationship":

> A successful [institutional] partnership is contingent upon trustworthiness of the principal stakeholders and a willingness from both parties to be accessible and approachable. . . . A mentorship collaboration at the institutional level cannot be reduced to regular standing meetings every other Wednesday during office hours. . . . Communication is imperative. But beyond that, successful mentoring at the institutional level depends in large measure on the effort put forth by the partners and the willingness to engage in supportive and mutually-beneficial collaborations. We were very lucky in this project to be surrounded by caring and committed individuals.
>
> *(NMHU)*

Conversations were facilitated in MSI collaborative meetings at different campus sites across the country, with "team time" and occasions for informal interaction over meals and events, and (as mentioned earlier) by several carefully planned information-gathering study tours of partner institutions focusing on specific programs and practices. Additional opportunities over the course of the project involved presentations at HACU meetings and planning at the Retention and Persistence Institute held by the Higher Education Research Institute at UCLA. This level of face-to-face interaction, augmented with conference calls and regular emails, created a level of respect and deep knowledge about the roles and responsibilities each held for facilitating change on campus. Over the course of the project, members mentioned "bonding" that occurred across teams and program areas among HSIs. In the words of one participant, "A very strong learning bond has been formed between [UdSC] and St. Mary's University Learning Assistance Center (LAC) . . . undeniably as a result of the three year reciprocal visits between both universities." Length of time of the project also contributed to these lasting relationships. One student affairs professional stated, "I know we will continue to stay connected and continue to advise one another into the future."

Changing Mindsets

Team members were constantly interacting in new environments. This facilitated links with others, who were becoming familiar faces, and provided opportunities for them to travel to other campuses with institutional members from their own campus and discuss next steps before returning to campus. Actually being *physically* "outside of the box," away from campus habits and routines, facilitated *thinking* "outside of the box." Further, having to explain organizational practices to another person (sensegiving) helps individuals to rethink their own rationale behind behavior (Kezar, 2014; Ravasi & Schultz, 2006) and campus practices. For both mentor and mentee institutions, there was a dynamic relationship between making practices explicit, observing what other HSIs do, and reflecting on one's own practice. One campus project leader observed,

> We have improved our own thinking and processes due to the fact that we must teach them to another institution. Mentoring has allowed us to examine our own practices and beliefs about student success and refine the way we carry out our roles at our university.
>
> *(CSUF)*

Campus visits served as a catalyst for revising thinking, gaining new perspectives on current and future programs and services, and extending professional networks and collaboration. The cross-campus site visits were particularly important because they allowed teams to understand how innovations develop in context, to recognize the challenges that each campus was facing, and to share values and beliefs that informed their practice. In several cases, the "tour" included conversations with students on partner campuses. This relevant, contextual-based type of learning is a form of authentic professional development.

In addition to cross-institutional relationships, project coordinators were able to increase collaboration and communications across divisions (student and academic affairs), departments, and program units on their respective campuses. Three aspects were important to increasing collaboration and convincing others on campus about the need for change: face-to-face interaction during campus visits, length of time of the project to build understanding of their work across campus, and flexible team membership for visits and meetings. UdSC offered that all "visits were very important for staff and faculty to see for themselves the implementation of new strategies and gave credibility and visibility to the [MSISSC] Project in our campus." Aside from witnessing what is possible, participants were able to cultivate new allies in promoting a student success agenda: "Being able to take different campus members on trips allowed us to spend meaningful time with campus colleagues and begin conversations on how to best collaborate to impact student success [on our own campus]" (StMU). Finally, alliances on campus also created a higher sense of regard for each other's work: "I think we also found support from one another, and affirmation that our goals are central and significant to the entire university" (CSUF).

Mutual Encouragement and Action

Mentee campuses were eager to learn, experiment, and implement new initiatives, as well as share their own challenges in the search for solutions. This impressed some mentor campuses, reflecting on their attitudes toward change and decision to act:

> When the project began we observed how "silo-ed" Sagrado was and gave them feedback on how to reduce it. They took that feedback and were able to make it work quickly, improving their orientation program and tutoring. That made us think about how open they were to change and we began to examine our own willingness to change. Their use of data was a strength, and we learned from them that we needed to capture and use data more effectively [for retention efforts].
>
> *(StMU)*

This mentor campus began to consider uses of technology and subsequently purchased platform software to improve communication, tracking interactions with students and student referral processes. In another case, after observations and interactions with a partner campus that has a higher proportion of Latina/o students, the mentor campus developed a committee to specifically target attention to Latina/o student success and their unique needs on a diverse campus. Having focused goals with a faculty-driven approach was also useful in supporting each other to move forward, in spite of obstacles, as in the case of the partnership between SBVC and CCD: "From the start, our two institutions had a strong plan of implementation and collaboration to develop learning communities [working with faculty to create a set of linked courses]. We had one specific goal to accomplish that made the work that much easier to get off the ground" (CCD). Independently, SBVC reported, "Through the relationships established both administratively and with faculty, the [collaborative] project was able to work through the challenges in a shorter time frame and with more success."

The Ripple Effect

Although each campus began with an initial proposal to change or develop specific programs and practices, over the course of the collaboration, numerous unanticipated effects and actions were reported by the six campuses. Success with initial programs triggered novel ideas for local campus implementation, such as online tutoring for college and local high school students at one campus and a peer-led, team learning freshman composition project at another. The project funds also supported students' social networks and engagement in meetings about retention. Several campuses sent students to the national HACU conference—many of whom had never been on an airplane or attended a banquet dinner—to engage with students from other HSIs. Students were asked to develop a plan for sharing what they learned with other students upon returning to campus.

Although student success was the primary focus of the project, academic and student affairs professionals saw benefits that could increase their own success on campus. Several participants talked about appreciating the "sense of community" developed with other MSIs (HBCUs and TCUs) as well as other HSIs in the collaborative beyond their HSI partner institution. As one campus project coordinator stated, "my professional network increased 100 fold! I was exposed to new models of success at fellow HSIs as well as at HBCUs and Tribal Colleges." Another professional offered, "We can honestly say we are only an email or phone call away from reaching an MSI expert/colleague for almost any issue [regarding student success]." Further, participants stated that they had acquired "a better understanding of data-driven decisions and strategic approaches to student success" and "reassurance that many institutions have similar struggles and there is really no need to reinvent the wheel." From our observations, some project coordinators increased their own visibility on campus as a change agent, and acquired recognition as a valuable source of knowledge regarding student success practices across the country.

Faculty benefitted in terms of support for faculty learning communities across several of the campuses, and training for the work that they do in teaching. The project also generated greater awareness among faculty about what it means to work at a HSI:

> CCD's HSI designation was more recognized and strengthened as a result of the project. In the past at CCD, student services played a larger role in our HSI designation and relationship with HACU. As a result of this grant [project activities], some faculty are more connected with HACU and aware of what it means to be an HSI. This has led to stronger relationships with student services and a stronger HSI committee on campus.

Conclusion and Implications

Several insights emerge from this story of organizational learning, institutional change, and student success work among HSIs. Given that colleges are typically slow to change (Kezar, 2014), the amount of institutional change and institutionalization of new practices in the HSIs was astonishingly fast. This was no doubt aided by a tailwind of state pressures to improve student graduation rates and basic skills, as well as activities set in motion by national interest in student progress. For example, the CSU system administration set goals and deadlines for individual campuses to improve their student retention and graduation rates; and the CSU Fullerton campus had launched a campus-wide task force to improve six-year graduation rates prior to the start of the project. For all of the campuses in the MSISSC, the grant-funded, collaborative project came at the right time to "piggyback" on ongoing efforts and provided additional discretionary funds for campuses to experiment and/or augment initiatives. External funding sources played an important role in the development of many novel initiatives across the campuses, and funds supported the collection of evidence on the success of programs and initiatives before diverting limited institutional resources. Foundation funds continue to play an important role in promoting innovation and institutional change among HSI campuses.

While the focus of the grant was on moving the needle on student success, it was the Alliance for Equity's initial proposal writing team's expertise and awareness of the challenges for MSIs that developed the cross-institutional mentoring model focused on using the assets within each MSI community as a way to build institutional capacity across institutions. The success of the collaborative mentoring model was also possible with the support of college presidents, all of whom rely on other administrators and grassroots leaders among faculty and staff to identify problems and implement solutions. One student affairs professional reported that, as a result of the project, he gained more knowledge about a range of student success practices and "renewed conviction to leadership principles that institutions do not make things happen, people do." While discretionary funds from the grant greased the wheels, it was actually up to each participant to take advantage of what became an authentic professional development opportunity. The project increased human capital within HSIs, empowering coordinators with new knowledge and facilitating their roles as change agents. Each campus had a unique set of challenges, no doubt complicated by structural, financial, and political obstacles—one participant stated that it was "important to understand that this change process was not easy or comfortable." How the change agents in these HSIs overcame obstacles and resistance to change has yet to be documented. More research is needed to understand the strategies used to overcome obstacles and resistance among individuals committed to student success (Kezar, 2014), especially within institutions that are redefining their identity to integrate a Hispanic-serving mission.

This action project contributes to the developing knowledge on organizational learning in postsecondary institutions, with a social justice focus (Bensimon, 2005). Instead of focusing on "fixing" the student, or changing student populations via admissions, a key assumption was that participants would identify ways to make the institution more responsive to students' needs and concerns (e.g., changing the structure of developmental education curriculum). This begins with exposing institutional actors to a new horizon of possibilities embedded in new approaches (e.g., academic and student affairs collaborations) and perspectives among peers charged with the responsibility for student success. This was accomplished through a collaborative mentoring model, characterized by a dialogic mentoring relationship and equity of voice. That is, mentees and mentors respected each other as professionals and, consequently, could question and influence respective assumptions and rationale for practices.

Organizational learning was facilitated by the introduction of new knowledge, using presentations and cross-institutional visits, which allowed participants to "see for themselves" how programs work. This was reinforced within an active community of practice across MSIs, and more specifically among HSIs, which widened actors' social networks regarding professionals and programs that serve large numbers of low-income and underrepresented students. Learning from others' experience, experimenting with new initiatives, and transferring the experienced-based knowledge to others on campus led to institutionalization and other forms of organizational change. In all cases, HSI campuses continued to innovate and take risks with new initiatives that required them to learn and then adapt based on their own contexts. Despite institutional culture, size, and resource differences, the collaborative mentoring model fostered lasting relationships and organizational change.

It is not an exaggeration to say that thousands of students were impacted by the new initiatives and expansion of existing initiatives accelerated through funding and focused efforts of the HSI collaboration. Further evaluation of new initiatives and the scaling-up of existing ones will determine their long-term effectiveness on student progress and degree attainment. However, the focus on organizational learning for student success serves as a reminder that we cannot expect college campuses to improve student success and degree attainment without attention to actors within institutions who do the work of educating students. Institution-wide change requires organizational learning and authentic forms of professional development that empower faculty (full- and part-time) and all levels of staff at HSIs to implement transformative practices that advance student success. We provided details about how an asset-based, collaborative mentoring model worked among HSIs and its impact. Based on information from participants in the project, our hope is that other campuses and communities of practice apply this mentoring approach to accelerate student success among low-income, first generation, and racial/ethnic minorities.

Acknowledgments

We would like to acknowledge all change agents who gave willingly of their time to make the project a success, and responded to questions and provided reports about their initiatives. Special thanks to project coordinators Rosalind Alderman (StMU), Gloria López Cólon (UdSC), Kandy Mink Salas (CSU Fullerton), Fidel Trujillo (NMHU), Lisa Silverstein (CCD), and Marc Donnhauser (SBVC), and also thanks to Carlos Rodríguez who served as the program evaluator during the primary grant period.

References

Arendale, D. (1997). Supplemental Instruction (SI): Review of research concerning the effectiveness of SI from the University of Missouri-Kansas City and other institutions from across the United States. *Eric Clearinghouse* document: ED 457 797. Retrieved from http://files.eric.ed.gov/fulltext/ED457797.pdf

Bauman, G.L. (2005). Promoting organizational learning to achieve educational equity in educational outcomes. *New Directions for Higher Education, 131*, 23–35.

Bensimon, E.M. (2005). Closing the achievement gap in higher education: An organizational learning perspective. *New Directions for Higher Education, 131*, 99–111.

Bokeno, R.M. & Gantt, V.W. (2000). Dialogic mentoring: Core relationships for organizational learning. *Management Communications Quarterly, 14* (2), 237–270.

Bonsangue, M., Caldwalladerolsker, T., Fernández-Weston, C., Filowitz, M., Hershey, J., Moon, H.S., . . . Engelke, N. (2013). The effect of supplemental instruction on transfer student success in first semester calculus. *Learning Assistance Review, 18*(1), 61–74.

Bragg, D., Baker, E., & Puryear, M. (2010). Follow-up of the Community College of Denver FastStart program. Champaign: University of Illinois, Office of Community College Research and Leadership. Retrieved from http://files.eric.ed.gov/fulltext/ED521421.pdf

California State University Fullerton. (2011). *University Learning Center.* Fullerton, CA: Author. Retrieved from http://www.fullerton.edu/sa/assessment/pdfs/Assessment Reports_UniversityLearningCenter/ULC_SIParticipantsLearningOutcomesSA_2011.pdf

Dill, D.D. (1999). Academic accountability and university adaptation: The architecture of an academic learning organization. *Higher education: Handbook of theory and research, 38*, 127–154.

DiMaggio, P.J., & Powell, W.W. (1983). The iron cage revisited: Institutional isomorphism and collective rationality in organizational fields. *American Sociological Review, 48*(2), 147–160.

Edgecombe, N., Jaggars, S.S., Baker, E.D. & Bailey, T. (2013). Acceleration through a holistic support model: An implementation and outcomes analysis of FastStart@ CCD. Eric Clearinghouse document, ED53910. Retrieved from http://eric.ed.gov/?id=ED539910

Ewell, P.T. (1997, December). Organizing for learning: A new imperative. *AAHE Bulletin*, 3–6.

Garvin, D.A. (1993). Building a learning organization. *Harvard Business Review, 71*(4), 78–84.

Hispanic Association of Colleges and Universities. (2012). *HACU legislative agenda.* Retrieved from http://www.hacu.net/images/hacu/govrel/2012_Legislative_Agenda.pdf

Hurtado, S., Álvarez, C. L, Guillermo-Wann, C., Cuellar, M., & Arellano, L. (2012). A model for diverse learning environments: The scholarship on creating and assessing conditions for student success. In J.C. Smart & M.B. Paulsen (Eds.), *Higher education: Handbook of theory and research, 27*, 41–122. New York, NY: Springer.

Kezar, A. (2014). *How colleges change: Understanding, leading and enacting change.* New York: Routledge.

Núñez, A.-M., & Bowers, A.J. (2011). Exploring what leads high school students to enroll in Hispanic-Serving Institutions. A multilevel analysis. *American Educational Research Journal, 48*(6), 1286–1313.

Ravasi, D., & Schultz, M. (2006). Responding to organizational identity threats: exploring the role of organizational culture. *Academy of Management Journal, 49*(3), 433–458.

Titus, M.A. (2006). Understanding the influence of the financial context of institutions on student persistence at four-year colleges and universities. *Journal of Higher Education, 77*(2), 353–375.

11

DO HISPANIC-SERVING INSTITUTIONS REALLY UNDERPERFORM?

Using Propensity Score Matching to Compare Outcomes of Hispanic-Serving and Non–Hispanic-Serving Institutions

Awilda Rodríguez and Emily Calderón Galdeano

While more Hispanics than ever before are attending college (Fry & López, 2012; Fry & Taylor, 2013), completion gaps in higher education persist. Only half of Hispanic students who started a bachelor's degree in 2006 completed it within six years, compared to 63% of non-Hispanic White students; 36% of Hispanics who started in 2008 completed an associate's degree within three years, versus 30% of non-Hispanic Whites (National Center for Education Statistics [NCES], 2013a). Given the need for a growing cadre of educated workers for the burgeoning knowledge economy, gaps in completion, particularly at four-year colleges, pose a challenge to the nation (Carnevale, Smith, & Strohl, 2010).[1] National demands for increased degree completion, as expressed by Complete College America, the Lumina Foundation's Goal 2025, the Bill and Melinda Gates Foundation, and President Barack Obama, cannot be met without improving the educational outcomes of Latina/o students. Due to the current and expected growth in the population, postponing a response to the challenge of improving education for Latinas/os is no longer an option (Gándara, 2003; Kelly, Schneider, & Carey, 2010).

By design, Hispanic-Serving Institutions (HSIs) are tasked with educating the nation's largest, youngest, and fastest-growing minority population.[2] Latina/o enrollment at HSIs continues to increase (Núñez & Bowers, 2011; Santiago, 2006). In 2010, 54% of Hispanics in higher education were enrolled in 311 HSIs, which comprised just 9% of postsecondary institutions that year (Hispanic Association of Colleges and Universities [HACU], 2011). In keeping up with the burgeoning population of Hispanic college-age students, the number of HSIs grew significantly (by 127%) between 1990 and 2010, as did the share of students they educate (HACU, 2013). Between 2000 and 2011, total student enrollment increased by 80% at HSIs, compared to 30% for all institutions (HACU, 2013). Due to increasing enrollment in higher education, and especially Latina/o student enrollment, the number of HSIs will continue to grow (Núñez, Hurtado, & Calderón Galdeano, chapter 1, this volume; Santiago, 2006, 2012; Torres & Zerquera, 2012). As HSIs are accountable for overall graduation rates, and not simply those of Latinas/os, understanding their overall degree production has become increasingly important to workforce needs and national degree attainment goals.[3]

Despite the instrumental role of HSIs in educating Latinas/os, the extant literature is unclear about their performance on college-going measures (Baez, Gasman, & Turner, 2008; Laden, 2004; Pascarella, 2006). Bridges, Cambridge, Kuh, and Leegwater (2005) concurred that there is a dearth of knowledge about HSIs and other Minority-Serving Institutions: "Although minority serving institutions prepare significant numbers of students of color, little is known about . . . their general overall educational effectiveness" (p. 29). The majority of literature on HSIs' outcomes has focused on the proportion of degrees earned by Hispanic students and how these institutions compare to other two- and four-year colleges and universities (e.g., Dayton, González-Vásquez, Martínez, & Plum, 2004; Gastic & Nieto, 2010; Laden, 2001, 2004; Núñez, Sparks, & Hernández, 2011; Stearns, Watanabe, & Snyder, 2002). In fact, a comparison of the graduation rates of HSIs and non-HSIs has led some researchers to conclude that "Hispanic-Serving Institutions do not perform as well as non-HSIs on some critical metrics" (Bensimon, Malcom, & Dávila, 2010, p. 3; Kelly et al., 2010). A simple analysis (Table 11.1) shows that, in 2011, six-year completion rates were lower at four-year public

TABLE 11.1 *Differences in Institutional Graduation Rates between HSIs and Non-HSIs by Sector, 2011*

	HSI		Non-HSI		*Difference*	*p*
	n	*Mean*	*n*	*Mean*		
Public four-year	59	0.37	514	0.47	0.10	***
		0.14		*0.17*		
Private four-year not-for-profit	66	0.38	1,129	0.55	0.17	***
		0.21		*0.21*		
Public two-year	147	0.19	807	0.23	0.04	***
		0.11		*0.13*		
Private two-year not-for-profit	9	0.53	63	0.51	−0.02	n.s.
		0.27		*0.03*		

*** *p* < .001, ** *p* < .01, * *p* < .05, n.s. (not significant).
Source: Authors' analyses of the 2011 Integrated Postsecondary Education Data System (IPEDS) database.
Note. Describes six-year cohort graduation rates for four-year institutions; three-year cohort graduation rates for two-year institutions. Excludes four-year and two-year institutions that were not found in 2005 or 2008 IPEDS survey files (respectively) or were missing data on key variables.

(10 percentage point difference) and four-year private not-for-profits HSIs (17 percentage point difference), as were three-year completion rates at two-year public HSIs (4 percentage point difference).

Without accounting for their institutional differences, comparisons of HSIs and non-HSIs may be inappropriate, as HSIs tend to have fewer resources and serve students who are at highest risk of not finishing their college education (Malcom, Dowd, & Yu, 2010; Merisotis & McCarthy, 2005; Núñez & Elizondo, 2012, and chapter 4, this volume). In fact, researchers have found that many of the institutional characteristics on which HSIs and non-HSIs differ greatly have direct implications for persistence and completion (García, 2013; Núñez & Elizondo, 2012). Table 11.2 illustrates the significant differences in institutional characteristics, student populations, and net costs, as well as the policies and offerings that promote credit accumulation. For example, in 2011, compared to public four-year non-HSIs, public HSIs on average enrolled 20% more undergraduates who were in greater financial need (40% more Pell Grant recipients), experienced 11% larger student–faculty ratios, and spent less of their budgets on instruction and academic support (12% and 9% less, respectively).[4]

The differences between four-year private not-for-profit HSIs and non-HSIs were somewhat similar, although HSIs in this sector had even fewer traditional age students and lower income students than their non-HSI counterparts. Two-year public HSIs served nearly twice as many students, on average, as two-year public non-HSIs. The differences between HSIs and non-HSIs were smallest in the two-year not-for-profit sector.

Despite the acknowledgement that HSIs and non-HSIs are different across many important institutional characteristics (Núñez & Elizondo, 2012), not enough attention is paid to differences between HSIs and other institutions within their respective sectors to know whether comparisons of outcomes are appropriate (Calderón Galdeano & Rodríguez, 2012). Examining HSIs' student outcomes in proper context is critical, especially when we consider that performance funding formulas in many states already use six-year student graduation rates to gauge institutional performance (Dougherty & Reddy, 2013). Furthermore, the federal government is proposing to implement a ratings system of postsecondary institutions that will likely be based on available data such as student body characteristics, net price of attending the institution, and institutional six-year graduation rates (Rodríguez & Kelly, 2014). Because this ratings system will purportedly be tied to colleges' ability to receive federal funding, how HSIs fare on graduation rate measures could have real implications for the amount of institutional resources they receive in order to serve their students (Núñez, 2014).

In short, if HSIs' outcomes are indeed being compared to colleges and universities that are dissimilar on important institutional characteristics, then researchers and policymakers may be penalizing HSIs unfairly. The purpose of this chapter is

TABLE 11.2 *Mean Differences between HSIs and Non-HSIs on Select Institutional Characteristics by Sector, 2011*

Four-Year Institutions

	Public			Private Not-for-Profit		
	HSI	Non-HSI	d	HSI	Non-HSI	d
	N = 59	N = 514		N = 66	N = 1,129	
Undergraduate enrollment	12,611	10,487	0.20	2,689	2,203	0.17
Percentage undergraduate enrollment age 18–24	71.8	76.0	-0.28	62.5	75.7	-0.65
Percentage of undergraduate students receiving Pell Grants	53.2	38.0	1.10	68.3	39.7	1.40
Student–faculty ratio	20.2	18.2	0.47	18.8	13.0	0.91
Percentage of tuition and fees covered by grant aid	53.2	38.0	1.10	68.3	39.7	1.40
Revenues from tuition and fees per FTE	$3,870	$6,283	-0.89	$10,286	$14,082	-0.55
Instruction expenses as a percentage of total core expenses	39.0	44.3	-0.61	42.3	41.6	0.07
Academic support expenses as a percentage of total core expenses	9.9	10.9	-0.24	10.9	10.1	0.17
Student service expenses as a percentage of total core expenses	8.8	9.6	-0.20	15.2	17.4	-0.30
Two-Year Institutions	N = 147	N = 807		N = 9	N = 63	
Undergraduate enrollment	12,021	6,520	0.65	484	420	0.15
Percentage undergraduate enrollment age 18–24	53.6	50.5	0.29	45.2	50.5	-0.23
Percentage of undergraduate students receiving Pell Grants	35.1	43.0	-0.52	72.9	53.7	1.04
Student–faculty ratio	25.6	19.8	0.89	17.3	13.7	0.58
Percentage of tuition and fees covered by grant aid	35.1	43.0	-0.52	72.9	53.7	1.04
Revenues from tuition and fees per FTE	$1,061	$2,084	-1.00	$7,171	$10,249	-0.41
Instruction expenses as a percentage of total core expenses	42.4	44.2	-0.21	33.6	35.5	-0.14
Academic support expenses as a percentage of total core expenses	8.1	8.6	-0.10	12.0	10.0	0.20
Student service expenses as a percentage of total core expenses	11.5	10.6	0.18	11	13	-0.17

Source: Authors' analyses of the 2011 Integrated Postsecondary Education Data System (IPEDS) database.

Note. Excludes four-year and two-year institutions that were not found in 2005 and 2008 IPEDS survey files (respectively) or were missing data on key variables. A *d* statistic between −.10 and .10 is considered a balanced sample (Austin, 2009).

therefore to further probe the differences between HSIs and non-HSIs with the following questions:

- Is it possible to find adequate comparison groups within each sector of non-HSI institutions?
- If so, what are the differences in completion by sector between HSI and non-HSI institutions?

This study contributes to the existing literature on HSIs and degree completion by accounting for differences in institutional characteristics between HSIs and non-HSIs, and by expanding our knowledge of the heterogeneity among HSIs as a whole. Further, this study's approach to comparing postsecondary outcomes between HSIs and non-HSIs has not been utilized before, and it therefore increases our understanding of the effectiveness of these vital postsecondary institutions.

Background on HSIs

To set the framework for this chapter, the review of literature is divided into two sections: (1) institutional predictors of completion and (2) HSIs and degree completion. For additional background on Hispanic-Serving Institutions, please see Chapter 1, Chapter 3, and Chapter 4 in this volume.

Institutional Predictors of Completion

Since student success can be defined in many ways, the bodies of empirical and theoretical literature exploring the factors that contribute to student success in college are voluminous. For example, researchers have produced substantial bodies of work explaining the impact of the college experience on academic, monetary, and social outcomes (Astin, 1993; Gurin, Dey, Hurtado, & Gurin, 2002; Myers, 2007; Rowley & Hurtado, 2002; Thomas & Zhang, 2005; Wolniak & Pascarella, 2005; Zhang, 2008). Other research has explored student success by explaining the factors that contribute to their departure from postsecondary institutions (Bowen, Chingos, & McPherson, 2009; Longerbeam, Sedlacek, & Alatorre, 2004). And, earlier in this book, in Chapter 6, Cuellar considered how HSIs contribute to student development on less traditionally considered measures of success. In order to narrow this large body of work, our review of the literature considers studies that use degree completion as an outcome of postsecondary student success.

Previous research points to individual characteristics that help explain the likelihood of postsecondary persistence and completion, such as race/ethnicity, age, and income (Arbona & Nora, 2007; Berger & Braxton, 1998; Berger & Milem, 1999; Cabrera, Burkum, & La Nasa, 2005; Carey, 2005; Hu & St. John, 2001; Ishitani, 2006; Lee & Rawls, 2010; Radford, Berkner, Wheeless, & Shepherd, 2010).

Research has identified race and/or ethnicity as an important student characteristic related to persistence and degree attainment: African American and Latina/o students are less academically successful than White and Asian American students, controlling for other factors (Berger & Braxton, 1998; Berger & Milem, 1999; Cabrera et al., 2005; Carey, 2005; Ishitani, 2006; Lee & Rawls, 2010).

Previous research has also linked age with the likelihood of degree attainment. Specifically, studies have reported that older students are significantly less likely to obtain degrees than younger students (Arbona & Nora, 2007; Hu & St. John, 2001; Radford et al., 2010). Researchers have argued, however, that age is a proxy for delayed entry into college, and it is delayed entry rather than a student's age itself that is negatively related to degree attainment (Arbona & Nora, 2007; Radford et al., 2010).

Research on Latina/o student success has also found that financial aid has a positive effect on persistence, rivaling or exceeding other factors (Bowen et al., 2009; Nora et al., 2005). There is also a strong positive relationship between family income and persistence to baccalaureate degree (Engle & Tinto, 2008; Mortenson, 2007; Terenzini et al., 2001), with Latinas/os experiencing more financial stress while attending college than non-Latinas/os (Nora et al., 2005).

Studies have also shown how institutional characteristics (e.g., sector, size, control, net cost, and expenditures) are determinants of college completion (Astin & Oseguera, 2005; Bound, Lovenheim, & Turner, 2010; Cabrera et al., 2005; Ishitani, 2006; Kim & Conrad, 2006; Lee & Rawls, 2010; Núñez & Elizondo, 2012; Radford et al., 2010; Titus, 2006a, 2006b). Research that has examined the relationships between institutional sector and students' persistence and degree attainment has generally shown that students who begin at four-year institutions are more likely to graduate from college than students who begin at two-year institutions (Cabrera et al., 2005; Lee & Rawls, 2010; Radford et al., 2010). There is also some evidence that attending a private rather than public college or university increases the likelihood of graduating from college (Astin & Oseguera, 2005; Ishitani, 2006). For African American students, who face postsecondary outcomes similar to Latinas/os (Lee & Rawls, 2010), research has also found that institutional size, measured by total enrollment, is positively related to degree attainment (Kim & Conrad, 2006).

HSIs and Degree Completion

Recent research on outcomes at Hispanic-Serving Institutions (HSIs) has focused on the proportion of degrees earned by Hispanic students and how these institutions compare to other two- and four-year non-HSIs (Bensimon et al., 2010; Núñez & Elizondo, 2012; Núñez et al., 2011; Vega & Martínez, 2012). Comparing the number of degrees conferred to Latinas/os by all U.S. institutions to the number of degrees conferred to Latinas/os by HSIs presents a particularly stark contrast. In 1999, HSIs conferred 36% of all degrees awarded to Hispanics nationally (Stearns et al., 2002). However, due to the increased growth of HSIs, in 2011 these institutions awarded 47% of all degrees to Latina/o students

(HACU, 2013). A review of degrees conferred to Latinas/os highlights the critical function HSIs provide in educating this particular group. Between 1990 and 2010, the number of degrees awarded by HSIs grew by 36%, while the number of degrees conferred by all institutions in the United States grew by only 13% (HACU, 2013).

While HSIs look favorable in comparison to non-HSIs when considering Latina/o degree *production* (i.e., the share of degrees conferred to Latina/o students enrolled at HSIs as a percentage of all degrees conferred to Latina/o students), the results are mixed when drawing comparisons along degree *completion* (i.e., the share of students that HSIs graduate, relative to the number of degree-seeking students who started at that institution six or three years prior). Some authors have demonstrated that HSIs have lower graduation rates than their non-HSI counterparts in their respective sectors. Bensimon and her colleagues (2010), for example, used data from the Integrated Postsecondary Education System (IPEDS) to examine six-year college graduation rates between HSIs and non-HSIs by sector. The authors concluded that although the Latina/o graduation rate of 44% at private HSIs was higher than the rate at all public institutions (39%), these HSIs still underperformed compared to private non-HSIs, which had a Latina/o graduation rate of 47% (Bensimon et al., 2010).

In contrast, other studies have asserted that HSIs have higher graduation rates than their non-HSI counterparts. Núñez and Elizondo (2012) compared IPEDS six-year graduation rate data and found that four-year HSIs had a Hispanic student graduation rate of 39%, compared to the 36% Hispanic graduation rate across all four-year institutions nationally found in previous studies (Radford et al., 2010). Additionally, Malcom (2010) found that Latina/o enrollment at four-year public institutions was related to six-year graduation rates. More specifically, HSIs with *less* than a 33% Hispanic enrollment rate had the highest rates of Latina/o graduates, and HSIs with *more* than a 33% Hispanic enrollment rate had the lowest six-year Hispanic graduation rates. Research has also shown that flagship institutions (which typically are non-HSIs) may not always be the best choice for Hispanic students and that some other four-year public HSIs are doing a better job of graduating Hispanics (Vega & Martínez, 2012).

The existing literature has contributed to our understanding of the differences between HSI and non-HSI completion rates. However, this chapter seeks to expand on the extant knowledge base in three important ways. First, most studies do not account for the well-documented differences in institutional characteristics between HSIs and non-HSIs. Núñez and Elizondo (2012, and chapter 4, this volume) have argued for HSI graduation rates to be assessed in an equitable manner that takes into account the unique characteristics of this set of institutions, yet few studies have considered comparisons of HSI and non-HSI outcomes by sector or other institutional characteristics, and those that have show mixed results (Bensimon et al., 2010; Malcom, 2010; Núñez & Elizondo, 2012; Vega & Martínez, 2012). Without accounting for these institutional differences, the oft-disadvantaged HSI group will seem to underperform. These large differences warrant an examination of whether comparison groups can even be formed.

Second, existing studies that have tried to account for institutional or student characteristics to explain the variation have used regression, which is limited in its ability to account for unobserved phenomena that may also contribute to completion rates (Malcom, 2010; Núñez & Bowers, 2011; Núñez & Elizondo, 2012; Núñez et al., 2011). Therefore, a different methodological approach such as propensity score matching is needed to better understand the extent of the gaps in completion rates between HSIs and non-HSIs. And third, due to HSIs serving a diverse student population (Johnson, Conrad, & Perna, 2006; Mercer & Stedman, 2008; Santiago, 2006), this study addresses overall graduation rates, as opposed to solely focusing on Latina/o student completion.

HSIs serve as the colleges of choice for the majority of Latinas/os, and in a previous study we found that Latina/o student graduation rate gaps between HSIs and non-HSIs were substantially reduced once adequate comparison groups were found (Rodríguez & Calderón Galdeano, 2014). Only one other study to date has used a matching technique to address institutional differences and selection bias. Using student-level data from Texas, Flores and Park (2014) used a propensity score matching approach to match students who attended four-year HSIs with students who enrolled in non-HSI four-year colleges who were statistically similar along various demographic and academic characteristics. Once these differences (and some institutional characteristics) were accounted for, there were no differences in students' likelihood of completion between those who attended HSIs and those who attended non-HSIs. While these are important findings, they are limited to the Texas context, and the analysis was performed at the individual student level. Matching at the institutional level has greater implications for policies that evaluate institutions on school-wide graduation rates. Likewise, in performance funding formulas, institutions classified as HSIs are judged for institutional performance based on graduation rates for all students versus only those for Latinas/os (Núñez, 2014; Rodríguez & Kelly, 2014). Thus, we have chosen to focus on overall institutional graduation rates in this chapter.

Analytic Methods

In order for us to compare graduation rates between HSIs that were similar to non-HSIs, we used a technique called *propensity score matching*. The following section describes the data we used and how we employed this approach to find comparable groups.

Data

We utilized survey data from the Integrated Postsecondary Education System (IPEDS), an annual survey administered to colleges and universities by the National Center for Education Statistics (NCES). The annual survey includes all institutions that receive Title IV funding. NCES collects information on institutional characteristics, finances, admissions, enrollment, and graduation rates (IPEDS, 2013). Three-year and six-year graduation rate data were pulled from the IPEDS Data Center for 2011 (the most recent available) for two-year and four-year institutions, respectively. The Hispanic Association of Colleges and Universities (HACU) provided official lists of four-year and two-year institutions identified as HSIs for 2011. Recognizing that institutional characteristics prior to 2011 would influence the six-year graduation rates of four-year institutions and three-year graduation rates of two-year institutions, we also pulled institutional characteristics from the IPEDS 2005 and 2008 files for four-year and two-year institutions, respectively.

Non-HSI institutions were defined as all institutions in the IPEDS dataset that were not Hispanic-Serving, Historically Black Colleges and Universities (HBCUs), or Tribal Colleges and Universities (TCUs). Since we used institutional characteristics from 2005 for four-year institutions and from 2008 for two-year institutions, we excluded from our analyses four-year institutions that were not present in the IPEDS 2005 files and two-year institutions that were not found in the 2008 IPEDS files. One institution was designated as both an HSI and an HBCU, and it was therefore excluded from the analyses. In total, 11% of public four-year, 22% of private not-for-profit four-year, and 3% of public two-year HSIs were excluded from the analyses due to incomplete data in IPEDS. The institutions were limited to degree-granting, currently active postsecondary institutions, and institutions that were not missing information on any of the explanatory variables. For-profit institutions were also excluded, as they are not eligible for HSI funding. These parameters yielded 59 public four-year HSIs, 66 private not-for-profit four-year HSIs, 147 public two-year HSIs, and 9 private not-for-profit two-year HSIs (Table 11.3).

TABLE 11.3 *Number of HSI and Non-HSI Institutions by Sector, 2011*

Sector	Present in IPEDS		Analytic Sample		Matched Sample	
	HSI	*Non-HSI*	*HSI*	*Non-HSI*	*HSI*	*Non-HSI*
Total	311	3,063	281	2,513	139	139
Public 4-year	66	633	59	514	25	25
Private 4-year not-for-profit	85	1,512	66	1,129	38	38
Public 2-year	151	825	147	807	76	76
Private 2-year not-for-profit	9	93	9	63	—	—

Source: Authors' analyses of the 2011 Integrated Postsecondary Education Data System (IPEDS) database.
Note. Authors employed listwise deletion to arrive at the analytic sample.

Analyses

In order to find an appropriate comparison group of non-HSIs for our first research question, we sought to reduce selection bias by using propensity score matching to find non-HSIs that were similar to HSIs within each sector. A regression adjustment approach is not recommended when the two groups (in this case, HSIs and non-HSIs) are very different, such as when the means of the propensity scores are greater than one-half of a standard deviation apart (Baser, 2007). Propensity score matching is a technique that allowed us to score non-HSI institutions on their similarity to HSIs based on their characteristics (e.g., size, percentage of Pell Grant students). Although we could not completely account for all of the differences between HSIs and non-HSIs, using this approach enabled us to identify institutions that were statistically similar to HSIs on the variables to which we did have access (Rosenbaum & Rubin, 1983).

We produced these propensity scores using a series of logistic regressions (one for each sector) with institutional characteristics as predictors of institutional completion rates that were identified in the literature (i.e., size, offered remedial services, revenues from tuition and fees per FTE, academic support expenses as a percentage of total core expenses), student population (i.e., percentage of students enrolled who received Pell Grants, percentage of African American undergraduate students, percentage of undergraduate enrollment age 18–24), as well as institutional policies that may improve credit accumulation (i.e., weekend/evening courses, on-campus day care for students' children, academic/career counseling services).[5] Because HSIs by definition are institutions that serve Latina/o students, we did not include the percentage of Latina/o undergraduate students. We did, however, include the percentage of African American undergraduate students, as we accounted for the types of students that institutions serve.

We then used a propensity score matching algorithm, greedy match (Parsons, 2001), to make one-to-one institutional matches for every sector. Institutions that were not matched were omitted from subsequent analyses. We examined density plots of propensity scores to better understand whether HSI and non-HSI institutions overlapped in characteristics. In addition, we compared institutions, after matching along the same institutional characteristics as in the first research question, to check if balance between HSIs and non-HSIs was met.

Our outcomes of interest were the six-year graduation rates for four-year institutions and three-year graduation rates for two-year institutions. Again, since HSIs enroll a diverse student body, we examined overall student graduation rates, as opposed to only those of Latina/o students. To address our second research question, we compared graduation rates between HSIs and non-HSIs by sector before and after matching, using the t test, to determine whether differences were statistically significant.

Findings

The density plots in Figure 11.1 show the overlap between the propensity scores of HSIs (solid) and non-HSIs (dashed). Areas where the two lines overlap are propensity scores where HSIs and non-HSIs were similar and where the propensity score algorithm was likely to find matches. Figure 11.1 illustrates that there was modest overlap between HSIs and non-HSIs, with variation across sectors. In particular, HSIs that were two-year private not-for-profits had very little overlap with their non-HSI peers. This figure reinforces the need to separate out analyses by sector, and also underscores how different HSIs and non-HSIs are, even within a particular sector.

Propensity Score Matching Improved Comparability of Groups

Conclusions from subsequent analyses are limited to only those institutions for which a match was found. The HSI samples lost institutions to varying degrees as a result of the matching process—58% of public four-year, 42% of private-not-for-profit four year, 48% of public two-year, and all of the two-year private

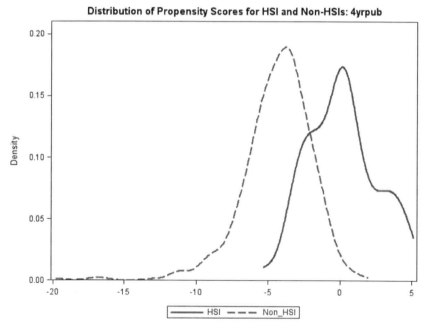

FIGURE 11.1   Continued

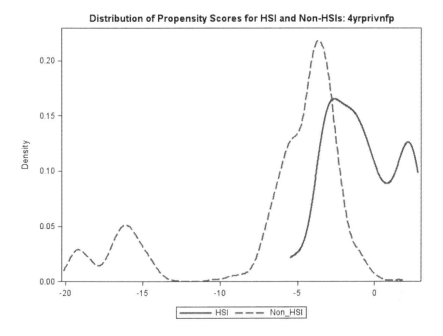

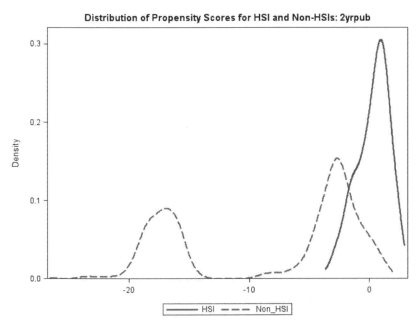

FIGURE 11.1   Continued

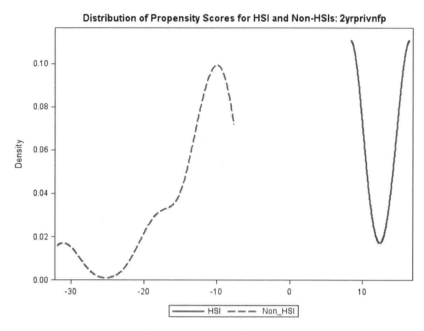

FIGURE 11.1 Distribution of Propensity Scores for HSIs and Non-HSIs by Sector

not-for-profits. As a result, we excluded from post-match analyses the private not-for-profit sector.

Through propensity score matching, we were able to reduce (but not eliminate) the differences in the observed variables for matched public four-year, private four-year, and public two-year institutions. A comparison between Table 11.2 and Table 11.4 shows that for the three sectors in the analysis, the d statistic values were dramatically reduced from the pre-match sample, although they were not all reduced to less than the 0.10 threshold for some of the covariates. For example, for private not-for-profits, the balance was improved after match for the covariates: undergraduate enrollment (from $d = 0.17$ to -0.08), percentage undergraduate enrollment age 18–24 (from $d = -0.65$ to 0.19), percentage of undergraduates who received Pell Grants (from $d = 1.40$ to 0.58), and student–faculty ratio (from $d = 0.91$ to 0.30). While we cannot say that these are equivalent comparison groups, we can say they are more balanced and therefore more appropriate comparison groups.

Once we found more comparable groups of non-HSIs for the three remaining HSI groups, we compared their institutional graduation rate averages (Table 11.5). In general, the gaps in overall graduation rates were greatly reduced after matching across the three sectors. The graduation rate gap between public four-year HSIs and non-HSIs declined by 3 percentage points. Once comparable private

TABLE 11.4 *Post-Match Mean Differences between HSIs and Non-HSIs on Select Institutional Characteristics by Sector, 2011*

	Public			Private Not-for-Profit		
	HSI	Non-HSI	d	HSI	Non-HSI	d
Four-Year Institutions	N = 25	N = 25		N = 38	N = 38	
Undergraduate enrollment	13,341	11,941	0.14	2,185	2,392	-0.08
Percentage undergraduate enrollment age 18–24	69.4	68.4	0.07	64.4	60.5	0.19
Percentage of undergraduate students receiving Pell Grants	47.0	39.0	0.62	55.9	45.0	0.58
Student–faculty ratio	19.2	18.7	0.10	15.3	13.8	0.30
Percentage of tuition and fees covered by grant aid	47.0	39.0	0.62	55.9	45.0	0.58
Revenues from tuition and fees per FTE	$5,062	$4,661	0.17	$13,755	$12,362	0.25
Instruction expenses as a percentage of total core expenses	39.1	40.6	-0.16	39.7	37.8	0.16
Academic support expenses as a percentage of total core expenses	10.0	10.1	-0.02	11.7	13.1	-0.19
Student service expenses as a percentage of total core expenses	8.0	9.6	-0.35	15.8	15.4	0.05
Two-Year Institutions	N = 76	N = 76		N = 0	N = 0	
Undergraduate enrollment	9,905	10,666	-0.10	—	—	—
Percentage undergraduate enrollment age 18–24	53.0	51.0	0.20	—	—	—
Percentage of undergraduate students receiving Pell Grants	33.4	34.5	-0.08	—	—	—
Student–faculty ratio	25.1	23.3	0.28	—	—	—
Percentage of tuition and fees covered by grant aid	33.4	34.5	-0.08	—	—	—
Revenues from tuition and fees per FTE	$1,253	$1,425	-0.17	—	—	—
Instruction expenses as a percentage of total core expenses	43.2	43.3	-0.02	—	—	—
Academic support expenses as a percentage of total core expenses	8.5	8.6	-0.03	—	—	—
Student service expenses as a percentage of total core expenses	11.3	11.1	0.04	—	—	—

Source: Authors' analyses of the 2011 Integrated Postsecondary Education Data System (IPEDS) database.

Note. Institutions were matched using predictors from the 2005 survey files for four-year institutions and the 2008 survey files for two-year institutions. Excludes four-year and two-year institutions that were not found in 2005 and 2008 IPEDS survey files (respectively) or were missing data on key variables. A *d* statistic between −0.10 and 0.10 is considered a balanced sample (Austin, 2009).

TABLE 11.5 *Post-Match Differences in Graduation Rates between HSIs and Non-HSIs by Sector, 2011*

	HSI		Non-HSI		Difference	p
	n	Mean	n	Mean		
Public four-year	25	0.35	25	0.42	0.07	n.s.
		0.15		0.21		
Private four-year not-for-profit	38	0.44	38	0.48	0.03	n.s.
		0.17		0.22		
Public two-year	76	0.19	76	0.22	0.03	n.s.
		0.10		0.11		
Private two-year not-for-profit	—	—	—	—	—	—

*** $p < .001$, ** $p < .01$, * $p < .05$, n.s. (not significant).
Source: Authors' analyses of the 2011 Integrated Postsecondary Education Data System (IPEDS) database.
Note. Institutional average was used instead of weighted student average, since the unit of analysis was the institution.

four-year not-for-profit institutions were found for HSIs, the completion gap dropped sharply from 17% to 3%. Public two-year institutions saw little difference before and after matching (from 4% to 3%). Finally, as noted earlier, no comparison could be made for private two-year not-for-profit HSIs.

Discussion and Implications

This study sought to understand differences in resources and student composition between HSIs and non-HSIs. We also sought to reveal whether adequate comparisons between these two types of institutions could be drawn by sector using propensity score matching, and whether gaps in completion rates could be reduced once we were comparing matched institutions.

There are three major findings in this study. First, HSIs and non-HSIs were quite different in terms of their student compositions, institutional resources, and finance structures. Descriptive analyses showed that, on average, most HSIs enrolled higher numbers of students, in general, and, in particular, more students with financial need; they also had higher student–faculty ratios than non-HSIs. Public HSIs also spent less on instruction and academic support than private not-for-profit HSIs. Given these important differences, which are often linked to college outcomes, the findings confirm that head-on comparisons of completion rates are inappropriate.

Second, an attempt to match HSIs with non-HSIs according to measures of student body composition, finances, and institutional resources through the use of propensity score matching yielded mixed results. With variation across sectors, there was some overlap between HSIs and non-HSIs. While we were not able to find statistically equivalent groups, we were able to reduce the differences between groups on many institutional characteristics for three out of the four sectors. In fact, for two-year private not-for-profits, no comparison group was found. And matching institutions for the other sectors came at some cost, as many HSIs were dropped from the analyses because the matching algorithm did not find comparable non-HSIs. Subsequent findings were limited to institutions for which matches were found. Nonetheless, one can still draw valuable insights from the comparison of the matched institutions because they represent about half of HSIs, excluding two-year private institutions.

Finally, there were no longer statistically significant differences in the gaps in completion rates for institutions that were matched. This suggests that the variables on which we matched institutions explain many of the differences in graduation rates between HSIs and non-HSIs. Stated differently, HSIs that had comparable matches graduated their students at similar rates to their non-HSIs counterparts. This finding goes against the notion that HSIs underperform and underscores how simple comparisons between HSIs with non-HSIs can be crude and unreliable.

There are some limitations associated with this study. First, HSIs are not a fixed set of institutions in the same way HBCUs are designated by their minority-serving status. The number of HSI institutions has increased 127% in the past 20 years (HACU, 2013). Therefore, aggregate measures of outcomes may be somewhat of a moving target depending on the set of institutions within a given year. Also, the variables available in IPEDS are limited, and while propensity score matching accounts for many observed institutional characteristics, there may be unobserved characteristics that have not been accounted for, such as various dimensions of campus climate (e.g., Hurtado, Álvarez, Guillermo-Wann, Cuellar, & Arellano, 2012), that may have a relationship with the observed outcomes. In addition, IPEDS data have a number of important fields with large amounts of missing data. In particular, private institutions are less likely to report on admissions and completion data that are not required by law (NCES, 2013b). Notwithstanding these limitations, the study's findings are compelling.

Since HSIs are the primary vehicle for educating the majority of Hispanics, this type of deeper understanding is essential for ongoing research on institutions classified as Hispanic-Serving and for increasing the quality and quantity of Hispanic college graduates. Research-based strategies that focus on improving student success in HSIs are efficient and effective in addressing the achievement gap for Hispanic students. A meaningful discussion on the transformation of Hispanic-Serving Institutions must include a grasp of what HSIs currently are and what they need to become.

Notes

1 The direction of completion gaps varies by sector. For example, Latina/o completion at public two-year colleges trails completion by White students (16% versus 23%, respectively).
2 The Latina/o population has grown dramatically within the past 20 years (125%) and is projected to increase to 25% of the total U.S. population between 2010 and 2060 (Passel, Cohn, & López, 2011; NCES, 2013a; U.S. Census Bureau, 2013). Most of the growth will be due to young Latinas/os. In fact, by 2023, the high school senior class is projected to increase in size by 40% (Prescott & Bransberger, 2012).
3 It is important to note that HSIs have experienced growth among all racial/ethnic populations. They serve a diverse student body and do not focus solely on Latina/o students (Johnson, Conrad, & Perna, 2006; Mercer & Stedman, 2008; Santiago, 2006).
4 Differences were calculated using Table 11.1 figures as follows: (HSI–non-HSI)/non-HSI. For example, the calculation for the difference in enrollment at public four-year colleges is (12,611–10,487)/10,487. Figures for Pell Grant recipients, student–faculty ratios, as well as instruction and academic support spending references were similarly calculated.
5 The models were slightly different for each sector due to data availability (e.g., not-for-profits tended to underreport some data) and variance (e.g., almost all two-year institutions provided remedial coursework). The final models are included in the appendix.

References

Arbona, C., & Nora, A. (2007). The influence of academic and environment factors on Hispanic college degree attainment. *Review of Higher Education, 30*, 247–269.

Astin, A.W. (1993). *What matters in college?* San Francisco, CA: Jossey-Bass.

Astin, A.W., & Oseguera, L. (2005). Pre-college and institutional influences on degree attainment. In A. Seidman (Ed.), *College student retention: Formula for student success* (pp. 245–276). Westport, CT: American Council on Education/Praeger.

Austin, P.C. (2009). Balance diagnostics for comparing the distribution of baseline covariates between treatment groups in propensity-score matched samples. *Statistics in Medicine, 28*(5), 3083–3107.

Baez, B., Gasman, M., & Turner, C.S.V. (2008). On Minority-Serving Institutions. In M. Gasman, B. Baez, & C.S.V. Turner (Eds.), *Understanding minority-serving institutions* (pp. 3–17). Albany, NY: SUNY Press.

Baser, O. (2007). Choosing propensity score matching over regression adjustment for causal inference: When, why and how it makes sense. *Journal of Medical Economics, 10*(4), 379–391.

Bensimon, E.M., Malcom, L., & Dávila, B. (2010). *(Re)constructing Hispanic-Serving Institutions: Moving beyond numbers toward student success* (EP3: Education Policy and Practice Perspectives No. 6). Ames, IA: Iowa State University.

Berger, J.B., & Braxton, J.M. (1998). Revising Tinto's interactionalist theory of student departure through theory elaboration: Examining the role of organizational attributes in the persistence process. *Research in Higher Education, 39*(2), 103–119.

Berger, J.B., & Milem, J.F. (1999). The role of student involvement and perceptions of integration in a causal model of student persistence. *Research in Higher Education, 40*(6), 641–664.

Bound, J., Lovenheim, M.F., & Turner, S. (2010). *Increasing time to baccalaureate degree in the United States*. Cambridge, MA: National Bureau of Economic Research.

Bowen, W.G., Chingos, M.M., & McPherson, M.S. (2009). *Crossing the finish line: Completing college at America's public universities.* Princeton, NJ: Princeton University Press.

Bridges, B.K., Cambridge, B., Kuh, G.D., & Leegwater, L.H. (2005). Student engagement at minority serving institutions: Emerging lessons from the BEAMS project. In G. Gaither (Ed.), *Minority retention: What works?* (New Directions for Institutional Research No. 125, pp. 25–43). San Francisco, CA: Jossey-Bass.

Cabrera, A.F., Burkum, K.R., & La Nasa, S.M. (2005). Pathways to a four-year degree: Determinants of transfer and degree completion. In A. Seidman (Ed.), *College student retention: Formula for student success* (pp. 155–214). Westport, CT: American Council on Education/Praeger.

Calderón Galdeano, E., & Rodríguez, A. (2012). *HSIs and non-HSIs: Understanding differences in retention and completion rates in an era of accountability.* Paper presented at the meeting of the American Association of Hispanics in Higher Education, Costa Mesa, CA.

Carey, K. (2005). *One step from the finish line.* Washington, DC: The Education Trust.

Carnevale, A.P., Smith, N., & Strohl, J. (2010). *Help wanted: Projections of jobs and education requirements through 2018.* Washington, DC: Georgetown University Center on Education and the Workforce.

Dayton, B., González-Vásquez, N., Martínez, C.R., & Plum, C. (2004). Hispanic-Serving Institutions through the eyes of students and administrators. In A.M. Ortiz (Ed.), *Addressing the unique needs of Latino American students* (New Directions for Student Services No. 105, pp. 29–40). San Francisco, CA: Jossey-Bass.

Dougherty, K., & Reddy, V. (2013). Performance funding for higher education: What are the mechanisms? What are the impacts? *ASHE Monograph, 39*(2). San Francisco: Jossey-Bass.

Engle, J., & Tinto, V. (2008). *Moving beyond access: College success for low-income, first generation college students.* Washington, DC: The Pell Institute.

Flores, S.M., & Park, T.J. (2014). The effect of enrolling in a Minority-Serving Institution for Black and Hispanic students in Texas. *Research in Higher Education.* Advanced online publication. doi:10.1007/s11162-014-9342-y

Fry, R., & López, M.H. (2012). *Hispanic student enrollments reach new highs in 2011.* Washington, DC: Pew Research Center.

Fry, R., & Taylor, P. (2013). *Hispanic high school graduates pass Whites in rate of college enrollment.* Washington, DC: Pew Research Center.

Gándara, P. (2003). Foreword. In G.J. Léon (Ed.), *Diversity in higher education, volume 3: Latinos in Higher Education* (pp. ix–xii). Boston: Elsevier Science.

García, G.A. (2013). *Challenging the manufactured identity of Hispanic Serving Institutions: Co-constructing an organizational identity* (Unpublished doctoral dissertation). University of California, Los Angeles, CA.

Gastic, B., & Nieto, D.G. (2010). Latinos' economic recovery: Postsecondary participation and Hispanic-Serving Institutions. *Community College Journal of Research and Practice, 34,* 833–838.

Gurin, P., Dey, E.L., Hurtado, S., & Gurin, G. (2002). Diversity and higher education: Theory and impact on educational outcomes. *Harvard Educational Review, 72*(3), 330–366.

Hispanic Association of Colleges and Universities. (2011). *HACU list of Hispanic-Serving Institutions (HSIs): 2010–11.* San Antonio, TX: Author. Retrieved from http://www.hacu.net/images/hacu/OPAI/2010%20Fed%20HSI%20list.pdf

Hispanic Association of Colleges and Universities. (2013). *HACU legislative agenda.* San Antonio, TX: Author. Retrieved from http://www.hacu.net/images/hacu/OPAI/2013_CF_Docs/HACU.2013.Legislative%20Agenda.pdf

Hu, S., & St. John, E.P. (2001). Student persistence in a public higher education system: Understanding racial and ethnic differences. *Journal of Higher Education, 72*, 265–286.

Hurtado, S., Álvarez, C.L., Guillermo-Wann, C., Cuellar, M., & Arellano, L. (2012). A model for diverse learning environments: The scholarship of creating and assessing conditions for student success. In J.C. Smart & M.B. Paulsen (Eds.), *Higher education: Handbook of theory and research* (Vol. 27, pp. 41–122). New York, NY: Springer.

Integrated Postsecondary Education System. (2013). *IPEDS Data Center*. Washington, DC: National Center for Education Statistics. Retrieved from http://nces.ed.gov/ipeds/datacenter/Default.aspx

Ishitani, T.T. (2006). Studying attrition and degree completion behavior among first-generation college students in the United States. *Journal of Higher Education, 77*, 861–885.

Johnson, J., Conrad, C., & Perna, L. (2006). Minority-Serving Institutions of higher education: Building on and extending lines of inquiry for the advancement of the public good. In C. Conrad & R. Serlin (Eds.), *The SAGE handbook for research in education: Engaging ideas and enriching inquiry* (pp. 263–279). Thousand Oaks, CA: SAGE.

Kelly, A.P., Schneider, M., & Carey, K. (2010). *Rising to the challenge: Hispanic college graduates as a national priority*. Washington, DC: American Enterprise Institute.

Kim, M.M., & Conrad, C.F. (2006). The impact of Historically Black Colleges and Universities on the academic success of African-American students. *Research in Higher Education, 47*, 399–427.

Laden, B.V. (2001). Hispanic-Serving Institutions. Myths and realities. *Peabody Journal of Education, 76*(1), 73–92.

Laden, B.V. (2004). Hispanic-Serving Institutions: What are they? Where are they? *Community College Journal of Research and Practice, 28*(3), 181–198.

Lee, J.M., Jr., & Rawls, A. (2010). *The college completion agenda: 2010 progress report*. New York, NY: The College Board. Retrieved from http://completionagenda.collegeboard.org/sites/default/files/reports_pdf/Progress_Report_2010.pdf

Longerbeam, S.D., Sedlacek, W.E., & Alatorre, H.M. (2004). In their own voices: Latino student retention. *NASPA Journal, 41*, 538–550.

Malcom, L.E. (2010). *Hispanic-serving or Hispanic-enrolling? Assessing the institutional performance of public 4-year HSIs and emerging HSIs*. Paper presented at the meeting of the American Educational Research Association, Denver, CO.

Malcom, L., Dowd, A., & Yu, T. (2010). *Tapping HSI-STEM funds to improve Latina and Latino access to STEM professions*. Los Angeles, CA: University of Southern California.

Mercer, C.J., & Stedman, J.B. (2008). Minority-Serving Institutions: Selected institutional and student characteristics. In M. Gasman, B. Baez, & C.S.V. Turner (Eds.), *Understanding minority-serving institutions* (pp. 28–42). Albany, NY: SUNY Press.

Merisotis, J., & McCarthy, K. (2005). Retention and student success at minority-serving institutions. In G. Gaither (Ed.), *Minority retention: What works?* (New Directions for Institutional Research No. 125, pp. 45–58). San Francisco, CA: Jossey-Bass.

Mortenson, T. (2007). *Bachelor's degree attainment by age 24 by family income quartiles, 1970 to 2005*. Oskaloosa, IA: Postsecondary Education Opportunity.

Myers, D. (2007). *Immigrants and boomers: Forging a new social contract for the future of America*. New York, NY: Russell Sage.

National Center for Education Statistics. (2013a). *Digest of Education Statistics 2013* (NCES 2014-015). Washington, DC: Author. Retrieved from http://nces.ed.gov/programs/coe/index.asp

National Center for Education Statistics. (2013b). *IPEDS 2012 Graduation Rate Survey* [Data File]. Available from http://nces.ed.gov/ipeds/datacenter/InstitutionByName.aspx

Nora, A., Barlow, E., & Crisp, G. (2005). Student persistence and degree attainment beyond the first year in college. In A. Seidman (Ed.), *College student retention: Formula for student success* (pp. 129–154). Westport, CT: American Council on Education/Praeger.

Núñez, A.-M. (2014). *Counting what counts for Latinas/os and Hispanic-Serving Institutions: A federal ratings system and postsecondary access, affordability, and success.* A knowledge essay commissioned by the President's Advisory Commission on Educational Excellence for Hispanics and presented at the Postsecondary Access and Completion for All: Latinas/os in America's Future Symposium, New York, NY.

Núñez, A.-M., & Bowers, A.J. (2011). Exploring what leads high school students to enroll in Hispanic-Serving Institutions. A multilevel analysis. *American Educational Research Journal, 48*(6), 1286–1313.

Núñez, A.-M., Sparks, P.J., & Hernández, E.A. (2011). Latina/o access to community colleges and Hispanic-Serving Institutions: A national study. *Journal of Hispanic Higher Education, 10*(1), 18–40.

Núñez, A.-M., & Elizondo, D. (2012). *Hispanic-Serving Institutions in the U.S. mainland and Puerto Rico: Organizational characteristics, institutional financial context, and graduation outcomes.* San Antonio, TX: Hispanic Association of Colleges and Universities. Retrieved from http://www.hacu.net/images/hacu/OPAI/H3ERC/2012_papers/Nuñez%20elizondo%20-%204yr%20hsi%20characteristics%20-%202012.pdf

Parsons, L.S. (2001). *Reducing bias in propensity score matched-pair sample using greedy matching techniques: Proceedings of the 26th Annual SAS Users Group International Conference.* Cary, NC: SAS Institute.

Pascarella, E.T. (2006). How college affects students: Ten directions for future research. *Journal of College Student Development, 47,* 508–520.

Passel, J., Cohn, D., & López, M.H. (2011). *Hispanics account for more than half of nation's growth in past decade.* Washington, DC: Pew Hispanic Center. Retrieved from http://www.pewhispanic.org/files/reports/140.pdf

Prescott, B.T., & Bransberger, P. (2012). *Knocking at the college door: Projections of high school graduates* (8th ed.). Boulder, CO: Western Interstate Commission for Higher Education.

Radford, A.W., Berkner, L., Wheeless, S.C., & Shepherd, B. (2010). *Persistence and attainment of 2003–04 Beginning postsecondary students: After 6 years* (NCES 2011-151). Washington, DC: U.S. Department of Education.

Rodríguez, A., & Calderón Galdeano, E. (2014). *What is working for Latinos? Understanding Latinos' postsecondary outcomes at HSIs versus non-HSIs.* Paper presented at the meeting of the American Educational Research Association, Philadelphia, PA.

Rodríguez, A., & Kelly, A.P. (2014). *Access, affordability, and success: How do America's colleges fare and what could it mean for the president's ratings plan?* Washington, DC: American Enterprise Institute.

Rosenbaum, P.R., & Rubin, D.B. (1983). The central role of the propensity score in observational studies for causal effects. *Biometrika, 70*(1), 41–55.

Rowley, L.L., & Hurtado, S. (2002). *The non-monetary benefits of an undergraduate education.* Ann Arbor, MI: University of Michigan Center for the Study of Higher and Postsecondary Education.

Santiago, D.A. (2006). *Inventing Hispanic-Serving Institutions (HSIs): The basics.* Washington, DC: *Excelencia* in Education. Retrieved from http://www.edexcelencia.org/sites/default/files/InventingHSIsFINALRv.pdf

Santiago, D.A. (2012). Public policy and Hispanic-Serving Institutions: From invention to accountability. *Journal of Latina/os and Education, 11*(3), 163–167.

Stearns, C., Watanabe, S., & Snyder, T.D. (2002). *Hispanic-Serving Institutions: Statistical trends from 1990–1999* (NCES 2002-051). Washington, DC: National Center for Education Statistics.

Terenzini, P., Cabrera, A.F., & Bernal, E.M. (2001). *Swimming against the tide: The poor in American higher education* (Research Report No. 2001–1). New York, NY: The College Board.

Thomas, S.L., & Zhang, L. (2005). Post-baccalaureate wage growth within four years of graduation: The effects of college quality and college major. *Research in Higher Education, 46*(4), 437–459.

Titus, M.A. (2006a). No college student left behind: The influence of financial aspects of a state's higher education policy on college completion. *Review of Higher Education, 29*(3), 293–317.

Titus, M.A. (2006b). Understanding college degree completion of students with low socio-economic status: The influence of the institutional financial context. *Research in Higher Education, 47*(4), 371–398.

Torres, V., & Zerquera, D. (2012). Hispanic-Serving Institutions: Patterns, predictions, and implications for informing policy discussions. *Journal of Hispanic Higher Education, 11*(3), 259–278.

U.S. Census Bureau. (2013). *2012 national population projections.* Washington, DC: Author. Retrieved from http://www.census.gov/population/projections/data/national/2012.html

Vega, A., & Martínez, R. (2012). A Latino scorecard for higher education: A focus on Texas universities. *Journal of Hispanic Higher Education, 11*(1), 41–54.

Wolniak, G.C., & Pascarella, E.T. (2005). The effects of college major and job field congruence on job satisfaction. *Journal of Vocational Behavior, 67*(2), 233–251.

Zhang, L. (2008). The way to wealth and the way to leisure: The impact of college education on graduates' earnings and hours of work. *Research in Higher Education, 49*(3), 199–213.

APPENDIX

TABLE A *Variables Included in Each Propensity Score Model*

Variables	4-Year Public	4-Year Private	2-Year Public	2-Year Private
Finance				
Tuition revenue[a]	X	X	X	X
Endowment	X			
Academic expenditures[b]	X	X	X	X
Instructional expenditures[c]	X	X	X	X
Student services expenditures[d]	X	X	X	X
Institutional Characteristics				
Geographic region			X	X
Degree of urbanization	X	X		
Total enrollment	X	X	X	X
Tuition and fees	X	X	X	X
Admissions rate	X	X		
Student Services				
Whether they offer remedial courses	X	X		
Whether they offer on-campus day care	X	X	X	X
Whether they offer weekend or evening courses	X	X	X	X
Whether they accept AP, dual enrollment, or credit for life	X	X		
Student Characteristics				
Percentage of African American students	X	X	X	X
Percentage of 18- to 24-year-olds	X	X	X	X
Percentage of students receiving aid[e]	X	X	X	X
Percentage of first-time full-time degree-seeking students	X	X		

Source: 2005 and 2008 IPEDS data were used for the four-year and two-year models, respectively.

[a] Tuition and fees as a percentage of core revenues.

[b] For four-year models, academic expenses per full-time equivalent (FTE); for two-year models, academic support expenses as a percentage of total core expenses.

[c] For four-year models, instructional expenses per FTE; for two-year models, instructional expenses as a percentage of total core expenses.

[d] For four-year models, student services expenses per FTE; for two-year models, student services expenses as a percentage of total core expenses.

[e] For four-year models, percentage of students receiving federal grant aid; for two-year models, percentage of students receiving Pell Grants.

CONTRIBUTORS

Anne-Marie Núñez, Ph.D., is an Associate Professor in the Educational Leadership and Policy Studies Department at the University of Texas at San Antonio. Her research focuses on how to promote equity in postsecondary access and success, particularly for Latina/o and first-generation college-going students.

Sylvia Hurtado, Ph.D., is Professor and Director of the Higher Education Research Institute at UCLA in the Graduate School of Education & Information Studies. An award-winning researcher, she has published numerous articles and books about student educational outcomes, campus climates, college impact on student development, and diversity in higher education.

Emily Calderón Galdeano, Ed.D., is the Director of Research for *Excelencia* in Education. Previously, she directed the Office of Policy Analysis and Information at the Hispanic Association of Colleges and Universities. Her research agenda focuses on the intersection of public policy and higher education, specifically related to Latina/o student success.

Laura J. Cortez, Ph.D., is a postdoctoral fellow at the University of Texas at Austin, where she earned a Ph.D. in educational administration. Her research focuses on college access, persistence, and degree completion, specifically of first-generation students at Hispanic-Serving Institutions.

Gloria Crisp, Ed.D., is an Associate Professor in the Educational Leadership and Policy Studies Department at the University of Texas at San Antonio. Her scholarship seeks to identify and understand the factors that promote success for students who attend community colleges and four-year broad access institutions.

Marcela Cuellar, Ph.D., is an Assistant Professor in the School of Education at the University of California, Davis. Her research focuses on access and equity, Latina/o students, and broad access institutions, including HSIs and emerging HSIs. She received her Ph.D. in Education from UCLA.

Diane Elizondo is a doctoral student in the Department of Educational Leadership and Policy Studies at the University of Texas at San Antonio. Her research examines how institutional organization, policy, and practice structure postsecondary opportunities and outcomes for underrepresented students, particularly for Latinas/os at Hispanic-Serving Institutions.

Joanna Frye is a research associate at the National Forum on Higher Education for the Public Good, and a Ph.D. candidate in the Center for the Study of Higher and Postsecondary Education at the University of Michigan. Her research interests are focused on higher education policy and politics.

Gina A. García, Ph.D., is an Assistant Professor of Higher Education at the University of Pittsburgh. Her research interests center on issues of equity and diversity within higher education, with an emphasis on the organizational identity of HSIs and the retention, success, and identity development of Latina/o college students.

Leslie D. Gonzales, Ph.D., is an Assistant Professor of Higher Education at Clemson University. Her research agenda concerns the academic profession, legitimization in academia, and how faculty (re)negotiate dominant conceptions of legitimacy. Dr. Gonzales is concerned with how the legitimization process impacts underrepresented scholars within academia serving in Hispanic-Serving Institutions.

René A. González is a consultant in higher education in program development and management. At the Hispanic Association of Colleges and Universities for twenty years he served as Senior Executive Director of Student Services and on several national task forces examining Hispanics in higher education.

Aurora Kamimura is a Ph.D. candidate in the Center for the Study of Higher and Postsecondary Education at the University of Michigan, and a research associate at the National Forum on Higher Education for the Public Good. Her research agenda examines the organizational resilience of postsecondary institutions, with a focus on Minority-Serving Institutions.

Christopher J. Nellum, Ph.D., is a Senior Policy Analyst in the American Council on Education's Center for Policy Research and Strategy. He received his Ph.D. from the Center for the Study of Higher and Postsecondary Education at the University of Michigan. His research examines public policy aimed at reducing educational disparities.

Noe Ortega is Assistant Director and Senior Research Associate for the National Center for Institutional Diversity at the University of Michigan. He is a Ph.D. candidate in the Center for the Study of Higher and Postsecondary Education, and his research examines organizational change and leadership for diversity in higher education.

Awilda Rodríguez, Ph.D., is an Assistant Professor at the University of Michigan's Center for the Study of Higher and Postsecondary Education. Her primary research interest focuses on understanding college access for traditionally underrepresented students. She received her Ph.D. in Higher Education from the University of Pennsylvania's Graduate School of Education.

Adriana Ruiz Alvarado, Ph.D., is a postdoctoral scholar with the Higher Education Research Institute at UCLA. Her research examines student mobility patterns, campus climate and intergroup relations, and college contexts that impact the persistence of underrepresented students.

Angela Vidal-Rodríguez is Director/Professor of the McNair Scholars Program at Northeastern Illinois University. She is a Ph.D. candidate in the Center for the Study of Higher and Postsecondary Education at the University of Michigan. Her research focuses on issues of organizational behavior and institutional policies that affect access and success of underrepresented students in higher education.

INDEX

Note: Page numbers in *italics* indicate figures.